S154 Science starts here
Science: Level 1

The Open University

Water for Life

Prepared by Ruth Williams, Linda Fowler, Sally Jordan
and Judith Metcalfe

This publication forms part of an Open University course S154 *Science starts here*. Details of this and other Open University courses can be obtained from the Student Registration and Enquiry Service, The Open University, PO Box 197, Milton Keynes MK7 6BJ, United Kingdom: tel. +44 (0)845 300 60 90, email general-enquiries@open.ac.uk

Alternatively, you may visit the Open University website at http://www.open.ac.uk where you can learn more about the wide range of courses and packs offered at all levels by The Open University.

To purchase a selection of Open University course materials visit http://www.ouw.co.uk, or contact Open University Worldwide, Michael Young Building, Walton Hall, Milton Keynes MK7 6AA, United Kingdom for a brochure. tel. +44 (0)1908 858793; fax +44 (0)1908 858787; email ouw-customer-services@open.ac.uk

The Open University
Walton Hall Milton Keynes
MK7 6AA

First published 2007. Second edition 2008

Edited and designed by The Open University.

Typeset by SR Nova Pvt. Ltd, Bangalore, India.

Printed and bound in the United Kingdom by Halstan Printing Group, Amersham.

ISBN 978 0 7492 1923 9

2.1

Contents

Chapter 1
Get ready ...

Have you ever asked yourself why ice floats on the surface of a pond rather than sinking to the bottom, or why sweating can cool you down? Have you ever wondered how camels can survive for long periods in the desert without water but humans cannot? These questions are all related to the theme of 'water for life' which you will explore in S154 *Science starts here.*

This topic has been chosen for a variety of reasons: first, it will introduce you to some fascinating science, spanning the main areas covered in Level 1 science courses – biology, chemistry, Earth sciences, physics and astronomy, and environmental science. Water is essential for life, and without water there would be no life. Water also has many special properties that single it out from other substances and that make it of interest to scientists in all areas.

A second reason for choosing the theme 'water for life' is that both water and life are subjects that are part of your everyday experience; you know a lot about them already. For example, water is the most common liquid on the Earth; it forms ice; it falls in the form of rain; all plants and animals need water to survive, and so on (see Figure 1.1, and the cover illustration). This knowledge provides a foundation on which you can build both in this course and when you progress to other Level 1 Open University courses.

(a)

(b)

Figure 1.1   Open University students, on excursions organised by the OU Geological Society, visiting regions where there is (a) plenty of water: a lake, ice and snow, and clouds in the Swiss Alps; and (b) water scarcity: the dried-up landscape of the Tabernas badlands in southern Spain may be familiar if you are a fan of the old 'spaghetti western' films such as 'A Fistful of Dollars'. Although this region is in Europe, it is classified as semi-desert and receives rain on an average of just four days a year.

Study comment

Boxes such as Box 1.1 below are used to break off from the main theme, usually to introduce a new skill. The best time to study a box is when you are first referred to it but you may also like to refer back to the box later in your studies. Note that all the boxes in the course are listed in the index at the end of this book. This may be the quickest way of locating the page on which a particular box starts, if you want to refer back to one.

Box 1.1 Numbering conventions

You are probably used to the way in which consecutive chapters in a book are numbered (Chapter 1, Chapter 2, and so on). In this book the sections within each chapter are numbered as well so that they can be referred to easily. If a section is subdivided, the subsections may be numbered, for example, 4.1.1, 4.1.2 and 4.1.3. Note also the convention for numbering figures, tables, questions and activities in this course. The first number refers to the chapter in which it appears; the second number to the order within that chapter. For example, Figure 2.1 is the first figure in Chapter 2; Activity 5.2 is the second activity in Chapter 5.

'Water for life' is a huge theme, and it would be possible to write a much longer course that focused on this one subject. However, the aim is to not cover the theme comprehensively in S154. Instead a range of topics have been chosen, from the use of water by individuals in the United Kingdom (the UK, i.e. England, Northern Ireland, Scotland and Wales) to the threat of water pollution on a worldwide scale, and from how desert organisms survive arid conditions to the survival of plants and fish in ponds in freezing conditions.

1.1   … get set …

You already have your course material and by now you should have looked through the *Course Guide*. The section on what to do before the course starts is particularly important for this chapter. It will be assumed that you have done the tasks in the bulleted list at the start of that section and, in particular, that you have registered with an Internet Service Provider (ISP) and familiarised yourself with connecting your computer to the internet and using a browser.

If you haven't yet done this, it is important to do so now as you will need to access the course website in Activity 1.1. There is more information about this in the *Course Guide*.

The aim of this first chapter of the book is to give you the tools you need to study the course material effectively. In particular it is important that you make contact with your tutor, via email, early on in this course. You may have already done this but, if you don't yet know how to do so, there is guidance on this in Activity 1.4, the final activity in this chapter.

It is important to keep on schedule with your work, so you will find out how to plan your study time. For example this chapter, including the activities both in this book and in the *Course Guide*, is designed to be studied over about a week before you move on to Chapter 2. It will also take you about a week each to study Chapters 2 to 4 and some of the activities in these chapters are designed to help you organise your study time with this in mind. Later chapters will take more variable amounts of time and there is another planning activity in Chapter 5 when you will plan your study time for the remainder of the course.

Chapter 2 looks at how water is used in the UK and considers why water is important for life. Chapter 3 explores the amount of water in different organisms and how organisms that live in deserts manage to survive. Usually we all think of water as a liquid but it can also occur as ice and as water vapour. Chapter 4 considers some of the properties of these three forms of water and their relevance for living organisms. Chapter 5 takes a break from the main theme of the book and introduces writing skills that are important for communicating your understanding of science to other people: at the highest level some scientific theories are very complex and the originators have to be able to explain them clearly so that other people can understand them. At a more mundane level, you need to be able to answer assignment questions clearly so that your tutor knows you have understood the material that the question is based on. At various points in the course you will look at planning your study time, and any practical work, for the next stage.

You will put these skills into practice while studying Chapter 6, which looks at water at the molecular level, and Chapter 7, which explores the way in which human societies exploit water together with the environmental consequences of this exploitation. Chapter 8 and Chapter 9 present two 'case studies': in one you will investigate the role that water plays in living material while in the other you will learn how scientists deal with the infinitesimally small and the astronomically large. The course concludes in Chapter 10 with a brief discussion of the activities and responsibilities of scientists and, in so doing, looks at what 'science' is all about.

As well as exploring topics related to the theme 'water for life', you will be developing several essential skills, including:

- organising and planning your study time
- learning how to communicate electronically with your tutor and fellow students
- practising your writing skills so that you can communicate your understanding of science to other people
- learning and revising mathematical skills, including the use of a calculator
- reading this book 'actively' and writing your responses to questions and activities
- learning to use other study materials, such as interactive questions and video sequences
- keeping a learning journal.

Where you concentrate your main efforts while studying this course will depend on your current strengths and weaknesses. You may have left school with a dislike of mathematics and no maths qualifications; if so, you'll find it worthwhile taking your time working through the maths and calculator sections. In many cases these sections are in 'boxes' with one or two questions beforehand to check your understanding: if you have already done a lot of maths and are skilled at using a calculator, you may be able to do these questions fairly easily. If this is the case, you can read through those boxes quickly or even skip them altogether. However, even if you are fairly competent at maths, you may be less confident in written communication. If this is the case, you'll need to study the sections about communication quite carefully.

If this is your first Open University course, you will need to spend some time planning how to organise your time and your study materials, and trying out different strategies for learning from the various course materials. A range of activities have been provided that will help you with this (Box 1.2). Many of the activities include an online component where you are encouraged to contact your tutor by email or to discuss aspects of the course with other students in your tutor group.

Box 1.2 The philosophy of activities

I hear and I forget, I see and I remember, I do and I understand.

(Proverb attributed to the Chinese philosopher Confucius)

You will find that you learn much better if you interact with the course material rather than simply read it. For example, many people find it helpful to annotate the course text or make notes and the course also includes questions for you to try and 'activities'. These activities require you to stop your study of the text in order to do something else, for example carry out some practical work, join an email discussion or watch a video.

Whenever you complete an activity you should keep a note of your responses or results but it is up to you how you do this: you may prefer to file loose-leaf A4 sheets in a ring binder that you use as an S154 study folder (this is covered in Activity 1.2) or you might find it more convenient to keep notes on your computer.

An icon in the book margin as shown here indicates the type of activity, and where you may be directed to other resources, for example the *Course Guide*, a video sequence or online via the course website. A calculator icon indicates where you should use your calculator for a particular calculation. A notebook and pen icon is where you need to note things down in your study folder, and a magnifying glass icon indicates an activity with practical work.

There are comments on many of these activities and you should always read them *after* attempting the activity for yourself. You will find them on the course website.

1.2   ... go!

Start by completing Activity 1.1 which introduces you to the course website and shows you how to access the useful resources there.

Study comment

You will be given guidance on the likely length of time you will need to complete activities but the actual time you take may depend on factors such as your computer skills or the speed of your internet connection. By the end of this chapter you should have a better idea of whether the given estimates are realistic for you personally.

Activity 1.1   Exploring the course website

You should allow about 20 minutes for this activity.

S154 has its own website which provides you with an online 'home' during your study of the course. You should aim to check the website twice a week at least.

Access the course website and make some brief notes about what you find. (*Note*: the *Course Guide* contains step-by-step instructions for accessing the course website.) You may want to print a copy of the homepage and file it in your study folder for future reference.

On the course website homepage you should see a link to 'Course resources' where you will find electronic copies of the majority of course resources, including electronic versions of the course book, the *Course Guide* and the assessment. Check that you can access this material.

Briefly explore other areas of the course website so that you become familiar with the locations of the various resources such as the course calendar, comments on activities and the links from 'Forums' which take you to your Open University (OU) electronic mailbox and your tutor group forum. You will look at the 'Forums' link in more detail in Activity 1.4. Now read the comments on Activity 1.1, by clicking on the link on the course website.

1.3   Planning for effective study

Now consider the following questions.

- When are you going to study: are you an early bird or a night owl?
- When will study time fit in with the rest of your daily life – work, family, leisure?
- How will you organise your study materials so that you can find them quickly and easily?

Your time spent studying S154 will be most effective if you are well organised and plan carefully. Before you move on to Chapter 2, spend a little time thinking about when and where you will study and where you will keep your Open University course materials. The following activities will help you to plan study time into your week. They will also help you to think about where you will find it best to study and, finally, give you some tips on how to keep your course materials organised and accessible so that you don't waste valuable study time looking for a particular item.

You have probably realised by now that when you study and where you study are highly important. As you work through the next activity, make notes on any thoughts you have about these issues. Later in this chapter there will be a series of activities for you to carry out online: Activities 1.2, 1.3 and 1.4. These will supplement and reinforce what you have done earlier in the chapter. Be sure to allow plenty of time for the online activities. You should start to plan your study and begin making the necessary practical arrangements by completing Activities 1.2 and 1.3.

Activity 1.2   When and where will you study?

You should spend about 5 minutes on this part of the activity and allow about 30 minutes for its continuation online later in this chapter.

As you will be spending about 10 hours a week studying S154, and around 16 hours a week if you move on to a 60-point course such as S104, it is important to plan how you will fit in at least 10 hours of study per week over the 10-week duration of this course. Your study periods will need to fit in with other commitments, for example work and family, or times when a shared computer is available. Your timetable will also be affected by personal preferences: perhaps you are an early riser, or maybe you enjoy working late in the evening. Consider for a moment when during the day, and during the week, you are likely to be able to study and make some brief notes about this. File your notes in your study folder. You will refer back to them and plan your study timetable in more detail later in the continuation of this activity.

Now that you have thought about when to study, the next thing to decide is the best place to study. Ideally, this would be a place that you can use whenever you want to study, where you can keep your materials spread out and read and write comfortably, where you won't be distracted by other people you may live with and where you won't interfere with their activities. If you have your own computer then you will probably prefer to study where you can use this as you work; otherwise you could find it helpful to agree times when you can use a shared computer. Unfortunately, the ideal isn't always attainable so you may have to compromise. Where do you think will be the best place(s) for you to study? Make some brief notes now and file them in your study folder.

You will probably want to keep your course materials and study folder handy for your study sessions, but they will need some organisation and exactly how you organise them, and where you keep them, is best planned early. The next activity gives some hints about how to do this.

Activity 1.3   Organising your study materials

You should spend about 5 minutes on this part of the activity and allow a further 15 minutes for its continuation online later in this chapter.

As well as the first mailing of course materials, you will already have received material from other parts of the OU, sent either by post or electronically. Unless you organise this material, you will be unable to find information easily when you need it. The amount of material you receive will quickly build up, so a filing system is necessary. Think about how you could sort the materials you have received so far, for example classifying them as 'S154 course material', 'general information about OU' or 'information from Regional Centre'. You may want to file them in labelled boxes or ring binders.

As suggested earlier, it may be easiest to keep some information in a ring binder. You will be told from time to time to file material in your study folder so, if you don't already have something suitable, you should buy one, perhaps with a set of file dividers to separate the sections. When you receive information electronically you may want to print it and file it or you may prefer to save it in a folder on your computer. Whatever you decide, it is well worth making sure you keep information properly organised so that you can retrieve it quickly and easily when you want it.

You also need somewhere to store your books and files, calculator and writing materials so that they are readily accessible.

There are suggestions on the course website about keeping an electronic study folder and you will be guided to these in the continuation of this activity later.

1.4   The Open University – a virtual university?

Although some students never visit the central campus of The Open University at Walton Hall in Milton Keynes (Figure 1.2), be assured that it does exist and is a lively place, despite not having any undergraduates studying on campus.

Figure 1.2   The Open University campus at Walton Hall.

1.4.1   Welcome to the virtual campus!

When something is described as 'virtual' in the context of computers and the internet it means something that is not 'actual' but exists in effect: for example, a virtual conversation would be one that took place by exchanging typed text messages, maybe on mobile phones, rather than by people speaking to each other face-to-face or on the telephone. A virtual café is where you can meet your fellow students and your tutor (although, sadly, you will have to make your own coffee).

Unlike students studying on university campuses, OU students very often study in isolation and, except during tutorials and residential schools, can't join in the everyday face-to-face discussions that form such a dynamic, informative and enjoyable part of university life. Because of this, you are encouraged to take part in online communication with your tutor and fellow students. As well as its real campus (Figure 1.2), the OU has a virtual campus that is accessible to all students and staff. Here there are areas for the different faculties: for example, there is a science area where you will find virtual meeting places to discuss different study programmes and courses – including S154. There is an OU Students' Association (OUSA) area where you can find out about the clubs and societies run by the students for the students, including several societies for enthusiasts of different areas of science.

The online communication that happens in these areas is generally in online discussion groups called forums. Although there is an instant messaging facility, the forums mainly use email postings to a message board that can be read and replied to when convenient by anyone who has access to the forum.*

Communication is immensely important for scientists: for example, they collaborate on research by communicating with each other, often by email, so that they can easily discuss their thoughts with colleagues around the world. When scientists want to make the results of their research known, they publish them as 'papers' in scientific journals: today these are usually available online and OU students and staff can access a wide range of scientific journal articles through the OU Library.

However, as another Chinese philosopher Lao Tse said, over two and a half millennia ago, 'the longest journey starts with a single step'. This is still true today and for now it is sufficient for you to start by taking the step of contacting your tutor and your tutor group. The related Activity 1.4 'Experiencing the virtual campus' at the end of this chapter will guide you through making this contact by:

- having virtual conversations with other students
- contacting your tutor by email.

Later in this course you will be asked to send information to your tutor or to discuss the results of an experiment with your fellow students. However, at this stage you don't need to do more than make contact, in the same way as you might if you met them on a university campus and said 'Hi!'

Next you will complete Activities 1.2 and 1.3 on planning your study, and then Activity 1.4, which involves accessing the online tutor group forum. These activities are all online, so you may want to do them together.

---

* A forum was the public square of an ancient Roman city where meetings and public business took place. The term is now applied to internet meeting places.

Activity 1.2   When and where will you study? (continued)

You should allow about 30 minutes on this part of Activity 1.2.

You will continue the work you did earlier in this chapter by exploring the online Study Support guidance that is available through the course website. There is advice to read and consider about when, and where, to study. After that you will be shown how to download a study planner that you can use when you plan your study of the rest of S154.

Detailed information on this activity is given in the *Course Guide*.

Activity 1.3   Organising your study materials (continued)

You should allow about 15 minutes on this part of Activity 1.3.

During this chapter you have been advised to use a study folder. This activity deals in more depth with keeping a study folder and contains useful guidance on accessing online materials such as templates that you can use. There are some examples of study folders which you can look at to give you an idea of what other students have found helpful.

Detailed information on this activity is given in the *Course Guide*.

Activity 1.4   Experiencing the virtual campus

You should allow about 15 minutes for this activity.

In the final activity of this chapter, you will make contact with the other students in your tutor group using your group's online discussion forum. You will also send an email to your tutor to say how you are getting on and what your study plans are for the coming week.

Detailed information on this activity is given in the *Course Guide.*

1.5   Summary of Chapter 1

Learning is most effective when you interact with material rather than simply reading it.

There is a course website where you can access course material and resources: you should aim to check this twice a week at least.

Planning when and where to study, and how to organise your material, is highly important.

A study folder is an excellent way to keep a permanent record of your study.

Although OU undergraduates do not study on campus they can interact with other students in the same tutor group by email through their tutor group forum and with other students generally through the forums run by the OUSA societies.

Email is a convenient way to keep in touch with your tutor.

Each chapter ends with a summary and a list of learning outcomes. The summary contains the important points and skills introduced in that chapter. These are the points that you should know and the skills that you should be familiar with. The learning outcomes indicate what you should be able to do and to understand at the end of your study of the chapter, and these may be assessed as part of the course.

Learning outcomes for Chapter 1

When you have completed Chapter 1 you should be able to:

- Understand the numbering conventions used in this book.
- Organise your time and study materials to study effectively.
- Find resources on the S154 course website.
- Communicate online with your tutor and fellow students.

Now that you have completed Chapter 1, you should be much more prepared to study the rest of S154 effectively. As you continue with the course, you will be reminded at various stages to email your tutor or to join in with a discussion in your online tutor group forum. You will also be prompted to carry out other activities, and some of these will count towards your assessment. In addition to these activities, when prompted to do so, remember to check StudentHome (your online homepage), the course website and your OU mailbox (for emails) regularly.

The course team hope that, even though it isn't a compulsory part of the course, you will also become an active member of the Open University's 'virtual campus' environment and enjoy the experience of being a student!

Certain important key points are highlighted in this way to emphasise them.

Remember to file any more notes you have made in your study folder before moving on to Chapter 2.

Chapter 2
Life in the desert?

The theme of this course is 'water for life'. This may conjure up a variety of images in your mind, but the image shown in Figure 2.1 is unlikely to be one of them! These dry bones, which were excavated in a desert location, give the very opposite impression to 'water for life'. However, this contrast emphasises that life, in all its known forms, critically depends on the presence of water. Where there is no water, there is no life.

In this chapter you will start your exploration of the theme 'water for life' by considering how the skeleton shown in Figure 2.1 came to be in this inhospitable desert location, where very little water is available. You will then see how the distribution of the world's population is related to the availability of water, and look at the pattern of water use in the UK and at different water-based fluids essential to keep the human body functioning properly.

Figure 2.1   Skeleton of an adolescent female discovered during an excavation of a ruined town in the Egyptian Sahara Desert.

In addition, this chapter will introduce several skills that should be useful throughout your study of science, such as reading information from diagrams and tables and using a calculator for arithmetic and for working out percentages. You will also be encouraged to think about the amount of time you are spending on your studies and how effectively you are spending that time. Chapter 2 should take you about 10 hours of study time. Remember that you will need to plan your time carefully to allow for periods when you will need to use your computer, for example in completing Activities 2.1 and 2.2 (near the beginning of the chapter), studying a video sequence in Activity 2.4 (at the end of the chapter) and attempting the online assessment questions relating to this chapter.

Activity 2.1   Keeping a learning journal

You should allow about 30 minutes for this activity initially and then about 10 minutes weekly updating your journal.

As you work through Chapter 2, you should keep a log of when you study, noting which days, what times of day and roughly how long you study for in each session. Then add any relevant comments: for example, reflect on whether the session went well or not, and the reasons for this. Did you study for as long as you had planned or for a shorter or longer time and, if so, why? A log of this sort is called a learning journal – see Box 2.1.

You may find it convenient to make notes in a notebook, but you should transfer these notes to your computer at least once a week.

Read through Box 2.1 first, and make your first entry in your learning journal. Detailed information on this activity is given in the *Course Guide*.

Box 2.1   Your learning journal

Throughout your study of this course, you should keep an online study diary or 'learning journal'. You should use it to record your thoughts and reflections on your studies. You may be asked to submit extracts of your learning journal to your tutor with your answers to an assessment question as evidence that you have demonstrated a particular learning outcome for the course.

The main purpose of your learning journal is to enable you to study in a methodical and productive way by:

- reflecting on the week or chapter of study you have just completed
- looking ahead and planning for the coming week or chapter

and your tutor will look for evidence of this in your comments.

Why keep a learning journal?

This can help you to develop your learning skills. If you have not done any formal studying for some time, this is especially important. Studying a university course is different from being at school or doing a training course at work. You will need to be more in control of your own learning and you will need to do a lot more thinking for yourself.

This makes it more challenging but also much more exciting. Keeping a learning journal makes you aware of your strengths and weaknesses, so that you can develop strategies to improve your learning and make it more enjoyable.

Will it take up a lot of time?

It need not. You can write as often as you like and as much as you like. However, you will learn more about your way of working if you write a few notes after each period of study, even if you spent only 15 minutes reading or watching a short video sequence.

What goes into a learning journal?

It is completely up to you. It would be useful to describe briefly the work that you did, but what is most important is to comment on how you think it went, whether you were able to do what you planned or met difficulties. Here are some topics you might find helpful, although you don't have to keep to these and may choose to include others instead or as well:

- Skills used
- What was good about it?
- Problems I encountered
- How I might resolve problems
- Action I need to take

What can I do about problems?

You may want to suggest some possible solutions to yourself. These could include choosing a different time of day to work, having more realistic objectives, discussing the topic with fellow students on the telephone or in your tutor group forum, or contacting your tutor.

For your learning journal to be useful, you need to be as honest as you can.

2.1 Bones in the desert

The skeleton shown in Figure 2.1 was discovered in the early 1980s by a French archaeological team when excavating a ruined town in the Egyptian Sahara Desert. It is the skeleton of an adolescent girl who lived about 4200 years ago. As Figure 2.2 shows, the Egyptian Sahara region is now an arid desert; there is no vegetation in sight. This is the driest part of the Sahara, with perhaps one or two centimetres of rain in a year.

Activity 2.2   Asking questions

You should allow about 15 minutes for this activity.

As a scientist you will need to ask questions. Suppose you had discovered the girl's skeleton. What questions might have occurred to you about how it came to be in a desert location?

Next time you access your tutor group forum, you should discuss your questions with your tutor and other students in your group.

Asking questions is an important step in the process of discovering more about the world around you, and your group's list might include questions that would occur to an archaeologist who unearthed a skeleton in an unlikely location. Archaeology is the scientific study of human antiquities, and archaeologists share many of the same scientific methods of working as the biologists, chemists, Earth scientists and physicists who will figure much more prominently in this course.

There have been extensive archaeological excavations in the Egyptian Sahara, and they have allowed archaeologists to build up a fascinating picture of the area. Of particular interest in the context of the 'water for life' theme is the fact that the Sahara has not always been a desert. Going back 20 000 years, to a time when northwest Europe was covered by a thick ice sheet, the Sahara was rich grassland that provided hunting grounds for prehistoric people. Stone tools from this period have been found in the desert, as well as remnants of ostrich eggs and evidence of early farming. However, about 10 000 years ago, as the Earth warmed and as the ice receded from Europe, the climate of North Africa changed to become the hot, dry desert climate that is now familiar. The human and animal populations moved either north to the Mediterranean coast, east to the Nile valley, or south, in each case to regions where water was available. The once-rich grassland was replaced by barren desert, punctuated in places by oases, where underground water allowed date palms and fruit trees to grow. It is thought that the place where the skeleton was found was such an oasis 4200 years ago.

Figure 2.2 Parched desert landscape in the Egyptian Sahara Desert.

Study comment

In the following paragraph two terms appear in **bold**. These are terms that you are expected to be able to explain the meaning of, and use correctly, both during your study of the course and at the end of the course. You will find definitions of these terms in the Course Glossary, which is in the 'Course resources' area of the course website.

The research that established the skeleton's origins illustrates the **scientific method**, a term used to describe the way in which knowledge and understanding advance in a wide range of scientific subjects. An archaeological discovery, such as the unearthing of the girl's skeleton, would generally be a new piece of information that had to be fitted into a jigsaw puzzle of existing knowledge about early civilisations in that area. This could lead archaeologists to develop an **hypothesis**, a tentative explanation, based on the available evidence, of the part the girl and her town played in those civilisations. In order to test the hypothesis, they would look for further evidence about the girl's lifestyle, possibly from additional excavations at the same site or at a different site, or by making some scientific measurements of the bones or objects found at the site. Subsequent discoveries might confirm part or all of the initial hypothesis, and might allow the hypothesis to be developed further. On the other hand, new evidence might cause the archaeologists to make some changes, or modifications, to their hypothesis, or even to reject the initial hypothesis and replace it with a completely new one. For example, new evidence about burial rituals might suggest that the girl had died elsewhere and been moved to the burial place where she was found.

Archaeologists are now very confident about their current hypothesis: the ruined town flourished in a desert oasis in Ancient Egypt's Sixth Dynasty, about 4200 years ago. However, it is always possible that some important future find, or some re-evaluation of previous work, will make archaeologists modify the hypothesis, or even reject it in favour of a completely different hypothesis. This constant process of re-evaluation is a characteristic of the world of science, and scientists should always be open to the possibility that new experiments, observations or discoveries may overthrow even a highly favoured hypothesis. That's one of the reasons why science is so exciting!

2.2 People don't live in deserts

The need for water to maintain human life, for both essential drinking water and cultivating food, means that human populations in desert areas are generally very low. Populations are very much higher where there are plentiful supplies of water. This is evident from comparing the two maps in Figure 2.3 but, before you do this, look at Box 2.2 'Reading illustrations', which introduces an important skill for studying science.

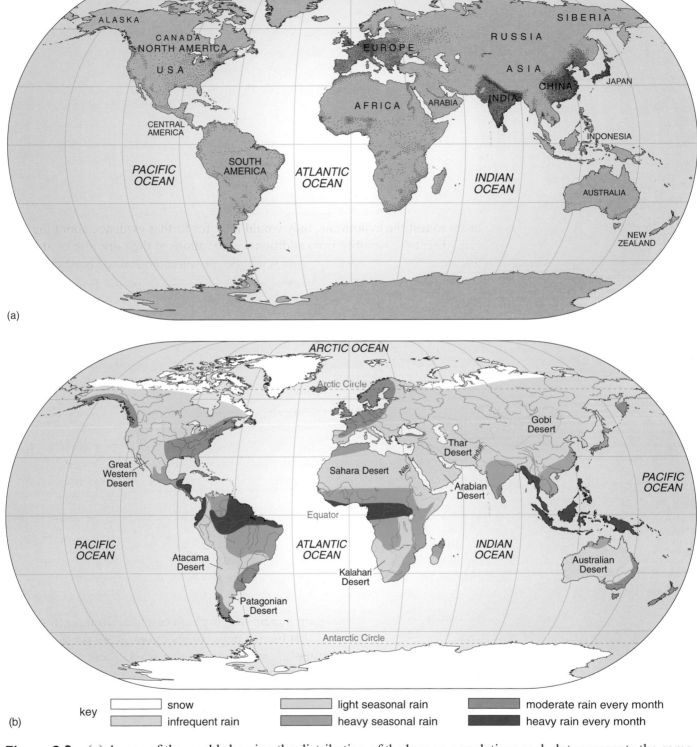

(a)

(b)

key

| snow | light seasonal rain | moderate rain every month |
| infrequent rain | heavy seasonal rain | heavy rain every month |

Figure 2.3   (a) A map of the world showing the distribution of the human population; each dot represents the same number of people. (b) A map showing world rainfall; the annual rainfall in different areas is indicated by the colour, and the meaning of each colour is shown in the key. A comparison of (a) and (b) shows that populations in desert areas are low unless abundant sources of water are available from elsewhere.

Box 2.2   Reading illustrations

Recall for a moment the layout of a novel. Almost certainly it consists of a few hundred pages of print, unbroken by any illustrations. Not all books are like that, of course. For example, both cookery books and do-it-yourself manuals are usually well illustrated with photographs, drawings, diagrams, etc.

■   The illustrations in cookery books and do-it-yourself manuals usually serve very different purposes. What are these?

☐   Those in a cookery book are largely to make the book look more interesting and to tempt you. They are normally photographs of a finished dish at its mouth-watering best. Those in a do-it-yourself manual are normally designed to help you see how to carry out a particular task.

Study comment

Questions like the one above are designed to make you stop and think about what you have just read and help you progress to the next step. The answer follows immediately, so you can reassure yourself that you are following the argument. However, you will get the most from the text if you cover up the answer while you try to answer the question for yourself.

The first two illustrations you saw in this chapter (Figures 2.1 and 2.2) are in the category of 'largely for interest'. They are there to lend some sense of reality to the notion of human bones found in a desert, and to break up a page or so of printed text. Figure 2.3 is different. It conveys important information and is an integral part of the teaching of Section 2.2, and this is why you will be asked to do some work on it. Most of the illustrations in this book, and in other scientific texts you will read, serve this purpose. You will not be asked to do some work on every illustration you meet, but you will be expected to 'read' all of them in order to understand how they clarify or add to what you are reading in the text.

Most of the illustrations have a figure number for identification and ease of reference – it's 2.3 for the maps that precede this box. As you read the text, you will find a reference to the figure number, and that is the best point at which to examine the figure. Along with the figure number there will be a figure caption (or title); this explains what the illustration is showing, and the caption is the best place to start 'reading' the illustration. So for Figure 2.3, the caption first tells you that there are two parts to the figure, (a) and (b), and they are maps that show world population distribution and world rainfall, respectively. It also tells you something about how these quantities are represented on the maps.

As you will appreciate, because the Earth is a sphere the views in Figure 2.3 are not those you would see if you could look down on the Earth from space. Figure 6.2 (in Chapter 6) is an example of a view from a satellite, and it shows only the part of the Earth that was facing the satellite when the photograph was taken. The advantage of maps like those in Figure 2.3 is that they allow the whole surface of the Earth to be shown in one picture. Scientists often use diagrams to represent particular aspects of an object, and these diagrams are rarely accurate representations of all aspects of the object. The population map, for example, shows the world as a flat sheet, with Alaska a long way from Siberia, whereas a look at a globe will show that they are close together.

However, as long as you bear in mind the limitations of this sort of map, it is a very useful way to convey information about the population of all regions of the world in a single diagram.

Figure 2.3a shows how densely populated the different areas of the Earth are. The population information is conveyed by the dots on the map, and the caption tells you that each dot represents the same number of people. This means that, where the dots are very close together, more people live in that region. In other words, there is a high **population density** in that region. England, for example, has a high population density overall, and the dots are close together there. If you live in a rural area, you may find this concept hard to comprehend, but the low population density in the countryside is balanced by a far higher population density in cities and towns. To read Figure 2.3a in the context of Section 2.2, you don't need to know how many people each dot represents. All you need to know is that the more dots there are in a given area, the more densely populated that area is. The impact is immediate.

■   From Figure 2.3a, which are the most densely populated areas of the world?

☐   You should have picked India, China, Japan and Europe. The dots are the closest together in these areas.

Figure 2.3b shows how rainfall (or snowfall) varies in different regions of the world. This time there is a **key** to show you what the different colours on the map mean. Hot desert areas where it seldom rains are yellow, and areas where there is heavy rainfall throughout the year are dark blue.

■   Consider the visual impact of Figure 2.3b. Do you think the colours used were chosen arbitrarily?

☐   No, the colours have associations. Blue is traditionally the colour of the sea, a watery environment: the darker the blue, the more watery the environment. Yellow is the colour of sand, which is associated with deserts. These sorts of associations make it easy to distinguish at a glance the wet areas from the dry areas.

Several features have been labelled in Figure 2.3b that were not labelled in Figure 2.3a, notably the locations of the Equator and the Arctic and Antarctic Circles. They were not labelled on Figure 2.3a because they were irrelevant to the discussion of the world population distribution. However, they are relevant to the consideration of world rainfall and deserts. You probably associate the Arctic Circle with cold temperatures and the Equator with hot temperatures. The closer to the Equator you are, in general, the higher the average annual temperatures and so the more likely you are to find hot deserts if there is little rain. Beyond the Arctic Circle, you are likely to experience snowfall rather than rainfall.

Later, in Chapters 3 and 4, you will explore the function of illustrations a little more. Meanwhile, as you encounter each new illustration you should stop to think about its function – is it largely for interest or is it an integral part of the teaching? Then write down, either in the book margin or in your study folder, the important points that you read from it.

It was said at the start of Section 2.2 that the populations in desert areas are generally very low. Regarding this as an initial hypothesis, you can see whether it is supported by evidence from the maps in Figure 2.3. Figure 2.3a shows how densely populated the different areas of the Earth are. If you look at this map, you will see that there are many areas where there are practically no dots at all, indicating that there are extremely few people living there.

■ Do these areas of low population density coincide with any of the desert areas that you know of?

☐ There is clearly a low population density in North Africa, which corresponds to the location of the Sahara Desert. Another low population density area is shown in Australia, where there are also large regions of desert. You may have identified others.

This information clearly supports the initial hypothesis that very few people live in desert areas, but now you can look a little deeper. Figure 2.3b allows you to make a comparison between population density and rainfall. Hot desert areas where it seldom rains are coloured yellow, and the names of many of the deserts are shown. Many of these areas are located in two bands on either side of the Equator.

■ Does a comparison of the two maps in Figure 2.3 confirm that very few people live in these hot desert areas? Are there any exceptions?

☐ Desert areas shown in the map in Figure 2.3b generally match up with the low population density areas shown in Figure 2.3a. Two clear exceptions that you might have noticed are along the Nile river valley in Egypt, and along the Indus river valley in Pakistan.

The Nile and Indus valleys have desert climates with little rainfall. The large rivers that give their names to these valleys bring water from the mountains, which can be used for drinking, crop irrigation, and so on, so that high populations can be supported in these areas. Therefore, the initial hypothesis has to be modified; a revised hypothesis is 'populations in desert areas are very low unless abundant sources of water are available from outside the region'.

The procedure that you have just followed illustrates the scientific method introduced in Section 2.1. An initial hypothesis is made based on a few observations; this hypothesis is tested by making further observations; and then it is revised to make it consistent with all of the observations.

The general conclusion to be drawn from these observations is that water is essential for humans, and human populations are concentrated in regions where they have access to the life-giving liquid.

Activity 2.3   Writing in your own words

You should allow about 10 minutes for this activity.

An effective way to check and reinforce your understanding of a key concept is to write a summary of that concept in your own words. Explaining the term *without looking back at the text* will indicate how much you have learned from the course. It will also mean that you are more likely to explain the concept in your own words. However, if you find this too difficult – and this is perfectly reasonable at this stage in the course – go back and read the relevant part(s) of the text, make a few notes and then *close the book* and write your response from your notes. This avoids the temptation to copy phrases from the book and is more likely to ensure that you use your own words.

(a) Try to write down, in a few sentences and without looking back at the text, what you understand by the term 'scientific method'.

(b) Look at the explanation of the scientific method in Section 2.1, make a few notes, then close the book and make any changes necessary to your answer to part (a).

Look at the comments on this activity when you next visit the course website.

2.3   How much water do you use?

All the information considered so far, such as that in the maps in Figure 2.3, has been **qualitative**. This means that it did not involve numerical information. In this section you will look at **quantitative** information, i.e. measurements with numbers attached to them.

Global water use has increased over the centuries not only because the world population has increased but also because water is now used in a huge range of additional ways that the girl in Figure 2.1 would never have dreamt of.

■   Name some of the ways water is used today that would have been unfamiliar to the girl who lived in the Egyptian Sahara 4200 years ago (Section 2.1).

☐   More water is used for washing and cleaning (baths and showers, washing machines and dishwashers, flushing toilets). In addition, water is used in manufacturing industries, in electricity generation and for recreational activities (e.g. swimming pools).

Table 2.1 (overleaf) shows information about the domestic use of water in the UK. The left-hand column of the table lists the main ways in which water is used, and beside each is indicated the average amount of water used each day for each person in the UK. Of course, these figures are estimates rather than precisely measured amounts. The water supply companies have no way of keeping track of how the tens of millions of households use all of the water that they supply. They base their estimates on surveys of a range of different types of households, carried out over extended periods of time to allow for seasonal variations, and they use the survey results to estimate typical values for the whole population. So it shouldn't be surprising if your use of water doesn't correspond to the pattern shown in Table 2.1 – you are not necessarily a 'typical' water user!

Tables of information are widely used in science and Box 2.3 explains some of the important points to look out for when interpreting data that have been presented in this way.

Table 2.1 Estimated daily domestic use of water per person in the UK*.

Use of water	Volume/ litres
baths and showers, etc.	50
flushing toilet	37
clothes washing	21
dish washing	12
garden watering	9
drinking and cooking	6
car washing	1
miscellaneous	14

* Source: based on figures published by the Environment Agency, 2001.

Box 2.3   Reading tables

Tables provide a neat and concise way of displaying and comparing information, and information given in a table can be referred to quickly, without having to read through large sections of text.

Note the following important features in Table 2.1, which are common to all tables of this type:

- a title
- a heading at the top of each column
- the 'volume' heading includes the **unit** of the measurement (litres in this case), so the unit does not have to be repeated after each number in the column.

Look at the data in Table 2.1. To discover the estimated amount of water used in washing clothes, for example, look down the first column to find the row that says 'clothes washing', and then read across this row to the number displayed, which is 21. But 21 what? The column heading makes it clear that the number means that 21 litres of water are used in washing clothes and the title of the table tells you that this 21 litres is the estimated amount of water used daily per person in the UK for washing clothes.

■ How much water, as an estimate, does each person in the UK use per day for baths and showers, etc.?

□ The answer is 50 litres. Remember to include units with your answer otherwise saying '50' doesn't make it clear that the amount is in litres – not gallons, pints or drops!

Note the way in which the volume column heading and its units are given as 'Volume/litres'.

Where appropriate, it is conventional to use 'quantity divided by units' (usually in the form 'quantity/units') in labelling the column headings in tables.

(You will discover in Chapter 3 that the 'quantity/units' convention is also used when labelling the axes of graphs, and the reason for this convention is explained in Box 2.5 'Fractions, percentages and ratios'.)

Question 2.1

To practise reading the information in Table 2.1, answer the following questions.

(a) How much water does the average person in the UK use each day in the home for flushing the toilet?

(b) What does the number 6 in the third row from the bottom of the table mean?

Study comment

The numbered questions should help consolidate your understanding of the text you have just read and so should be tackled when you reach them. You should write your answer in the book margin or in your study folder. You should do this *before* referring to the answers given at the end of the book.

Table 2.1 gives data only for domestic water use; commercial and industrial use of the mains supply is excluded. In addition, many industrial and agricultural users of water get their supply directly from rivers or the ground, without going through the treatment works or distribution system of the public water supply, and the dominant source of water for agriculture in the UK – for growing crops – is the direct precipitation of rain and snow. Also, power stations and industries that use large amounts of water are often sited on the coast or on river estuaries, and use seawater for cooling purposes. Cooling water is generally returned to its source – river, estuary or sea – albeit a few degrees warmer. The water returned to a river from a power station may well be removed again further downstream to be used for industry, agriculture or domestic consumption.

To make more sense of the numbers in Table 2.1, you will need to do some calculations involving the addition, subtraction, multiplication and division of these numbers. You will probably want to use your calculator (or the calculator program on your computer) for some or all of these calculations. The course website gives details of the types of scientific calculator recommended for this course but, unfortunately, different calculators operate in slightly different ways, so comprehensive instructions on how to use *your* calculator cannot be provided. However, at key points where you need to use your calculator for a specific purpose, some guidelines are provided on the most likely buttons to use. These guidelines, combined with the manufacturer's operating instructions, should enable you to use your calculator effectively, and you should check that you can when advised to do so. If you cannot use your calculator to get the expected result, you should contact your tutor as soon as possible.

To check that you are confident at doing calculations, both with and without a calculator, you should try Question 2.2. If you are not sure how to do the calculations in this question – or if you get them wrong in any way – you are strongly advised to study Box 2.4, before moving on.

Question 2.2

Do the following calculations *without using your calculator*. Then check that you can also get the correct answers using your calculator.

(a) $3 \times 10 \div 2$

(b) $8 + 2 \times 5$

(c) 3×2^2

(d) $(5 + 3) \div 2$

(e) $(2 + 3)^2 \times 2$

(f) 10 litres + 5 litres − 2 litres

Box 2.4 Doing calculations, with or without a calculator

For this course it is assumed that you can add, subtract, multiply and divide whole numbers.

■ Check that you can do the following four calculations without using a calculator: $9 + 3$; $9 - 3$; 9×3; $9 \div 3$.

☐ You should have obtained the following answers: $9 + 3 = 12$; $9 - 3 = 6$; $9 \times 3 = 27$; $9 \div 3 = 3$.

Check that you can use your calculator to obtain the same answers as before. You are likely to need to enter the numbers and symbols in a simple sequence from left to right (e.g. '9' then '+' then '3') and then to press the '=' key. However, some calculators use the symbol '*' instead of '×' for multiplication and '/' instead of '÷' for division, and at least one requires the user to press 'Enter' instead of '=' to get the answer. Check your calculator now!

Many scientific calculations are rather more complicated than those discussed above, in that they involve several steps. In some of these calculations, for example $9 + 3 + 5 + 2$, $3 + 4 - 2$, $5 \times 2 \times 7$, $6 \times 2 \div 3$, you simply need to start at the left and work through to the right. So in the first example, adding 9 and 3 gives 12, adding another 5 gives 17 and adding another 2 gives the final answer of 19.

■ Check that you can do the following three calculations both without and with a calculator: $3 + 4 - 2$; $5 \times 2 \times 7$; $6 \times 2 \div 3$.

☐ You should have obtained the following answers: $3 + 4 - 2 = 5$; $5 \times 2 \times 7 = 70$; $6 \times 2 \div 3 = 4$.

Question 2.3

Use your calculator to find answers to the following.

(a) $38 + 92 - 61$

(b) $24 \times 32 \times 8$

(c) $24 \times 32 \div 8$

Doing calculations in the right order

Now consider the calculation $3 + 2 \times 4$. If you simply work from left to right in this case, adding 3 and 2 gives 5, then multiplying by 4 gives 20, *but this is the incorrect answer.*

There is a rule, applied by mathematicians and scientists everywhere, which states: multiplication and division should be carried out before addition and subtraction.

Applying this rule to the calculation $3 + 2 \times 4$, the multiplication of 2 and 4 should be done first, giving 8, then the 3 is added to give the correct final answer of 11. Most modern calculators 'know' this rule (which is known as a rule of **precedence**, where precedence means 'priority'), so entering $3 + 2 \times 4$ into your calculator in exactly the order in which it is written should give the correct answer of 11. Check this now.

Question 2.4

Do the following calculations *without using your calculator.* Then use your calculator to check the answers.

(a) $3 \times 4 + 2$

(b) $2 + 4 \times 3$

(c) $4 \times 2 - 21 \div 7$

What about powers?

Most people are familiar with the fact that 5×5 can also be written as 5^2 (said as 'five squared') and $4 \times 4 \times 4$ as 4^3 (said as 'four cubed'). This shorthand notation can be extended indefinitely, so $2 \times 2 \times 2 \times 2 \times 2 \times 2$ becomes 2^6 (said as 'two to the power of six', or more usually just as 'two to the six'). In this example, the 2 is called the **base number** and the superscript 6 (indicating the number of twos that have been multiplied together) is variously called the **power**, the **exponent** or the **index** (plural **indices**).

■ Use your calculator's instruction booklet to find out how to enter a base number raised to a power, such as 2^6.

☐ You may have a button labelled 'x^y', in which case you should press '2' then 'x^y' then '6'. Alternatively, you may have a button labelled '$^\wedge$' in which case you should press '2' then '$^\wedge$' then '6'. (Note that $2^6 = 64$; your calculator may calculate this value straight away.)

If you are asked to calculate, say, 5×3^2 there is another rule of precedence.

Powers should be calculated before multiplication, division, addition or subtraction.

So, in the example of 5×3^2 the 3^2 should be evaluated first:

$$3^2 = 3 \times 3 = 9$$

then

$$5 \times 3^2 = 5 \times 9 = 45$$

(Note that the instruction 'to **evaluate**' simply means to work out the value of an expression.)

Question 2.5

Do the following calculations *without using your calculator*. Then use your calculator to check the answers.

(a) 3^3

(b) 3×5^2

(c) $3^2 + 4^2$

The role of brackets

Sometimes you need to do the addition or subtraction in a calculation before the multiplication, or to add two numbers together before raising to a power. The way to override the standard rules of 'multiplication before addition' and 'powers before multiplication', etc. is to use brackets.

Brackets in a calculation mean 'do this first'.

So, in the calculation $(3 + 2) \times 4$, you should add the 3 and the 2 first (to give 5), then multiply by 4, i.e. $(3 + 2) \times 4 = 5 \times 4 = 20$. Similarly, in the calculation $(3 + 4)^2$, you should add the 3 and the 4 first before squaring. So $(3 + 4)^2 = 7^2 = 49$. Note that these give different answers from the calculations *without* brackets: for example, $3 + 2 \times 4 = 3 + 8 = 11$.

You can do calculations including brackets on a scientific calculator by using its brackets keys. Try the calculation $(3 + 2) \times 4$ on your calculator now, and make sure that you can get an answer of 20 not 11.

If you have a calculation which involves nested brackets, work out the innermost sets first. For example:

$$20 \div [(3 - 1) \times (3 + 2)] = 20 \div [2 \times 5] = 20 \div 10 = 2$$

Note that using different symbols for the brackets, for example ( ), [ ] and { }, makes the calculation clearer than using the same symbol throughout the calculation.

Strictly speaking, brackets are only needed to override the other rules of precedence, and they are not needed in calculations such as $3 + (2 \times 4)$. In the absence of the brackets, you or your calculator would follow the rule and do the multiplication first in any case. However, brackets are often used in calculations for clarity, even when they are not strictly necessary. For example, the calculation $6 \times 4 + 12 \times 5$ is more understandable and 'readable' if it is written as $(6 \times 4) + (12 \times 5)$, even though the brackets are not essential here. You are encouraged to write brackets in your calculations whenever they help you to express your working more clearly.

So far in this course, the four arithmetic operations have been written as +, −, × and ÷. However, in scientific calculations, division is more usually written as a fraction (see Box 2.5 for more about fractions). Twelve divided by three could equally accurately be written as $12 \div 3$, 12/3 or $\frac{12}{3}$.

In a slightly more complicated example, $(8 + 4) \div 3$ could equally accurately be written as $(8 + 4)/3$ or as $\frac{8 + 4}{3}$.

Note that the bracket, used to indicate that the addition should be done before the division in this case, has been omitted from the final statement of this expression. This is because the horizontal line used to indicate division acts as an 'invisible bracket', i.e.:

$$\frac{8+4}{3} = \frac{(8+4)}{3} = \frac{12}{3} = 4$$

BEDMAS

Fortunately, there is an easy way to remember the correct order in which arithmetic operations should be carried out. The rules are neatly summed up in the mnemonic* **BEDMAS**. The letters in BEDMAS stand for Brackets, Exponents, Division, Multiplication, Addition and Subtraction and the order of the letters gives the order in which the operations should be carried out. You should work out the Brackets first, then the Exponents (otherwise known as indices or powers), then any Divisions and Multiplications, and finally the Additions and Subtractions. You may see BIDMAS (where the 'I' stands for 'Indices') or BODMAS instead of BEDMAS; the three expressions are equivalent.

There is one final point to make about the order in which arithmetic should be done. When faced with a calculation that includes a series of multiplications and divisions (or a series of additions and subtractions), you should work through the calculation *from left to right in the order in which it is written*.

___

*A mnemonic (pronounced 'nem-on-ick') is a set of letters or a phrase that make up some memorable word or name that helps you remember the correct order of a sequence. For example, ROY G BIV is a mnemonic that tells you the order of the colours in the rainbow: red, orange, yellow, green, blue, indigo and violet. Another popular 'rainbow' mnemonic is 'Richard Of York Gave Battle In Vain'.

Question 2.6

To practise the BEDMAS rules, try the following calculations both in your head and with your calculator.

(a) $150 \div 10 \times 3$

(b) $(2 \times 3)^2$

(c) 2×3^2

(d) $[(10 - 5) \times (3 + 1)] + 4$

(e) $\dfrac{18 + 6}{3}$

(f) $\dfrac{18}{3} + 6$

What your calculator doesn't tell you – the unit of the answer

In considering the figures for water use given in Table 2.1, often the results of calculations need to include units of measurement in addition to numbers. However, calculators deal only with the numbers; how do you decide what the unit of the answer to a calculation should be?

The answer comes from the fact that *the unit must be the same on both sides of an equation*, just as the numbers are. For example, if you want to add 3 litres and 5 litres, a calculator (or mental arithmetic) will tell you that $3 + 5 = 8$. Then, since the unit must be the same on both sides of the equation, the answer must be 8 litres, i.e. 3 litres + 5 litres = 8 litres. An important consequence of this requirement is that you can't add or subtract quantities unless both quantities have the same unit. You can't add 2 litres and 5 gallons; the total amount is neither 7 litres nor 7 gallons. To find the total amount, you need to convert 5 gallons into litres (or 2 litres into gallons) so that you are adding amounts measured in the same unit. Units are discussed further in Box 3.2 'Units of measurement' and throughout the course.

The online interactive questions for Chapter 2 will give you more practice in the skills developed in Box 2.4.

Question 2.7

Use the information in Table 2.1 to calculate:

(a) the total domestic use of water per person per day in the UK

(b) the difference between the total daily domestic use per person (your answer to part (a)) and the amount used outdoors (for garden watering and car washing)

(c) the volume of water used per person *per week*, and per person *per year*, for baths and showers.

Question 2.8

Write down an arithmetical expression for each of the following situations, and then use your calculator to work out the answers. As an example, suppose you had been told that the daily domestic use of water by a particular family of four is typically 440 litres, and asked to find the annual use per person. The annual use must be 365 times the daily use, and the use per person is found by dividing the family use by four. So an arithmetic expression is 440 × 365 ÷ 4. Then since 440 × 365 ÷ 4 = 40 150, the annual use per person is 40 150 litres.

(a) Three people sharing accommodation each use 145 litres of water in a day. They use 15 litres, 25 litres and 40 litres, respectively, for baths and showers. How much water do they together use for all other purposes?

(b) What is the estimated daily volume of water used for baths and showers, flushing toilets, and in washing clothes by a family of four 'typical' people?

Activity 2.1   Keeping a learning journal (continued)

You should allow about 10 minutes for this part of Activity 2.1.

Have you brought your journal up to date yet? If not, spend a few minutes completing it for your study of Chapter 2 so far. Look back at Box 2.1 'Your learning journal' and use the suggestions there if you are unsure about what to include.

2.4   Saving water

In Section 2.3 you considered the daily domestic water use per person in the UK. The numbers given in Table 2.1 are estimates for the whole population, averaged over the year. Clearly, there will be seasonal variations in domestic water use, and when droughts lead to water shortages there can be dramatic changes to the levels and patterns of water use. In this section you will look at some of the savings that could be made in water consumption to cope with drought conditions (or to reduce water bills that are based on the amount of water supplied).

■ In a serious drought, in which categories of domestic water use shown in Table 2.1 would your household be likely to reduce its water consumption?

☐ Only you know the answer to this question – it is obviously very subjective. However, if you have a garden or a car, savings in outside use may be top of your list (the use of hosepipes and sprinklers is often first to be prohibited in a drought). You may also have considered savings in water use for baths and showers or for flushing the toilet (some water companies provide free devices for their customers to use in toilet cisterns to reduce the volume of water used per flush).

To illustrate the savings that might be made, you will consider the strategy adopted by a hypothetical household, the Browns. They agree to reduce their normal pattern of water use, shown in Table 2.2, by:

- not using any water outside
- reducing water use for baths and showers to two-thirds of normal
- putting a 1-litre 'save-a-flush®' bag in their 10-litre flush cistern. (This sealed bag contains a couple of tablespoons of grains of super absorbent polymer and silica sand. The bag allows water through and the grains swell up with water from the cistern expanding the bag to a volume of 1 litre.)

Table 2.2 Average daily water use by the Brown household before they implemented water-saving measures.

Use of water	Volume/litres
flushing toilet	120
bath and shower	96
washing machine	54
dishwashing	24
outside use (e.g. garden, car washing)	20
miscellaneous (including, drinking, cooking, cleaning)	86

The water savings that the Browns make by adopting this three-point strategy are explored in the questions that follow. In answering these questions, you will need to express the Browns' savings as fractions, percentages and ratios and to complete Table 2.3 in order to decide which of these forms makes it easiest to compare the savings. If you are not familiar with calculating fractions, percentages and ratios you may find it helpful to study Box 2.5 before attempting Questions 2.9 to 2.12.

Question 2.9

(a) What is the daily saving in the Browns' water consumption if they don't use any water outside? Express your answer as a fraction and as a percentage of the initial total average daily water use. (Enter your answer in Table 2.3.)

(b) What saving would result from their strategy to reduce their water use for baths and showers to two-thirds of the normal use? Express your answer in litres and then as a fraction and a percentage of the family's initial total average daily water use. (Enter your answer in Table 2.3.)

(c) Now consider the savings from their third strategy. What fraction of their normal use for flushing the toilet will be saved, and what is this saving as a percentage of the normal use for flushing the toilet?

(d) What total daily saving results from their strategy of reducing their water use for flushing the toilet? Express your answer in litres and as a fraction and a percentage of the initial total daily water use. (Enter your answer in Table 2.3.)

Table 2.3 The Browns' water savings relative to initial total use. To be completed as part of Question 2.9.

Use of water	Fraction	Percentage
outside use	*1/20*	5%
bath/shower	66 litres 2/25	8%.
flushing toilet	12 litre. 3/100	3%.

Question 2.10

Which of the two ways (fractions and percentages) used in Table 2.3 to express the relative savings makes them easiest to compare?

Question 2.11

Use the information in Table 2.2 and your answers to Question 2.9 to give, in the simplest possible form, the ratio of the Browns' water use for baths and showers to that for flushing the toilet (a) before and (b) after the family implemented their water-saving measures.

Question 2.12

The Browns' neighbours, the Patels, manage to make daily savings of 70 litres on their normal use of 500 litres. By comparing the information given for the Browns and the Patels, decide which household makes the greater percentage savings.

Box 2.5 Fractions, percentages and ratios

Fractions, percentages and ratios are all ways of expressing proportions, i.e. they show the relationship between two or more numbers.

Fractions

The term **fraction** means that a quantity is part of a whole, and is the result of dividing a whole amount into a number of equal parts. So if you say that you can eat one-quarter of a cake, written as $\frac{1}{4}$, then you are considering that the cake has been divided into four equal parts and saying that you can eat one of those parts. After you take your $\frac{1}{4}$ of the cake, three of the four quarters will remain, so the fraction remaining is three-quarters or $\frac{3}{4}$. The numbers $\frac{1}{4}$ and $\frac{3}{4}$ are examples of fractions.

Fractions are characterised by a **numerator** (the number on the top) and a **denominator** (the number on the bottom). So in the fraction $\frac{3}{4}$, the numerator is 3 and the denominator is 4.

Note also that fractions can be written in two different ways: three-quarters can be written as $\frac{3}{4}$ or 3/4. Both forms are used in this course. The first is used when writing out a calculation, but the second way is sometimes more convenient in a line of text.

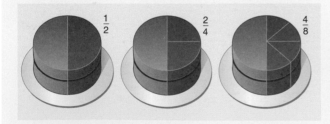

Figure 2.4 Sharing out half a cake.

The pictorial representation in Figure 2.4 makes it obvious that it is possible to have fractions which have different numerators and denominators, but are nevertheless equal. The cake can be divided

into two and the shaded half further subdivided into two-quarters or four-eighths, but half the cake still remains shaded. So the fractions $\frac{1}{2}$, $\frac{2}{4}$ and $\frac{4}{8}$ all represent the same amount of the original cake, and can therefore be described as **equivalent fractions**. This can be written as

$$\frac{1}{2} = \frac{2}{4} = \frac{4}{8}$$

Note that multiplying both the numerator and denominator of $\frac{1}{2}$ by two gives $\frac{2}{4}$ and repeating this multiplication gives $\frac{4}{8}$:

$$\frac{1}{2} = \frac{2}{4} = \frac{4}{8}$$

Similarly, dividing both the numerator and the denominator by two takes you from $\frac{4}{8}$ to $\frac{2}{4}$ and repeating the division gives $\frac{1}{2}$:

$$\frac{4}{8} = \frac{2}{4} = \frac{1}{2}$$

These are examples of a fundamental rule associated with fractions.

The value of a fraction is unchanged if its numerator and denominator are both multiplied by the same number, or both divided by the same number.

Fractions are usually expressed with the smallest possible whole numbers in the numerator and denominator. The numerator and denominator of $\frac{4}{6}$ can both be divided by two to give $\frac{2}{3}$, the numerator and denominator of $\frac{6}{9}$ can both be divided by three to give $\frac{2}{3}$, the numerator and denominator of $\frac{10}{15}$ can both be divided by five to give $\frac{2}{3}$, and the numerator and denominator of $\frac{2000}{3000}$ can both be divided by 1000 to give $\frac{2}{3}$. Thus:

$$\frac{2000}{3000} = \frac{10}{15} = \frac{6}{9} = \frac{4}{6} = \frac{2}{3}$$

These fractions are all equivalent, and $\frac{2}{3}$ is the simplest form in which they can be expressed.

Working out an equivalent fraction with the smallest whole numbers can be done step by step. It's best to start by seeing whether you can divide by simple numbers, such as 10, 2 or 5. If the numerator and denominator both end in zero, you can divide them both by 10; if they are both even numbers, you can divide them by 2; and so on. The process of dividing the top and bottom of a fraction by the same quantity is often referred to as **cancelling**, because it is commonly shown by striking through the numbers being divided. For example: $\frac{5}{15}$ can be simplified by dividing the numerator and denominator by 5, which can be shown as

$$\frac{\overset{1}{\cancel{5}}}{\underset{3}{\cancel{15}}}$$

To express $\frac{10}{40}$ in the simplest possible form, you would divide the top and the bottom by 10. This division can be illustrated by 'cancelling out' the zeros:

$$\frac{1\cancel{0}}{4\cancel{0}} = \frac{1}{4}$$

If there are more zeros, more cancelling is possible. But remember – you cancel the same number of zeros in the denominator as you do in the numerator. Thus:

$$\frac{3\cancel{00}}{20\cancel{00}} = \frac{3}{20}$$

■ How would the fractions $\frac{450}{1050}$ and $\frac{420}{660}$ normally be expressed?

□ $$\frac{45\cancel{0}}{105\cancel{0}} = \frac{\overset{9}{\cancel{45}}}{\underset{21}{\cancel{105}}} = \frac{\overset{3}{\cancel{9}}}{\underset{7}{\cancel{21}}} = \frac{3}{7} \; ; \; \frac{42\cancel{0}}{66\cancel{0}} = \frac{\overset{21}{\cancel{42}}}{\underset{33}{\cancel{66}}} = \frac{\overset{7}{\cancel{21}}}{\underset{11}{\cancel{33}}} = \frac{7}{11}$$

In the first case, the fraction was divided in turn by 10, by 5 and by 3; in the second case, the fraction was divided by 10, then 2 and then 3.

Question 2.13

Write each of the following fractions in the simplest possible form. Which of the fractions are equivalent?

(a) $\frac{6}{8}$

(b) $\frac{3000}{4000}$

(c) $\frac{6}{12}$

(d) $\frac{75}{100}$

(e) $\frac{3}{8}$

Now it isn't just numbers that you can cancel when simplifying fractions; you can often do the same with the units. Suppose you want to know what fraction of domestic water use in the UK is for dish washing; then, using information from Table 2.1 and the answer to Question 2.7(a), you have to divide 12 litres by 150 litres:

$$\frac{12 \;\cancel{litres}}{150 \;\cancel{litres}} = \frac{\overset{6}{\cancel{12}}}{\underset{75}{\cancel{150}}} = \frac{\overset{2}{\cancel{6}}}{\underset{25}{\cancel{75}}} = \frac{2}{25}$$

So $\frac{2}{25}$ of domestic water use is for dish washing. Note that in the first step above, the unit of litres was cancelled, since this was the same in the numerator and denominator of the fraction.

This cancellation of units explains the convention used when expressing units in the headings of tables, etc., for example 'Volume/litres' in the heading of Table 2.1. Consider one entry from this table, the '37' used to indicate the fact that on average people in the UK use 37 litres of water per day for flushing the toilet. The volume can be written as:

Volume = 37 litres

Dividing this by litres and cancelling gives:

$$\frac{\text{Volume}}{\text{litres}} = \frac{37 \;\cancel{litres}}{\cancel{litres}} = 37$$

table heading ↗ ↖ entry in table

So if you take the volume in litres and divide it by litres, you end up with a simple number, which is the number that is entered in the table. The $\dfrac{\text{Volume}}{\text{litres}}$, usually written as 'Volume/litres', goes in the table heading while the '37' goes in the body of the table.

When reading the number from the table, you know that for this example

$$\frac{\text{Volume}}{\text{litres}} = 37$$

To find the volume, you need to *multiply* both sides of the equation by the units (litres in this case) to give:

$$\frac{\text{Volume}}{\text{litres}} \times \text{litres} = 37 \times \text{litres}$$

or simply Volume = 37 litres.

Until now you have only considered fractions in which the number on the top is smaller than the number on the bottom, so these fractions are part of a whole. However, it is possible to have a fraction in which the numerator is *larger* than the denominator, such as $\frac{5}{4}$ or $\frac{13}{8}$, which is sometimes called an **improper fraction**. The fraction $\frac{5}{4}$ simply means five quarters (of a cake, or whatever); only four quarters can come from a whole cake, so the fifth quarter must come from another cake. The fraction $\frac{5}{4}$ can also be written as $1\frac{1}{4}$ but, for most purposes in this course, it is better to leave values expressed as improper fractions.

The addition, subtraction, multiplication and division of fractions are discussed in Chapter 9, Box 9.2.

Question 2.14

Use the information from Table 2.1 and the answer to Question 2.7(a) to find the fraction of domestic water use in the UK that is for baths and showers. Express your answer in the simplest possible form.

Percentages

You have probably met percentages in various contexts, such as a 3% pay rise, 10% interest on a loan, or 20% off goods in a sale. A **percentage** is a fraction expressed in hundredths. So $\frac{1}{2}$, i.e. one-half, is $\frac{50}{100}$, or fifty-hundredths, and this is expressed as 50 per cent, which is usually written as 50%. This literally means 50 in every 100. The advantage of using percentages is that it is always talking about hundredths, so percentages are easy to compare, whereas fractions can express arbitrary numbers of parts, eighths, sixteenths, fiftieths, or whatever is chosen. It is not immediately obvious that $\frac{19}{25}$ is larger than $\frac{15}{20}$, but if these fractions are expressed as percentages, i.e. 76% and 75%, respectively, it is easy to see that the former number is the larger of the two. But how are fractions converted into percentages, or percentages into fractions?

To convert a fraction into a percentage you should *multiply* the fraction by 100%. So to convert $\frac{1}{2}$ to a percentage:

$$\frac{1}{2} \times 100\% = 1 \div 2 \times 100\% = 50\%$$

Three-quarters, $\frac{3}{4}$, converts to:

$$\frac{3}{4} \times 100\% = 3 \div 4 \times 100\% = 75\%$$

To convert a percentage into a fraction, you need to remember that a percentage is a fraction expressed in hundredths and then cancel as appropriate. So:

$$75\% = \frac{\overset{15}{\cancel{75}}}{\underset{20}{\cancel{100}}} = \frac{\overset{3}{\cancel{15}}}{\underset{4}{\cancel{20}}} = \frac{3}{4}$$

(dividing the numerator and the denominator of the fraction by 5, then by 5 again), and

$$15\% = \frac{\overset{3}{\cancel{15}}}{\underset{20}{\cancel{100}}} = \frac{3}{20}$$

(dividing the numerator and the denominator by 5).

Question 2.15

Convert the following fractions to percentages.

(a) $\dfrac{7}{10}$

(b) $\dfrac{13}{25}$

(c) $\dfrac{3}{2}$

Question 2.16

Convert the following percentages to fractions of the simplest possible form.

(a) 60%

(b) 64%

(c) 67%

Calculating fractions and percentages of numbers

Now consider how you would work out what a certain fraction or percentage of a given number is: for example, what $\frac{3}{4}$, or 75%, of 12 is. First, think about what $\frac{3}{4}$ of 12 means. First of all 12 can be divided into four equal parts or quarters ($12 \div 4 = 3$). Then, since you want three-quarters, which is three times as big, you multiply one of these parts by three ($3 \times 3 = 9$). So $\frac{3}{4}$ of 12 is 9. This calculation can be written as

$$\frac{3}{4} \times 12$$

which is the same as

$$3 \times \frac{12}{4}, \text{ or } \frac{3 \times 12}{4}$$

So '$\frac{3}{4}$ of' a number means multiply $\frac{3}{4}$ by that number. If you see 'of' think 'multiply'.

Note that fractions in printed text are usually written so that they are equally spaced above and below the middle of the line, e.g. as $\frac{3}{4}$. However, when multiplying by a fraction it is the numerator not the denominator that should be multiplied; in finding $\frac{3}{4} \times 12$ it is the three that should be multiplied by 12, not the four. It is important to make this clear when writing fractions by hand, so the first two expressions below are both correct, but the third is not.

■ What is $\dfrac{2}{3}$ of 18?

☐ $\dfrac{2}{3}$ of 18 means $\dfrac{2}{3} \times 18$, which is 12.

Working out 75% of a number can be done in a similar way if you remember that $75\% = \dfrac{75}{100}$. So 75% of 40 is:

$$\frac{75}{100} \times 40 = 30$$

Some modern calculators will convert directly between fractions and percentages and find the percentage of a number at the press of a button. However, it is worth making sure that you understand the *meaning* of fractions and percentages before letting your calculator do the work for you. This will enable you to check that the answer you obtain is reasonable: for example, 48% of a quantity should be just less than half of it.

Question 2.17

Calculate the following.

(a) $\dfrac{2}{5}$ of 20

(b) $\dfrac{7}{8}$ of 24

(c) 15% of 60

(d) 60% of 5

Ratios

Another way of expressing the proportion of one quantity to another is to consider the **ratio** of the two numbers. Suppose that a class of 25 children has 15 girls and 10 boys. The ratio of girls to boys is 15 to 10, which is usually written as 15 : 10, i.e. with a colon (:) between the two numbers, and can be simplified to 3 : 2 (by dividing both 15 and 10 by 5, in the same way as fractions can be simplified by dividing the numerator and denominator by the same whole number). Ratios are usually expressed in their simplest possible form and should never include units.

■ From Table 2.1, you know that the average daily water use in the UK for baths and showers is 50 litres per person per day, compared with 12 litres per day for dish washing. What is the ratio of water use for baths and showers to that for dish washing? You should express the ratio in its simplest possible form.

☐ Since *both* quantities are expressed in 'litres per person per day', you can ignore the units in the ratio and express it in simple numbers as 50 : 12. Dividing both numbers by two allows the ratio to be simplified 25 : 6.

You need to take care when asked to give the ratio of two numbers, as the following example shows.

■ Suppose 2 out of 10 people in the UK drink bottled water. What is the ratio of people who drink bottled water to those who don't?

☐ The ratio is 2 : 8, which can be expressed as 1 : 4 (by dividing both numbers by two).

Did you fall into the trap and answer 2 : 10 or 1 : 5? This is the ratio of people who drink bottled water to the *total* number of people. Of course, if you had been asked what is the ratio of people who don't drink bottled water to those who do, the answer would have been 8 : 2 or 4 : 1. So, always read the question carefully.

Ratios are particularly useful where the relative proportions of two or more parts of a whole are being considered. For example, the ratio of males to females in the general population of the UK is about 1 : 1. Ratios can be used to compare more than two quantities, so if you use 150 grams of flour, 150 grams of sugar and 100 grams of fat in making a cake, these quantities are in the ratio 150 : 150 : 100, which simplifies to 15 : 15 : 10 and then to 3 : 3 : 2. However, for the remainder of this course, you will only be asked to consider ratios of a quantity to one other quantity.

Question 2.18

In a group of Open University students, 15 were men and 8 were women.

(a) What was the ratio of women to men in the group?

(b) What fraction of the total group were women?

The online interactive questions for Chapter 2 give you more practice in the skills developed in Box 2.5.

If you have not already done so, you should complete Questions 2.9 to 2.12 before moving on. The answers to these questions should convince you that percentages are usually more convenient than either fractions or ratios for comparing proportions.

2.5 Water for life

You calculated earlier (Question 2.7) that the domestic usage of water in the UK is equivalent to about 150 litres per day for every person in the population. That's a lot of water. When non-domestic use is included, the UK water use figure rises to around 1000 litres per person per day, and when the amount of water used in other countries in the production of goods consumed in the UK is also included, the total figure is more than 3000 litres per person per day. This is discussed further in Chapter 7. Domestic use is only around 5% of the total figure, but it nevertheless amounts to a huge quantity of water. Life in the world's most developed areas has come to depend on such plentiful supplies of water being available at the turn of a tap. In Section 2.4 you calculated some reductions in water use that might be made in drought conditions in the UK, and in recent years domestic appliances such as washing machines have been designed to use less water. However, the savings made are relatively small. Just imagine how your lifestyle and your use of water would change if every day you had to carry 150 litres of water, weighing 150 kilograms, from a well or a tap that was some distance away from where you live. Your water use would undoubtedly decrease to an amount that was much closer to the few litres a day that are really essential to maintain life – just a small fraction of the 150 litres currently used.

The ultimate test of how essential water is for life comes when people are deprived of water. Survival times without water depend critically on the prevailing conditions; somebody who is stranded in the hot sun of the Sahara Desert would not survive for nearly as long as a person shut in a cool, dark cellar. The record for surviving without water is possibly held by a young Austrian man, who in 1979 was put into a holding cell and then forgotten by the police. He was discovered 18 days later, close to death. However, it is unusual for a person to survive for more than 7–10 days without water, and the survival time would be far shorter in a hot desert.

The reasons that humans are so dependent on water are readily apparent if you think about the range of different water-based fluids in the body and the essential roles that they fulfil.

■ What fluids can you think of that are found in, or on, the human body?

☐ You may have thought of blood, urine, sweat, tears, saliva, digestive juices, and mucous fluid in the nose and lungs.

A wide range of essential bodily functions depend on these water-based fluids. It is fortunate, therefore, that in normal circumstances bodies have a remarkable ability to regulate their fluid levels so that all of these functions continue to operate efficiently. So, for example, when the water content of your body is too low then you feel thirsty and will find something to drink; and when you drink large volumes of liquid your body will increase production of urine to remove the excess liquid. However, when the body is deprived of water, the many functions that depend on water-based fluids are disrupted, and the consequences become increasingly severe as water deprivation increases.

Plants also contain large amounts of water-based fluids, as is discussed in more detail in Chapter 4, and they too need regular supplies of water for their growth. The Egyptian Sahara Desert (Figures 2.1 and 2.2) is now inhospitable to humans, not only because of the lack of water for drinking, but also because water is not available for growing food. However, although humans cannot live in the desert without taking water supplies, there are organisms that can exist on the meagre amounts of water that are naturally available in these regions, and you will see how they manage this in the next chapter.

2.6 Summary of Chapter 2

Humans and other organisms need water to live; human populations are therefore low in desert areas where there is a lack of water.

The scientific method describes the way in which scientific knowledge and understanding develop by revising or replacing existing hypotheses in response to new observations and discoveries.

Illustrations in the text can be used to convey important information, and should be 'read' carefully.

Tables are a clear, concise way to display information. A table should have a title, and should have column headings that include information about the units of all measured quantities.

BEDMAS is a mnemonic for remembering the order of carrying out mathematical operations in a calculation. You should work out the **B**rackets first, then the **E**xponents (otherwise known as indices or powers), then any **D**ivisions and **M**ultiplications, and finally the **A**dditions and **S**ubtractions. For any part of a calculation that involves just divisions and multiplications, or just additions and subtractions, you must work from left to right.

Fractions, percentages and ratios are convenient ways of comparing relative amounts of two quantities. It is easier to compare two proportions expressed as percentages rather than as fractions or ratios.

Learning outcomes for Chapter 2

When you have completed Chapter 2 you should be able to:

- Keep a learning journal.
- Read illustrations.
- Rewrite text in your own words.
- Read data from tables.
- Do calculations in the correct order.
- Express quantities as fractions, percentages and ratios.

    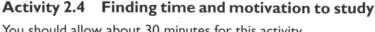

Activity 2.4   Finding time and motivation to study

You should allow about 30 minutes for this activity.

This activity involves watching a 5 minute video sequence *Finding the Time and Motivation to Study* and then sending a message to your tutor group forum.

Video activities require more than just watching the screen and listening to the words; they have much in common with studying text – you need to concentrate on what is being said and try to follow the argument. You will find that it usually helps to make notes while you watch. Of course, you can pause the clip at any point or look at part of it again, in the same way that you would reread a demanding piece of text.

In this video sequence, four Level 1 students are discussing their study strategies with their tutor. You should watch the sequence once, and then, while viewing it a second time, stop at appropriate places and note down useful tips that the students provide about:

- how they find time for study
- when they study
- for how long they study at a session
- how they find motivation for study.

Information on how to access the video sequence *Finding the Time and Motivation to Study* is given in the *Course Guide*.

When you have viewed the video sequence, look back at your learning journal to see whether you have had any similar problems to these students and whether you had ideas for solving them. Note down your thoughts and then send an email to your tutor group forum either

(a) about a problem you had and the way you solved it

or

(b) what motivates you to study.

You may find it interesting and helpful to read, and perhaps reply to, contributions from other students in your group.

Activity 2.1   Keeping a learning journal (continued)

You should allow about 15 minutes for this activity.

Access your learning journal to review what you have written so far, compare it with the study planner you completed during Activity 1.2 and then consider the following questions.

(a) When did you study – which days and at what times of the day? Did you find that certain days and/or times suited you better than others? Enter your comments in your learning journal.

(b) For how long did you study at a time? What determined the length of each study period – was it the amount of time available, your ability to concentrate, or the nature of the particular task? Enter your comments in your learning journal.

(c) How long have you spent studying Chapter 2 overall? It has probably taken you about 10 hours to reach this point in Chapter 2. How did your study time compare with this – longer, shorter or about the same?

(d) Look at the summary and learning outcomes for this chapter. Do you feel that you have achieved all the outcomes or are there one or two that you need to spend a little more time on?

Note down your answers in your learning journal.

Chapter 3
Water in living organisms

One characteristic that all living organisms have in common is that they contain water. This may not be obvious, because the fluids that are obtained from animals and plants are not pure water. Blood, urine and sweat from animals and the sap from plants all contain a variety of substances, and they look, taste and smell quite different from water. However, many experiments on these fluids, and on those from a huge range of other organisms, have demonstrated that water is the major component in every case.

In this chapter you will investigate *how much* water is present in living organisms. You will start by seeing how water content is measured, and then you will be able to do the first practical work for the course – an experiment to measure the water content of a potato. (Alternatives such as sweet potato or yam can be used instead.)

This will provide an interesting, and perhaps surprising, result which can be compared with data on the water content of a variety of plants and animals, including humans. The water content of humans and potatoes are not much different from the water content of camels and cacti, even though the latter organisms can survive in hot, dry desert conditions. At the end of this chapter you will discover how camels and cacti manage to survive in conditions that are so inhospitable from the human viewpoint.

Interwoven with the theme of 'water in living organisms' is the development of a variety of skills. The experiment will introduce skills associated with practical work in science, including planning, measuring, recording and analysing data, and critically evaluating what you have done. Using these skills is part of scientific inquiry. You will also look at the skill of identifying key points (see Box 3.1) and developing science skills associated with units of measurement and reading information from graphs, and the maths skill of using decimals. However, you should begin by continuing the work on planning your study that you started in Chapter 1.

Activity 3.1   Planning your study

You should allow about 20 minutes for this activity initially, with a further 20 minutes for reviewing and updating your plan later in this chapter.

In addition to the study components that you used in Chapter 2 – this book and the online activities – there is some practical work to do in this chapter (in Activity 3.2). Try to plan now the day and time you will carry out the practical work, using the advice and study planner provided for Activity 1.2. Remember to keep a log of the time actually spent studying Chapter 3, and note this in your learning journal.

To help you plan when you will do the practical work in Chapter 3, you should read the information in Activity 3.2 in this book and briefly survey the section on 'planning the experiment' in the additional information given for Activity 3.2 in the *Course Guide*. As you will see, there is more than one way of doing the experiment and how you decide to do it will influence your plan of work. You will find it easier to do the practical work (which requires an estimated study time of an hour and a half) after completing your study of Section 3.1. There is also an associated online activity to do (Activity 3.3) and you need to allow about 25 minutes for this. It would be best to do this activity immediately after completing the experiment, or at the beginning of the subsequent study session, as it relates to the practical work. So read the notes for Activity 3.2 now and note down in your learning journal when you plan to do the practical work. You also need to allow some time for assembling the materials and equipment before doing the experiment.

Finally, you need to bear in mind any decisions you made as a result of Activities 2.1 and 2.4. Do you need to allow more time for Chapter 3 than the course team's estimate of 11 hours? Are you going to try a different study pattern? For example, you may decide to work for some short periods of 30 minutes in addition to longer stretches of, say, 2 hours. You will need to access your learning journal and record:

- when you plan to do the practical work (Activity 3.2)

- when you plan to discuss your results (Activity 3.3)

- how long you estimate this will take.

Before you return to the theme of this chapter, Box 3.1 introduces active reading and identifying key points – skills that help you learn and study more effectively.

Box 3.1   Active reading and identifying key points

Reading can be a passive process, but it can also be an active one. The questions and activities that are built into this course are designed to encourage you to think about the text as you study. Answering the questions and doing the activities in Chapter 2 should have convinced you that doing something associated with the text is far more effective than just reading it.

It is important to realise that this course book is a workbook rather than a textbook, and you should feel free to write and draw in it as you study. As you read, you should try to identify the key points in the text. You could use a highlighting (fluorescent) pen to pick out words and phrases that correspond to main ideas or key points, i.e. those phrases that carry the crucial explanation of a point or a definition of something. Alternatively, you may prefer to underline the important words and phrases. In addition, you will find that constantly asking yourself 'what are the key points?' will help you to grasp the content of the text. The highlighted words and phrases will also be useful for summarising and revising.

What you choose to highlight (or underline), and how much, rather depends on you. At first you might be tempted to highlight the majority of the text, but try to be selective and just highlight the key points. You should start to identify key points as you study Sections 3.1 and 3.2. Activity 3.5 in Section 3.3 will help you to develop your technique.

3.1 Water – the vital ingredient

The presence of water in all known living organisms has led scientists to accept the hypothesis that every living thing contains water. Remember, though, that an hypothesis is an explanation provisionally adopted to account for certain observations. The hypothesis that all living organisms contain water is consistent with all of the many experiments and observations that have been carried out. However, if someone discovered a form of life that did not contain water, whether on Earth or on some other planet, this hypothesis would have to be abandoned. Until that happens, you should assume that the hypothesis is correct. Now you will look more closely at the *amount* of water in living things.

It is not easy to measure the amount of water in a *living* organism (or in part of it), but it is straightforward to do it immediately after the organism has died or, in the case of plants, been harvested. In the case of plants that are gathered for food, water contents have been measured to provide dietary information. The amount of water in cabbage, for example, has been determined by weighing raw cabbage leaves, drying them to remove all of the water that they contain, and then weighing them again.

■ Suppose that 800 grams of cabbage leaves are slowly dried in an oven, and then found to weigh only 100 grams. How much water did the leaves contain?

☐ The amount of water is the difference between the initial 800 grams and the final 100 grams, assuming that only water is released when the leaves are dried. So the cabbage leaves contained 700 grams of water.

Note the assumption that has been made here: that only water is released in the drying process. This is not strictly true, since small amounts of other substances will also be released, but it is a good enough approximation for present purposes. Scientists are often willing to make simplifying assumptions, which is acceptable as long as these assumptions are clearly stated.

The number 700 in the answer above is accompanied by the appropriate unit, grams. Units are essential information about any measured quantity, and here, as in the rest of this course and in science generally, the metric unit of mass is used. Box 3.2 reviews the basic metric units of mass, length and time, which you will meet continually as you study science.

Box 3.2   Units of measurement

If you were told that the length of a piece of string was 37, you would be rather baffled: 37 what? Is it 37 metres, 37 centimetres, 37 feet, or even 37 miles? Similarly, if somebody says that a friend weighs 100, what does this mean? These examples highlight both the importance of both having an agreed system of units to make measurements with and the importance of quoting the units when you want to communicate what you have measured.

In science, the units used are known as **SI units**, which is an abbreviation for 'Système Internationale d'Unités' (International System of Units).

In 1960, an international conference formally approved this set of metric units as standard, so replacing the many different national systems of measurement that had been used in science up to that time. The advantage of having a standard set of units is that everyone uses them, and there is no need to convert laboriously from one system to another to compare results in different countries. So although in everyday life in the UK people may still buy milk and beer in pints, and measure distances between towns in miles, in the scientific community SI units are used almost exclusively. Mixing imperial and metric units of measurement can have disastrous consequences. The loss of the Mars *Climate Orbiter* in 1999 on reaching Mars, after a nine-month journey, was the result of some scientists working in metric units while others worked in imperial units. The spacecraft had been erroneously navigated on a trajectory bringing it down to only 50 km above the surface rather than a safe altitude of 80 km (50 miles).

So what are SI units? At this stage, only the SI units of length, time and mass will be introduced.

- The basic SI unit of length is the **metre**, which is abbreviated to m.
- The basic SI unit of time is the **second**, which is abbreviated to s.
- The basic SI unit of mass is the **kilogram**, which is abbreviated to kg.

Although a metre is a conveniently sized unit for measuring the height of a person or the width of a room, it is an inconvenient size to use for quoting the distance between London and Edinburgh, or the breadth of a pinhead. Therefore, it is conventional and convenient to use larger and smaller multiples of the metre when appropriate; note that these are also SI units. So, for example, large distances can be measured in kilometres (km), and small distances or lengths can be measured in millimetres (mm). The prefix **kilo** means 'one thousand', so a kilometre is one thousand metres. The prefix **milli** means 'one-thousandth', so a millimetre is one-thousandth of a metre. Put another way, one metre is one thousand millimetres. Therefore, $1 \text{ km} = 1000 \text{ m}$, $1 \text{ mm} = \frac{1}{1000} \text{ m}$ and $1 \text{ m} = 1000 \text{ mm}$.

■ How many millimetres are there in 1 kilometre?

□ $1 \text{ km} = 1000 \text{ m}$ and $1 \text{ m} = 1000 \text{ mm}$,

so $1 \text{ km} = 1000 \times 1000 \text{ mm} = 1000\,000 \text{ mm}$.

Another common prefix that you may have met is **centi** (as in centimetre, abbreviated to cm), which means 'one-hundredth'. So $1 \text{ cm} = \frac{1}{100} \text{ m}$, which means that:

$$100 \text{ cm} = 100 \times \frac{1}{100} \text{ m} = \frac{100}{100} \text{ m} = 1 \text{ m}, \text{ i.e. } 1 \text{ m} = 100 \text{ cm}$$

■ How many centimetres are there in 25 metres?

□ Since $1 \text{ m} = 100 \text{ cm}$, $25 \text{ m} = 25 \times 100 \text{ cm} = 2500 \text{ cm}$.

If you didn't know how many millimetres there were in a centimetre, you could use the definitions to work this out. From the definitions, 1 m = 100 cm = 1000 mm.

So, if each of these equal lengths is divided by 100,

$$\frac{1}{100} \text{ m} = \frac{100}{100} \text{ cm} = \frac{1000}{100} \text{ mm}$$

which gives

$$\frac{1}{100} \text{ m} = 1 \text{ cm} = 10 \text{ mm}$$

This means that there are 10 millimetres in 1 centimetre. Alternatively, if you want to know how many centimetres are equivalent to 1 millimetre, you can start from the equation 1 cm = 10 mm and divide these equal lengths by ten, so

$$\frac{1}{10} \text{ cm} = 1 \text{ mm, or } 1 \text{ millimetre} = \frac{1}{10} \text{ centimetre}$$

■ How many centimetres are there in 350 millimetres?

□ Each millimetre is equal to $\frac{1}{10}$ cm, so you need to multiply the number of millimetres (350) by $\frac{1}{10}$ cm. So

$$350 \text{ mm} = 350 \times \frac{1}{10} \text{ cm} = \frac{350}{10} \text{ cm} = 35 \text{ cm}$$

In general, the abbreviations for units are used in all calculations, like the ones above. Within the main text, the full word or sometimes the abbreviation is used, although as the course progresses the abbreviations will be used more frequently. Most importantly, you can also see from these examples that the abbreviations for units are both singular and plural, so 'm' means metre or metres.

The relationships between the four units of length that have been introduced are summarised in Table 3.1.

Table 3.1 The relationships between km, m, cm and mm.

1 km	=	1000 m	=	100 000 cm	=	1000 000 mm
$\frac{1}{1000}$ km	=	1 m	=	100 cm	=	1000 mm
$\frac{1}{100\,000}$ km	=	$\frac{1}{100}$ m	=	1 cm	=	10 mm
$\frac{1}{1000\,000}$ km	=	$\frac{1}{1000}$ m	=	$\frac{1}{10}$ cm	=	1 mm

The basic SI unit of time – the second (s) – will be familiar from everyday life. Longer time intervals may be measured in minutes, hours, days or years, but these are not SI units. Shorter times are measured in sub-multiples of the second. Thus, a millisecond (ms) is one-thousandth of a second, just as a millimetre is one-thousandth of a metre.

You may have been surprised that the kilogram is the SI unit for mass, rather than the unit for weight. After all, in everyday usage, a person's weight is said to be so many kilograms. However, in scientific use, the term **weight** means the downward pull on an object due to gravity, e.g. the downward pull that makes an apple fall to the ground. This means that your weight would decrease if you went to the Moon, where gravity is only about $\frac{1}{6}$ as strong as on Earth. Your **mass**, however, is determined by the amount of matter in your body and, since this doesn't depend on gravity, your mass is the same wherever you are in the Universe. Weighing scales are always marked in units of mass, e.g. kilograms, so to be scientifically correct you should say that somebody has a *mass* of 55 kilograms, rather than their *weight* is 55 kilograms.

You may also have been surprised to learn that the basic SI unit of mass is the kilogram not the gram. This is because, in general, the kilogram is of a more convenient size for measuring the masses of everyday objects, although you will have seen the number of grams quoted on all kinds of packaged food. Just as the *kilo*metre is equal to *one thousand* metres, so the *kilo*gram is equal to *one thousand* grams, i.e. 1 kilogram = 1000 grams. Very small quantities are measured in milligrams, where one milligram (mg) is one-thousandth of a gram, 1 milligram = $\frac{1}{1000}$ gram. So, using abbreviations, 1 kg = 1000 g, and 1 mg = $\frac{1}{1000}$ g.

Question 3.1

Complete the blanks in the following relationships between units.

(a) 5 km = ...5000.... m = ...500,000... cm = ...5000,000... mm

(b) ....30.... kg = 3000 g = ..3000,000.. mg

(c) 25 s = ..25,000.. ms

Before leaving this discussion of units, there is one other important point to remember about the relationship between units. Suppose you had to add together 100 cm and 2 m, what would be the first step you would need to take? You could convert 100 cm to 1 m, so the calculation becomes 1 m + 2 m = 3 m. Alternatively, you could convert 2 m to 200 cm, so 100 cm + 200 cm = 300 cm. The same is true for all units, not just the units of length.

Question 3.2

Try the following calculations, which all involve changes to units.

(a) 7 kg + 4000 g

(b) 55 cm − 40 mm

(c) 20 s − 1000 ms

Units are discussed further in Box 9.1.

Earlier the result was given of one particular measurement of the water content of cabbage leaves, in which 800 g of cabbage leaves were found to contain 700 g of water. However, if a series of experiments were done to determine the water content of cabbage leaves, it is unlikely that each experiment would start with exactly the same mass of raw cabbage leaves, and so a different dry mass would probably be determined each time. In each case there would be a different mass of water in the leaves. Generally it is not the mass of water that is really of interest, but the fraction – or better still the percentage – of the leaves that is water.

■ If 800 g of cabbage leaves are slowly dried in an oven, and then found to weigh only 100 g, what fraction of the original mass of the leaves was water? What percentage was water? (You may want to refer back to Box 2.5.)

☐ Since the 800 g of leaves lost 700 g of water when they were dried, the fraction that was water is $\dfrac{700 \text{ g}}{800 \text{ g}}$, which after cancelling the zeros and the units is the same as $\frac{7}{8}$. To express this as a percentage you multiply the fraction by 100%. Thus the percentage of water is $\dfrac{7}{8} \times 100\%$, which is 87.5%.

This number, 87.5, is a decimal number. Box 3.3 reviews the important facts about this type of number, including how to convert between fractions, percentages and decimal numbers. Try Questions 3.3 to 3.6 if you want to check whether you need to study this box in detail.

Box 3.3   Decimal numbers

A fraction such as $\frac{1}{2}$ can also be written as 0.5; $\frac{1}{2}$, 50% and 0.5 have the same meaning and the number 0.5 is an example of a **decimal number**. Decimal numbers are used throughout science, and you need to become proficient at adding, subtracting, multiplying and dividing them. Fortunately, your calculator will take the pain out of the calculations, so you can concentrate on understanding what the numbers mean.

Decimal numbers consist of two parts separated by what is called a **decimal point**. When printed, a 'full stop' is used for the decimal point. Here are four examples, with words in brackets indicating how the numbers should be said: 0.5 ('nought point five'), 2.34 ('two point three four'), 45.875 ('forty-five point eight seven five'), and 234.76 ('two hundred and thirty-four point seven six'). Note that the part of the number before the decimal point is spoken as a whole number, and the part after the point is spoken as a series of individual digits. Also note that in some countries, a comma is used instead of a full stop in decimal numbers.

What do these numbers mean? Well, the part of the number before the decimal point represents a whole number, and the part after the decimal point represents the fraction, something between nought and one, that has to be added on to the whole number. Thus if you divide 13 by 2 you get $6\frac{1}{2}$ if you use fractions, but 6.5 if you use a calculator; the 0.5 is equivalent to the half. Note that when there is no whole number, i.e. the number is less than one, it is usual to print or write a zero in front of the decimal point, otherwise the decimal point might be overlooked. (Your calculator, however, may not always show the zero.) If you divide 13 by 4, with fractions you get $3\frac{1}{4}$ and with a calculator you get 3.25, so a quarter is the same as 0.25.

Conversion of any fraction to a decimal number is straightforward with a calculator. All you have to do is divide the number on the top of the fraction by the number on the bottom. Try this for yourself: with the fraction $\frac{15}{40}$, you should obtain the decimal number 0.375.

Now, just as each digit that is on the left of the decimal point has a precise meaning that depends on where it comes in the order, so also does each digit that is after the decimal point. These meanings are summarised in Table 3.2 for the number 7654.321.

Table 3.2 The meaning of each digit in the number 7654.321.

Thousands	Hundreds	Tens	Units	Point	Tenths	Hundredths	Thousandths
7	6	5	4	.	3	2	1
7×1000	6×100	5×10	4×1		$3 \times \frac{1}{10}$	$2 \times \frac{1}{100}$	$1 \times \frac{1}{1000}$
$= 7000$	$= 600$	$= 50$	$= 4$		$= 0.3$	$= 0.02$	$= 0.001$
	total = 7654					total = 0.321	

The 4 immediately *before* the decimal point means 4 units (or 4 ones), which is simply 4; the 5 signifies 5 tens, or 50; the 6 signifies 6 hundreds, or 600; and the 7 signifies 7 thousands, or 7000. So 7654 means $7000 + 600 + 50 + 4$.

In a similar way, the 3 *after* the decimal point means 3 tenths, or $\frac{3}{10}$, the 2 means 2 hundredths, or $\frac{2}{100}$, and the 1 means 1 thousandth, or $\frac{1}{1000}$. Also, just as 7654 means 7 thousands plus 6 hundreds plus 5 tens plus 4 units, so 0.321 means 3 tenths plus 2 hundredths plus 1 thousandth. So

$$0.321 = \frac{3}{10} + \frac{2}{100} + \frac{1}{1000}$$

Now, to add fractions, first you have to convert them into equivalent fractions with the same denominator as each other. (The addition of fractions is discussed further in Box 9.2.) In this case, the first two fractions would be converted to equivalent fractions each with a denominator of 1000.

Since $\frac{3}{10}$ is an equivalent fraction to $\frac{300}{1000}$, and $\frac{2}{100}$ is equivalent to $\frac{20}{1000}$,

$$0.321 = \frac{300}{1000} + \frac{20}{1000} + \frac{1}{1000} = \frac{(300 + 20 + 1)}{1000} = \frac{321}{1000}$$

Here, the numerators have been added together to get the total number of 'thousandths', but the denominators haven't been added since these just indicate that 'thousandths' are being added in each case.

This shows that converting a decimal number to a fraction is really quite straightforward; you just take the numbers after the decimal point (321 in the example above) and divide by 1 followed by the same number of zeros as there were digits after the decimal point (three in this case), so

$$0.321 = \frac{321}{1000}$$

Question 3.3

Convert the following fractions to decimal numbers.

(a) $\dfrac{3}{8}$

(b) $\dfrac{7}{10}$

(c) $\dfrac{3}{100}$

Question 3.4

Convert the following decimal numbers to fractions, and convert each fraction to its simplest form.

(a) 0.7
(b) 0.2
(c) 0.222 $\frac{111}{500}$ Why not $\frac{H}{=}$

Question 3.5

Convert the following percentages to decimal numbers.

(a) 79%
(b) 35%
(c) 3%

(*Hint*: you may find it helpful to start by converting the percentages to fractions.)

A calculator does arithmetic with decimal numbers in the same way as it does with whole numbers, including carrying out operations in the right order. The only difference is that you have to key in the decimal point, using the decimal point key on the calculator, at the appropriate place in decimal numbers. As an example, try multiplying 2.36 and 43.7 and the result, 103.132, should appear in the display.

Question 3.6

Work out the following decimal calculations.

(a) 24.31 − 13.94

(b) 3.05 × 2.2

(c) 499.56 ÷ 27.6

If you calculate the percentage of water in a vegetable using the method described in Activity 3.2, your calculator may display a final answer such as 86.58715683 and it might be tempting to write this number down as your answer. (Some calculators may display fewer digits than the example given here so the last few digits will not appear on the display.) But this would not be very sensible because it might imply that you know that the percentage of water is exactly 86.587 156 83%, which is unlikely to be the case. In order to give a more meaningful answer, this number must be rounded to a more appropriate number of decimal places, or to the nearest whole number. Decimal places and rounding are discussed in Box 3.4. Try Question 3.7 at the end of this box if you want to check whether you need to study the box in detail.

Box 3.4   Decimal places and rounding

The number of digits after the decimal point in a number is termed the number of places of decimals, or simply the number of **decimal places**. So, for example, 0.745 is expressed to three decimal places, 7 is in the first decimal place, 4 is in the second decimal place and 5 is in the third decimal place.

■ To how many places of decimals is 86.587 156 83 expressed?

☐ Eight; there are eight digits after the decimal point.

Often when you do a calculation your calculator will display an answer with perhaps seven or even nine decimal places: for example, it may indicate that $\frac{1}{3}$ is 0.333 333 333. In most cases, it is not necessary to give all of these digits. It is probably sufficient to know that $\frac{1}{3}$ is about 0.33, and to forget about the thousandths, the ten-thousandths, and so on. Sometimes it is enough

to know that $\frac{1}{3}$ is about 0.3. If you approximate in this way, you are **rounding** the number. However, rounding is a little more complicated than just chopping off the unwanted digits.

If you want to round 1.2645 to two decimal places, you need to look at the first digit to be removed – in this case, 4. If the first digit removed is 0, 1, 2, 3 or 4, the last remaining digit – in this case, 6 – is *left unchanged*. So the answer is 1.26.

However, if the first digit to be removed is 5, 6, 7, 8 or 9, the last remaining digit is *increased by one*, a process described as 'rounding up'. So, for example, if 1.2645 is rounded to one decimal place, the answer is 1.3 – the first digit removed is 6, so the 2 is rounded up to 3.

The reason for rounding up when the first digit removed is 5 or greater is clear if you bear in mind that the number that is midway between 1.2 and 1.3 is 1.25. So all numbers between 1.25 and 1.3 are closer to 1.3 than they are to 1.2. Therefore, it makes sense to round up the last remaining digit whenever it has been followed by a digit between 5 and 9. Note that, by convention, the digit 5 is rounded up.

- Round 86.587 156 83 to the nearest whole number.

☐ The first digit to be removed is the 5 immediately after the decimal point thus the number is rounded up to 87.

Sometimes, rounding a decimal number will produce a zero as the final digit; for example, both 1.803 and 1.798 become 1.80 when rounded to two decimal places. Don't be tempted to ignore the final zero in these cases though, because it contains important information about the decimal number. Quoting a

length as 1.80 metres tells you that the measurement is between 1.7950 metres and 1.8049 metres because numbers within this range are equal to 1.80 metres when rounded to two decimal places. On the other hand, quoting the length as 1.8 metres means that it is between 1.750 metres and 1.849 metres, which is a much larger range.

Question 3.7

Round each of the following numbers to one decimal place, to two decimal places, and to three decimal places.
(a) 0.2648
(b) 0.825 51
(c) 21.1184

Measurements of the percentage of water in cabbage leaves demonstrate that this type of plant material contains a very large proportion of water: the value calculated earlier was 87.5%. How typical is this value? Does all vegetable matter contain such a large percentage of water? To extend your understanding of water content, you should now do an experiment (Activity 3.2) to find out the percentage of water in a potato. The potatoes that you eat are tubers, enlarged parts of the stem that grow underground, so your experiment will indicate whether tubers and leaves contain different percentages of water.

Before tackling this experiment, write down your best estimate, or guess, for the percentage of water that you think potatoes contain. When you have completed your experiment, you will have a measured percentage, and you will be able to compare this with your initial estimate.

Estimate/guess of the percentage of a potato that is water: …………%

Measured percentage of a potato that is water (to the nearest whole number): …………%

Activity 3.2   How much water is there in potatoes?

You should allow about 90 minutes for this activity.

One of the key activities of scientists is carrying out experiments to discover more about the natural world. In this first experiment of the course you will measure the water content of some potatoes. This activity will introduce a variety of skills associated with practical work.

The aims of the experiment are:

- To determine the percentage of water in potatoes.

- To develop skills associated with experimental design, planning and making measurements, recording and analysing results, and thinking critically about experimental work.

You will determine the percentage of water in potatoes by weighing some potatoes on kitchen scales, drying them in an oven or airing cupboard to remove the water, and then reweighing the potatoes. You will check that all of the water has been removed by taking a series of measurements of mass, until the mass no longer decreases.

The experiment should take about 90 minutes of your active time in total. You will need an initial 10 minutes to read through the instructions and about 20 minutes for working out the results and thinking critically about the experiment. The experiment itself will take about an hour, but the spread of that time will depend on the method you use to dry the potatoes. There are detailed notes for planning and carrying out the experiment in the *Course Guide* and you should turn to these now.

Activity 3.3   Reviewing the potato experiment

You should allow about 25 minutes for this activity.

On completing an experiment, it is good practice to review what you have done and this activity will help you to do this. There are two parts to the activity: first you will email your tutor with your experimental results, your conclusion, and any reflections on the way you carried out the experiment. Then you will discuss your results with other students in your group.

Task 1

Email your tutor about your experimental results.

In the email you should:

- Include the final conclusion that you wrote to your experimental work and any changes you made to how you wrote this after you read the comments on Activity 3.2. You should also state the value you obtained for the percentage of water in potatoes.

- Mention anything that you would do differently in order to try to improve the result. You should ask yourself whether the equipment, or the method used, could be improved and, if so, what sort of improvements could be made.

Task 2

- Visit the wiki for your tutor group (via the link to "Activities for Chapter 3" from the Course Calendar) and post your value for the percentage of water in potatoes.

- Look at the values posted by other students.

Before you complete the rest of this activity, you may have to wait for others in your group to post their results. Then consider:

- How your value compares with the results obtained by other students in your group.
- Whether the results vary from student to student. This is likely to happen. Consider what the reasons are for this variability.
- Whether you would get an identical result if you were to repeat the experiment.

You may like to log on to your tutor group forum (for how to do this, see Activity 1.4 in the CG) and discuss your thoughts with the other students in your group.

Activity 3.1 Planning your study (continued)

At this point make sure your learning journal record of the time spent studying Chapter 3 is up to date.

3.2 How much water?

The result of your measurement of the percentage of water in a potato may have surprised you. By far the largest component of a potato is water, although the percentage of water in a potato is smaller than in cabbage leaves. Are these two results typical of plant matter, or do other plants have quite different water contents? Also, how do the water contents of animals compare with those of plants? These questions will be answered in this section.

First, look at some results from an experiment with different plant material, namely a cucumber (Figure 3.1). Cucumbers are commonly referred to as

Figure 3.1 (a) Cucumbers growing; (b) a sliced cucumber showing its green skin and pale flesh and seeds.

(a)

(b)

vegetables because they are not particularly sweet, but they contain seeds, just like an apple, and therefore a biologist would classify them as fruit.

■ Do you think that the percentage of water in a cucumber is higher or lower than in a potato? Explain why.

☐ Cucumber is very moist and almost slimy, which suggests that its water content is higher than in a potato.

An experiment to determine the water content of cucumber was carried out with a microwave oven, using the method suggested in the notes for Activity 3.2. The results obtained were initially recorded in a table, but there is an alternative way of displaying the results. Scientists often choose to present their results as a **graph**. With a graph, it is usually much easier to take in the general pattern of the measurements than it is with a table of data. This is because graphs give a direct picture of the relationship between measured quantities (between mass of cucumber and time, for example). Figure 3.5 on page 52 shows the results of the experiment to determine the water content of cucumber, now plotted as a graph. However, before studying this graph in detail, you may find it helpful to read through Box 3.5, which explains some of the important points to be borne in mind when reading data from any graph of this kind. Try Questions 3.8 and 3.9 at the end of this box if you want to check whether you need to study this box in detail.

Box 3.5   Reading information from a graph

Graphs are used to illustrate the relationship between two quantities; for example, Figure 3.2 (overleaf) shows the way in which the height of a girl changes as her age increases.

As with most illustrations, all graphs should have a title (in this case 'Height of Marie, from birth to 18 years old.') and, when reading information from a graph, this is a good place to start. It tells you, at a glance, what the graph is about.

Next, look at the vertical and horizontal axes of the graph ('axes' is the plural of '**axis**'), reference lines which carry the **scale** of the graph and so help you to locate points on the graph and to read values from it. Note that the vertical axis is labelled 'height/cm' and the horizontal axis is labelled 'age/years'. Axes should always be labelled in this way, with the unit (if there is one) given in the same way as in the column headings of tables (Box 2.3).

Where appropriate, it is conventional to use 'quantity divided by units' (usually in the form 'quantity/units') in labelling the axes of graphs.

In the case of Figure 3.2, both scales start from zero. The point where both scales are zero (which is not included on all graphs) is known as the **origin** of the graph.

On Figure 3.2, the combination of the label and the scale on the vertical axis indicates that the numbers correspond to height in centimetres, i.e. 0 cm, 20 cm, 40 cm, etc. So, moving vertically upwards on the graph, the girl's height increases by 20 cm for each 1 cm on the graph paper. Look at Figure 3.3, which shows an enlarged version of the small section of the vertical scale between 20 and 40 cm on Figure 3.2. Because the horizontal lines on the graph in Figure 3.3 are equally spaced, you can work out what values of height correspond to each of the lines. The 20 cm difference between 20 cm and 40 cm has been divided into 10 small equal divisions, so each small division represents $\frac{20\ cm}{10} = 2$ cm. So the horizontal lines on the enlarged graph have been marked 22, 24, 26, and so on. The point on the axis indicated by arrow 'A' corresponds to 28 cm, and the point indicated by arrow 'B' corresponds to 36 cm. A point that is halfway between the lines marked 34 and 36 corresponds to 35 cm.

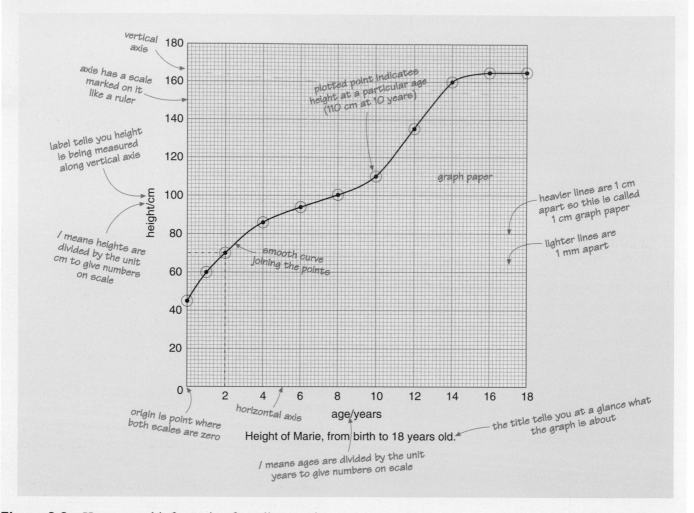

Figure 3.2 How to read information from line graphs.

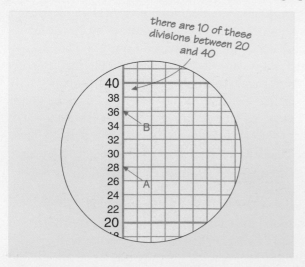

Figure 3.3 Enlarged part of the vertical scale of Figure 3.2.

The horizontal axis in Figure 3.2 has a scale numbered 0, 2, 4, 6, … 18; these numbers correspond to the age in years. The successive numbers are separated by 1 cm, so this is also a uniform scale. For every 1 cm that you move from left to right on the graph, the age of the girl increases by 2 years.

■ How much does the age of the girl increase for each small division?

☐ Since 10 small divisions represent 2 years, one small division (1 mm) represents

$$\frac{2 \text{ years}}{10} = 0.2 \text{ years. This is about 10 weeks.}$$

The combination of title, axes, axis labels, scales and graph paper give a framework for displaying the results of measurements, which are represented by the circled points on the graph in Figure 3.2. The position of a point on the graph represents a pair of related measurements; the horizontal position of a point represents the girl's age, and the vertical position corresponds to her height *at that age*.

To work out the height for a particular point, you can draw a horizontal line from the point to the vertical axis, and read off the appropriate number from the scale.

■ What is the height for the third point from the left on the graph in Figure 3.2?

☐ The answer is 70 cm; you can find this value by drawing a line horizontally from the third point to the vertical axis.

The corresponding age is read by drawing a line vertically downwards from the point to the horizontal axis.

■ What is the age for the third point from the left in Figure 3.2?

☐ The answer is 2 years, you can find this value by drawing a line vertically downwards from the third point to the horizontal axis.

An alternative to drawing lines on the graph is to lay a ruler on the graph, horizontally or vertically, to help your eye follow a line from a point on the graph to the axis.

The eleven circled points on the graph represent measurements of the girl's height at different ages. The points have been joined together with a smooth curve to represent the overall trend of the measurements, which gives an immediate visual picture of how the height has changed.

■ What is the trend of the girl's height with increasing age?

☐ The girl's height increased rapidly in the first four years, and her growth then slowed down – the curve becomes flatter. There was another growth spurt corresponding to the onset of puberty, between 10 and 14 years, and her height then remained almost constant at about 165 cm. (This last height is $2\frac{1}{2}$ divisions above 160 cm and, since each division is 2 cm, the height must be $2\frac{1}{2} \times 2$ cm $= 5$ cm above 160 cm.)

The smooth curve allows the girl's height to be estimated at ages between those at which the actual measurements were made. So, to estimate her height at 7 years, find 7 years on the age axis, follow a vertical line upwards from here to the curve, and then follow a line from this point on the curve to the vertical axis, and read the appropriate value for the height from the scale on the axis; it's about 97 cm. This process of determining intermediate values between the plotted points is known as **interpolation**.

Question 3.8

Use Figure 3.2 to estimate the girl's height at 11 years.

Question 3.9

To practise reading graphs, study Figure 3.4 and answer the following questions.

(a) What is the subject of this graph?

(b) What quantity is plotted on the vertical axis, and in what unit is it measured?

(c) What is plotted on the horizontal axis, and in what unit is it measured?

(d) What was the water flow of the stream at 12.00 hours?

(e) What was the maximum flow of the stream and at what approximate time did it occur?

(f) Describe in words the way in which the water flow changed over the period plotted on the graph.

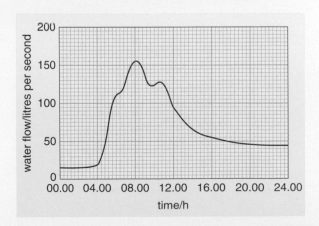

Figure 3.4 The volume of water in a stream flowing past a fixed point per second, monitored over a 24-hour period, during a flood after heavy rainfall. This is the type of graph produced by a continuously recording instrument so there are no individual plotted points.

Now look at Figure 3.5, which shows the results of the experiment to determine the water content of cucumber. On this graph, time is plotted horizontally with units of minutes and mass is plotted vertically with units of grams. The measured values of the cucumber's mass at various times are represented by the points, and a smooth curve has been drawn through these points. The curve shows at a glance that the mass decreases fairly steadily as the time increases for the first 15 minutes, and then it becomes almost constant after about 20 minutes. This is probably similar to the pattern for the change in mass that you observed in the potato experiment.

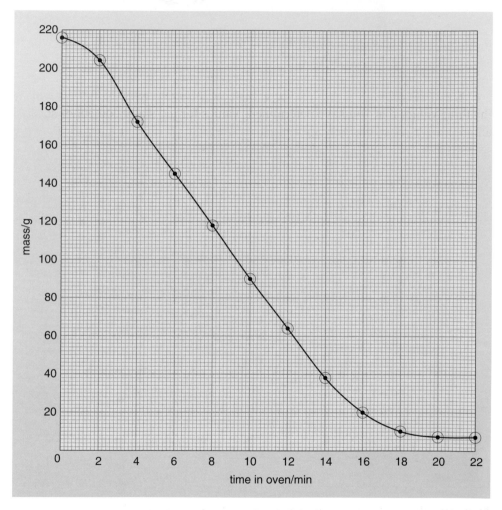

Figure 3.5   Results of an experiment in which cucumber slices were heated in a microwave oven to determine their water content. The mass of the cucumber was measured after successive periods of time in the oven.

Question 3.10

Use the graph in Figure 3.5 to work out (a) the mass of the cucumber after 6 minutes, and (b) how long it took for the mass of the cucumber to fall to 82 grams.

The graph in Figure 3.5 shows that there is a large drop in the mass of the cucumber as the water is driven out. However, to make a comparison with the results of the potato experiment, you need to determine the *percentage* of water in the cucumber, and you can do this next, again using information from the graph.

Question 3.11

(a) From Figure 3.5 determine the initial mass of the cucumber, the mass of the dried cucumber and, hence, the mass of water in the cucumber.

(b) From these values determine the percentage of the mass of the cucumber that is water.

You have now determined values for the percentages of water in potato, cabbage and cucumber, the first from your own experiment and the other two from the data in this book. The water contents of a selection of other vegetables and fruit are shown in Table 3.3 for comparison, and there are spaces for you to write in the three values that you have determined. Values for the water content of several animals are also shown. The information in the table shows that, apart from peanuts and weevils, all of the items listed contain over 60% water, and lettuce and jellyfish contain 95% or more. Clearly, water really is a major component of living organisms.

Table 3.3 Water content of various plants (or parts of plants) and animals. To be completed as part of Section 3.2.

Plant	Water content/% total mass	Animal	Water content/% total mass
lettuce	96	jellyfish	95
tomato	93	cod fish	82
melon	92	earthworm	80
apple	85	frog	78
mango	82	chicken	74
banana	71	herring	67
peanut	5	dog	63
cabbage	87.5%	cockroach	61
potato	78.2%	bean weevil	48
cucumber	97	human	65

Now consider the human animal again and what percentage of water *we* contain. Of the animals listed in Table 3.3, we are most like dogs, since humans and dogs are mammals – the scientific term for the class of animals that have fur (or hair) and milk-producing mammary glands for suckling their young. You might expect, therefore, that human water content is similar to a dog's. This expectation is confirmed by the available data: the typical water content of humans is about 65%; enter this value in Table 3.3 now.

Of course, this value of 65% of the total mass for the water content of humans is a value for the whole body. Different parts of plants contain different percentages of water, and the same is true for our bodies. The 'driest' parts of the body are hair, containing 3% water, and tooth enamel, containing 4%, and the parts with the highest percentages are the grey matter of the brain and the testes, which each contain about 84% water, and blood, which is 83% water. In between these are bone with about 50% water, muscle with 76% and most other body tissues with between 70% and 80%.

Activity 3.4 Constructing a table of data

You should allow about 15 minutes for this activity.

The previous paragraph contains some useful information about the water content of various parts of the human body, but this is obscured by a lot of words. In this activity you should construct a table that displays this information (the percentage content of various parts of the human body) more clearly.

In constructing your table of data you will need to consider:

- what title you will give the table
- how many columns you need and what information each column will contain
- what headings you will use for the columns
- the order in which you will present the information in the columns.

This will require you to read the paragraph above again, and you may also find it useful to refer back to Box 2.3 'Reading tables'. Having decided how you will lay out your table, draw up the appropriate columns and headings, and enter the information from the paragraph. File your table in your study folder – compare yours with the one in the comments on the activity next time you access the course website.

The overall percentage of water in the human body varies from time to time. For example, think of a person who goes to the pub and rapidly drinks 4 pints (about 2.25 litres) of beer without losing water by sweating or urinating. The percentage of water in their body will increase temporarily by about 2%, but a healthy person will rapidly get rid of even this large excess of water. In certain circumstances, however, the rapid intake of large amounts of water can have fatal effects. For example, there have been several tragic cases of teenagers who died after taking a drug at a party and then drinking large amounts of water to avoid becoming dehydrated. The cause of death was excess water in the body, which caused the brain to swell so that it was 'crushed' within the skull. The drug was indirectly responsible because it inhibited the kidneys from getting rid of the excess water in the normal way.

There are a variety of medical conditions that result in abnormal amounts of water being retained by the body tissues. The medical term for this water retention is 'oedema' and it results in swelling of the body. It is an unwelcome complication of pregnancy for some women, and, among other causes, a possible result of kidney disease.

The girl in Figure 2.1 must also have been about 65% water when she was alive about 4200 years ago. However, the water has long since disappeared from her body. All of the soft tissues have completely disappeared – food for a variety of organisms – and only the bones remain. The bones have also become dehydrated in the hot, dry ground; the water has escaped, just as it did from the potato in your experiment, so that the bones no longer contain the 50% of water that would have been present when the girl died.

3.3   Camels and cacti

Activity 3.5   Identifying key points

You should allow 5 minutes for this part of the activity in addition to the reading time for Section 3.3.

At the beginning of this chapter it was suggested that, as you read, you should try to identify key points and highlight or underline them. This activity is designed to help you develop this technique. As you read the paragraph overleaf on cacti, pick out – by either highlighting or underlining – those words and phrases that are concerned with particular aspects of *how* cacti *obtain*, *store* and *conserve* water. Be selective and don't be tempted to highlight too many words and phrases. At the end of Section 3.3, you will be reminded to compare your highlighted or underlined words with those in the comments on this activity.

Two living organisms that are associated in many people's minds with hot, dry deserts are camels and cacti (Figure 3.6).

(a)

(b)

Figure 3.6   (a) Camels in the desert; (b) barrel cacti growing in desert conditions.

Camels – sometimes referred to as 'the ships of the desert' – are mostly confined to Arabia, North Africa, India and Central Asia. Cactus plants, of which there are about 1000 different kinds, are mostly native to North America, particularly the desert areas in the southwest USA and in Mexico. In common with all other living organisms, camels and cacti need water to sustain life, but they can get very little of it in the desert regions where they live. Moreover, the problems associated with the lack of water are made worse in some deserts by the extreme heat during the day.

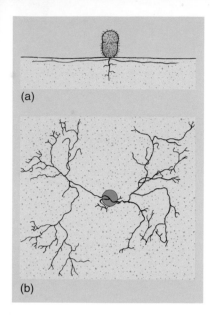

Figure 3.7 The shallow but extended root system of a barrel cactus (a) viewed from the side and (b) viewed from above. In each diagram the sand has been 'removed' to expose the root system.

■ What might be the consequence of the high air temperatures for living organisms?

☐ They may lose water from their surfaces, for example by sweating in the case of animals.

Hence, to survive in deserts, organisms have to be able not only to manage for long periods without water but also to ensure that water loss from their surfaces is kept to a minimum. So how do they cope with these conditions? Cacti will be considered first.

Cacti are very efficient at storing water in their thick, fleshy stems. For this reason they are often described as 'succulents', meaning 'juicy and fleshy'. A large barrel cactus (of the type shown in Figure 3.6) with a height of 1 m and a width of 0.8 m, can readily release up to two litres of drinkable water. On the infrequent occasions when rain falls in the desert, cacti use an extensive system of shallow roots (Figure 3.7) to take up water very rapidly before it can run away or evaporate. As well as having very effective water collection and storage systems, cacti are highly efficient at conserving their stored water. Their surface layer is exceptionally waterproof. Most other types of plant have leaves which lose large amounts of water from their surfaces in hot, dry conditions. In cacti, the leaves are reduced to spines or bristles; this not only minimises water loss but the spines also protect the cacti from being grazed by animals.

Activity 3.5 Identifying key points (continued)

You should allow about 10 minutes for this part of the activity.

You have been highlighting, or underlining, words and phrases in this section that reveal how cacti obtain, store and conserve water. Compare your highlighted words with those suggested in the comments on this activity, when you next access the course website.

Now consider camels, which are famous for their ability to make long, arduous journeys across waterless deserts. Camels conserve water by several mechanisms. Unlike humans, camels do not sweat very much. Before they start to sweat, their body temperature can rise by about 2 degrees Celsius (the Celsius temperature scale is described in Section 4.1.3). This increase in temperature would produce a severe fever in humans. When humans sweat most of the water comes from their blood. If the lost water is not replenished, the blood becomes too viscous (thick), and the heart has difficulty pumping it around the body. In contrast, the water lost when camels sweat comes from throughout the body tissue, and only small amounts come from the blood. To understand the significance of this, consider the following values. When humans lose 4% of their body mass through sweating, their blood volume is reduced by 10%. However, when camels go without water for a long period, they can lose about 20% of their body mass before their blood volume is reduced by 10%. In other words, compared with humans, camels have to lose a five times greater percentage of their body mass before their blood volume drops by 10%. Also, humans will be near death if they lose body water equal to about 12% of their body mass, but camels can survive a loss of body water equal to 40% of their body mass.

Another way in which camels conserve water is by excreting relatively small amounts of water as urine and in their faeces. Urination is the way in which various waste products leave the body dissolved in water, and it's also the way in which the body eliminates any excess amounts of water. To minimise water loss, desert animals produce urine that is very concentrated – typically it contains less than half as much water for a given quantity of waste material as human urine. Faeces are solid waste products, but they do contain a certain amount of water. The faeces produced by desert animals are generally very dry.

As well as minimising the amounts of water they lose from their bodies, camels can quickly replace any water lost by drinking enormous quantities – over 100 litres at a time – when it is available. However, they do not drink more than is required to make up the amount of water they have lost.

Camels also get part of their water intake from their food but, in addition, they have remarkable humps, which are rather like portable larders. It is important to note that these humps are fat stores, *not* water tanks as many people think. When a camel is starved, it breaks down fat from its hump (just as humans break down fat when starved or dieting), and water is produced in this process, as well as energy being released.

What has emerged from this brief discussion of camels and cacti is that water is just as essential for their continued life as it is for humans. They contain similar percentages of water to other organisms, but they have characteristics that enable them to live in hot, dry desert environments, where water is not available all of the time. This observation that different types of animals and plants are adapted to different environments is one of the wonders of science.

3.4 Summary of Chapter 3

All living organisms contain water. Whole plants and whole animals generally contain over 60% water, and some contain as much as 95%. The human body contains about 65% water, but there is a wide variation between the percentages of water in different parts of the body.

Some animals and plants are adapted to living in hot, dry desert environments. They minimise water loss and are very efficient at taking in water when it is available.

Scientific measurements are expressed in SI units. The basic SI unit for length is the metre (m), for time it is the second (s), and for mass it is the kilogram (kg). It is often convenient to use multiples and sub-multiples of the basic SI units; these larger and smaller units are usually indicated by prefixes to the name and symbol of the basic unit and are also regarded as SI units.

Decimals are a way of representing numbers that involve fractions. The number of digits after the decimal point is known as the number of decimal places.

Carrying out experiments (including planning, measuring, recording and analysing data, and critical evaluation) is an important part of scientific inquiry.

Graphs give a pictorial representation of the relationship between two sets of numbers, and are frequently used by scientists to display results of experiments. They show up any trends in the results.

Highlighting the text keeps your reading active and helps you to follow the argument.

Learning outcomes for Chapter 3

When you have completed Chapter 3 you should be able to:

- Plan your studies.
- Do calculations involving SI units.
- Express quantities as decimals.
- Round numbers appropriately.
- Plan and carry out an experiment, record data and analyse the results.
- Read and interpret information from graphs.
- Construct a table of data.
- Identify key points in the text.

Activity 3.1 Planning your study (continued)

You should allow about 20 minutes for this part of the activity.

You should now review your work plan and the time log you have been completing for Chapter 3. This will help you plan how to tackle Chapter 4.

Look at your learning journal to review your work plan and calculate the total amount of time you spent on Chapter 3, including the practical work, and compare this with the amount of time you estimated for this chapter. This will reveal the extent to which you need to modify the estimates in future to match your own study needs.

(a) Were you able to carry out the practical work at the times you had planned? If not, why did your plans have to change? Make a note of the changes you would make to how you plan or prepare for the practical work.

(b) If you tried a different study pattern this week from the previous week, perhaps by varying the time of day and/or the length of time that you studied at a stretch, make a note of what was successful for you.

(c) How does the total time spent on Chapter 3 compare with our estimated time of 11 hours?

Make a note of your responses in your learning journal before continuing with Chapter 4.

Chapter 4
Properties of water

This chapter will broaden the discussion of water to include the solid and gaseous forms – ice and water vapour – both of which play important roles in the story of life. You will look in some detail at the floating of ice on water, the evaporation of water to form water vapour, the capacity of water to dissolve substances, and at the consequences for living organisms. Then at the end of the chapter you will look at the overall recycling of water that occurs on Earth – the water cycle.

Most of the study time for this chapter will be dedicated to learning about important properties of water and their significance for life. You will also develop more maths skills, particularly those relating to handling negative numbers and calculating areas, volumes and densities, and you will learn more about effective study and the use of diagrams. This chapter contains more scientific concepts than the previous ones, so you may need to spend more time on it than you did on the others. However the first study skill introduced in this chapter is reading by scanning (Box 4.1). This technique enables you to get a quick sense of the content before you start reading in any depth.

Box 4.1   Scanning a chapter

The introductory paragraphs above give a brief overview of the science and skills covered in this chapter, and you will find that there are similar 'introductions' at the start of each chapter in this book. However, to give yourself a more complete view of what a chapter contains, you should quickly scan through it before studying it more thoroughly. Your aim should be to identify the main topics and the key ideas. You should ignore the questions and activities, and not worry about highlighting or making notes. Pay particular attention to the title and the first and last paragraphs in each section (e.g. Section 4.1) because these often give a good indication of what the section is about. Make sure that you read the summary at the end of the chapter too, as it contains the most important points.

Activity 4.1   Reading to learn: scanning a chapter

You should allow about 10 minutes for this activity.

Scan through this chapter, and note down the main topics in your study folder, before you start to study it in detail.

4.1 Water, ice and water vapour

The discussion in this book so far has concentrated on liquid water. This is not surprising, since the most obvious signs of the huge quantities of water on the planet are liquid – rivers, lakes, seas, oceans and rain. Moreover, when water is playing its most important roles in living organisms, it is a liquid. Indeed, the word 'water' generally conveys a picture of a liquid. However, if you were shivering on a polar ice-cap, the most obvious form of water all around you would be snow and ice, that is, you would see plenty of evidence for water being a *solid*. On the other hand, if you were to boil water in a kettle, you would generate water vapour, which is a *gas*, and if the water were left boiling for long enough, all of the liquid water in the kettle would be converted to water vapour. The hot water vapour that emerges from the spout is not visible, but it cools as it meets the cold air and condenses into tiny droplets of *liquid* water, rather like a hot mist or cloud (Figure 4.1). As these water droplets move further away from the spout, they evaporate to become water vapour once more.

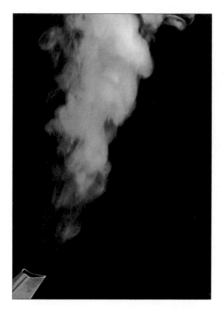 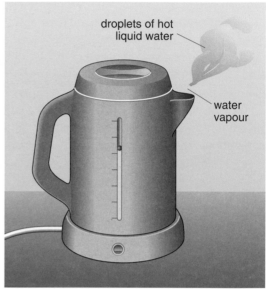

Figure 4.1 Conversion of boiling liquid water to water vapour (evaporation), then to liquid water droplets (condensation).

It is worth noting in passing that scientists use the word 'steam' to describe the *gaseous* form of water. So it is steam that emerges from the spout, and it is steam that is formed again when the cloud evaporates. The intermediate stage, where you can see a cloud of tiny water droplets, is *not* steam according to the scientific use of the word. This is rather different from the everyday use of the word: most people think of the cloud of liquid water droplets as being steam, but this is not the correct scientific use of the word.

You will find examples of other words in this book that have a precise scientific meaning but that are used more loosely in everyday language (recall the use of the words 'mass' and 'weight' in Box 3.2). You need to be aware of the scientific meaning of such words and make sure that you use them correctly in your own writing. Newspapers quite often use scientific words incorrectly and, as you become more familiar with scientific language, you will be able to spot when words are misused.

However, some scientific terms are generally used correctly in everyday language. For example, the processes of **evaporation** and **condensation**, both of which are shown in Figure 4.1, are terms that refer to the changes from a liquid to a gas and from a gas to a liquid, respectively. The conversion of a liquid into a gas is also often called **vaporisation**. The terms 'evaporation' and 'vaporisation' are frequently used interchangeably.

In fact, the air around you contains water vapour all of the time. It is not visible to the human eye, so you might wonder how we know that it is there. Its presence can be detected with scientific instruments, but you may be able to think of some observations or experiments that provide further evidence for the presence of **water vapour** in the air.

Condensation of water on cold objects is evidence for the presence of gaseous water in the air. If you take a can or bottle out of the refrigerator, drops of liquid water – condensation – will appear on its sides. This water must have come from the air. When water vapour in the air comes into contact with a cold surface, it tends to condense as liquid water on that surface. There is an important reason for this occurrence: cold air cannot hold as much water vapour as warm air. The chilled can cools the surrounding air so that it is not capable of holding as much water vapour and the 'rejected' water condenses as a liquid on the cold surface of the can. You will also have observed condensation on the inside of windows when the temperature is low outside.

Mist, fog, clouds, rain and snow are also consequences of water vapour being present in the air. All are formed when moist air cools. As the air temperature falls, the air cannot hold all of the water vapour it contains and some of it condenses into very tiny droplets. If these droplets are very small, they remain suspended in the air, either as clouds if at high altitudes (Figure 4.2), or as mist or fog if near the Earth's surface.

Thus, ice, water vapour and water are different forms of the same substance. In science, the three different forms – **solid**, **liquid** and **gas** – are called the different *states* of substances. The observation of these three states raises three questions.

- What are the differences between the solid, liquid and gaseous states?
- Are ice, liquid water and water vapour composed of the same substance?
- What determines whether water exists as a solid, liquid or gas?

The full answer to these questions is beyond the scope of this course; however, some preliminary answers will be given.

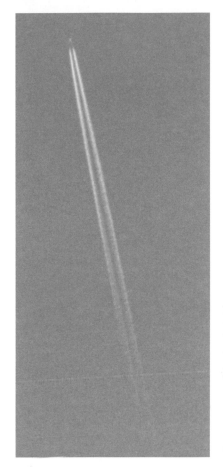

Figure 4.2   The long white vapour trails (contrails) from aircraft seen high in the sky are the result of water vapour in the exhaust gases freezing in the very cold temperatures at high altitudes.

4.1.1 What are the differences between solid, liquid and gaseous states?

Think about how solids, liquids and gases could be defined so that you can distinguish between them easily. A good definition of each state should be applicable to any solid, liquid or gas that you can think of, but it will simplify matters if you take familiar examples of each state and think about their properties.

Question 4.1

Think about a piece of iron, some cooking oil and the air and note down the main features of a solid, a liquid and a gas that allow each to be distinguished from the other two. It may help to think about how permanent the shapes of solids, liquids and gases are, and how easy it is to change their shape or the volume of the space they occupy.

Since water is the theme of this book, you will now consider how the descriptions of solids, liquids and gases apply to ice, liquid water and water vapour. An ice cube has a fixed shape and volume whatever type of glass you put it in. When it melts, however, the resulting liquid water flows so that it adapts to the shape of the bottom of the glass. However, the volume of the liquid water doesn't change when you swirl it around in the glass or when you tip it into the sink. Leave the liquid water for long enough, though, and it will evaporate. If this happened within a sealed room then the gaseous water would be uniformly spread out through the air in the whole room. In other words, gaseous water does not have a fixed volume – it fills any space into which it is put. This property distinguishes a gas from a liquid.

You have probably experienced the capacity of a gas to expand to fill its container without realising it. When a person wearing perfume enters a room, you can smell the perfume almost straight away. You do not have to be very close to the person wearing the perfume to get the benefit. This observation should tell you that the gas that has evaporated from the liquid perfume pervades the room very quickly.

4.1.2 Are ice, liquid water and water vapour the same substance?

How can you be sure that the liquid known as water does not change into a different substance as water freezes into ice or as water is boiled to produce water vapour? There are various chemical experiments that prove that ice, liquid water and water vapour are all composed of the same substance, but how could you convince yourself without doing experiments?

Ice brought out of a freezer into a warm room soon turns to water and, if the water is put back into the freezer, it becomes ice again. Likewise, the substance that escapes into the air as a gas when water boils can condense on a cold surface such as a window and become liquid water again. You could convince yourself of this by holding a cold spoon over the spout of a kettle while the water is boiling; you would soon see droplets of water on the spoon.

These changes from one state to another and back again do not demonstrate beyond doubt that ice, liquid water and water vapour are all made of the same substance. However, scientists generally assume that *the simplest explanation of the facts is correct until some new evidence disproves it.* The fact that ice, liquid water and water vapour share a lack of colour, smell and taste is also consistent with the view that they are all the same substance.

4.1.3 What determines whether water is a solid, liquid or gas?

A major factor that determines the state of water is the **temperature**. When ice is taken out of a freezer, it warms up until it reaches a temperature at which the ice melts to form liquid water. If the liquid water is then heated in a saucepan, it eventually reaches a temperature at which the liquid boils and, if heated long enough, it is completely transformed into water vapour. The same is true of other substances. If you heat a lump of fat or a block of iron, they will eventually reach temperatures at which they melt to become liquids and, if heated further, they will boil and be converted to fat vapour and iron vapour, respectively. However, the temperatures at which ice, fat and iron melt are different, and the temperatures at which the three substances boil are also different.

There are many different scales of hotness or coldness, and any of them gives a measure of temperature. Perhaps the commonest **temperature scale** is degrees Celsius, abbreviated to °C, which was named in honour of a Swedish astronomer, Anders Celsius, who devised the scale in 1743. He defined the freezing temperature of pure water as 0 °C on this scale and the boiling temperature of pure water as 100 °C. The **Celsius scale** is widely referred to as the centigrade scale, because there are 100 divisions – or degrees – between the freezing and boiling temperatures of pure water. However, the correct scientific name of the scale is Celsius. On this scale, the normal human body temperature is around 37 °C, although this varies slightly between individuals.

It is now known that the freezing and boiling temperatures of water are not fixed temperatures – water boils at about 71 °C at the top of Mount Everest, for example. To define the Celsius scale the conditions under which the water freezes or melts have to be specified more precisely. Thus 0 °C (spoken as 'zero degrees Celsius' or 'zero degrees C') is the temperature at which water freezes at sea level under normal atmospheric conditions, which is called the *normal* **freezing temperature** of water. Similarly, 100 °C is the temperature at which water boils at sea level under normal atmospheric conditions, which is called the *normal* **boiling temperature** of water (Figure 4.3).

The most familiar way of converting water to a gas is by heating the liquid up to the normal boiling temperature and this produces vapour at 100 °C. However, liquid water does not have to be heated to its boiling temperature to convert it to gas.

(a)

(b)

Figure 4.3   (a) A glass thermometer with calibration marks in units of °C. The red alcohol thread shows the temperature of iced water to be 0 °C. (b) A digital thermometer showing the temperature of boiling water to be 100 °C.

For example, a puddle in the road does not last forever; the water evaporates and the road becomes dry again, and the higher the temperature, the more rapidly the water evaporates. The most familiar way of converting water to a solid is by cooling the liquid down to below the freezing temperature, which produces ice at 0 °C. Ice is considered in more detail in Section 4.2.

The Celsius scale is not limited to the range between 0 °C and 100 °C; for example, the temperature of the surface of the Sun is about 5500 °C, and air temperatures frequently drop well below 0 °C in winter. A wide range of Celsius temperatures is shown in Figure 4.4. When temperatures fall below zero, they are represented by **negative numbers**; the lower the temperature, the larger the number after the minus. At the lowest temperature shown, −196 °C (i.e. 196 degrees below zero), nitrogen gas, which is the main component of the air that you breathe, condenses and becomes a liquid.

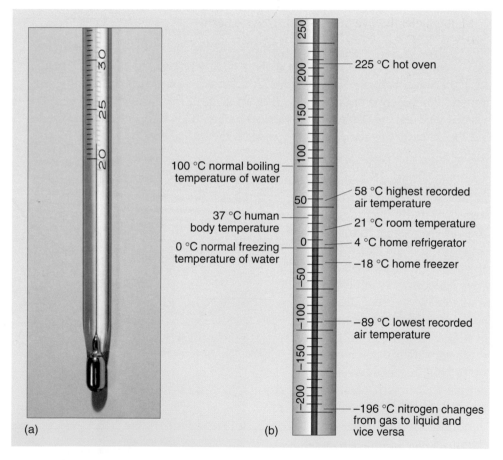

Figure 4.4 (a) A glass thermometer with a silver mercury thread showing a room temperature of 21.5 °C. (b) Some notable temperatures on the Celsius scale. Note that a minus sign is always used to denote negative temperatures but a plus sign is not used in front of positive temperatures.

Try Questions 4.5 and 4.6 if you want to check your understanding of the use of negative numbers in the context of the Celsius temperature scale. If you are not familiar with negative numbers, you may find it helpful to study Box 4.2 before attempting these questions.

Box 4.2 Negative numbers

Negative numbers arise in any situation where there are values that are less than some agreed reference point (labelled zero), such as 0 °C on the Celsius temperature scale. When the temperature falls five degrees below 0 °C, it is called 'minus five degrees Celsius', or −5 °C, and if it falls even further to 10 degrees below zero then it is −10 °C. So the minus sign in front of a temperature tells you that it is 'less than zero' and the number tells you how many degrees less than zero. In other words, the larger the number that follows the minus sign, the further the temperature is below zero degrees. Mathematically, five degrees below zero means 0 °C − 5 °C and, if you do to the subtraction '0 − 5' on your calculator, you will see that the answer is −5.

If you are not used to thinking about negative numbers, it may help to think in terms of money. If your bank account is overdrawn by £50, it has '£50 less than nothing' in it, and your balance is −£50. You would have to add £50 to bring the balance up to zero. In a similar way, if the temperature is −50 °C (i.e. 50 °C 'less than nothing'), you would have to increase the temperature by 50 °C to bring it up to zero. If your balance is −£100, you are overdrawn by £100 and so in greater debt than if you were overdrawn by just £50. Similarly, −100 °C is colder than −50 °C.

Question 4.2

Arrange the following temperatures in increasing order, i.e. starting with the lowest temperature and ending with the highest temperature.

210 °C, 0 °C, −27 °C, 1750 °C, −85 °C, −26 °C, −210 °C, 85 °C

Calculating with negative numbers

There are several simple rules which can be applied when you need to carry out arithmetic operations (addition, subtraction, multiplication and division) involving negative numbers. These rules are given below, with examples of each.

> Adding a negative number is the same as subtracting the corresponding positive number.

So, for example:

$$5 + (−3) = 5 − 3 = 2$$
$$(−5) + (−3) = (−5) − 3 = −8$$

Subtracting a negative number is the same as adding the corresponding positive number.

So, for example:

$$5 − (−3) = 5 + 3 = 8$$
$$(−5) − (−3) = (−5) + 3 = −2$$

Note the way in which brackets have been used in the examples to make it clear how the numbers and signs are associated.

If you are struggling to see why subtracting 3 from −5 should give −8, whereas adding 3 to −5 gives −2, you may find it helpful to revisit the financial analogy. If your account is £5 overdrawn and you spend a further £3, you will end up with an overdraft of £8. However, if your account is £5 overdrawn and you repay £3, your overdraft will be reduced to £2.

> If you multiply or divide two numbers which have *the same* sign, the answer is *positive*.

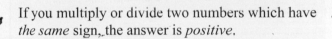

So, 5 × 3 = 15, as you already know, but also (−5) × (−3) = 15.

8 ÷ 4 = 2, as you already know, but also (−8) ÷ (−4) = 2.

> If you multiply or divide two numbers which have *different* signs, the answer is *negative*.

So, 5 × (−3) = −15 and (−8) ÷ 4 = −2.

Question 4.3

Do the following calculations, *without using your calculator*.

(a) (−3) + (−4)

(b) (−10) − (−5)

(c) 6 ÷ (−2)

(d) (−12) ÷ (−6)

Make sure that you know how to input negative numbers into your calculator. With some makes of calculator you can enter expressions like those in Question 4.3 more or less as they are written, with or without brackets. With other makes you may need to use a key labelled something like +/– or ± to change a positive number into a negative one.

Question 4.4

Making sure that you input all the signs, use your calculator to work out the following calculations.

(a) $117 - (-38) + (-286)$

(b) $(-1624) \div (-29)$

(c) $(-123) \times (-24)$

(a)

Question 4.5

In each of the following pairs of temperatures, which value would correspond to the warmer object?

(a) 57 °C and 65 °C

(b) 57 °C and –65 °C

(c) –57 °C and –65 °C

(d) –57 °C and 65 °C

Question 4.6

Nitrogen is part of the air we breathe – it is a gas at room temperature. It condenses to a liquid at –196 °C and freezes at –210 °C. What is the difference between the temperature at which nitrogen condenses and the temperature at which it freezes?

4.2   Why does ice float?

This section looks at a property of water which you probably take for granted, but which is, in fact, exceptional and has important consequences for life. This property is the fact that ice floats on water. Put some ice cubes in a glass of water and they float at the top; they don't sink to the bottom. On a much larger scale, icebergs float in the open seas when they break away from the ice shelf. You may never have thought of this as being particularly strange, but the solids formed when most liquids are frozen will sink when placed in the liquid from which they were formed. Figure 4.5 compares the behaviour of ice with that of virgin olive oil.

(b)

Figure 4.5   Ice cubes float but oil cubes sink! The cubes in (a) were formed by placing liquid water in a freezer and they are shown floating on liquid water; the cubes in (b) were formed by placing virgin olive oil in a freezer and they are shown at the bottom of a glass of the same olive oil.

How can you tell whether a solid will float on a liquid? Most types of wood float on water, but steel does not. You might think that the reason for this is that steel is heavier than wood but, although that is the start of an explanation, you need to be more precise. After all, a small steel screw will sink in water but a large tree trunk will float. It isn't the mass of the steel screw that is important, it's the fact that the screw is heavier (it has a greater mass) than the amount of water that has the same volume as the screw. Conversely the tree trunk floats because it is lighter (its mass is less) than the amount of water that has the same volume as the tree trunk.

Before looking at floating in more detail, you need to be clear about the concepts of area and volume and the units that are used to measure them (the information about water use in Chapter 2 was given as volumes of water, measured in litres, but these terms were not properly defined). Check your understanding by trying Question 4.7. If you have any problems with this question, you should study Box 4.3 before proceeding.

Question 4.7

A domestic water tank is 978 mm long, 622 mm wide and 610 mm high.

(a) What is the volume of the tank in m^3? You should give your answer to three places of decimals.

(b) What is the volume of the tank in litres? You should give your answer to the nearest whole number.

Box 4.3 Area, volume and more on units

Area is a measure of the size of an object's surface. For squares and rectangles, the area is found by multiplying the length by the width. So, if a rectangular garden pond (Figure 4.6) has one side 4 m long and another side 2.5 m long, the numerical value of the area is given by multiplying 4×2.5, which is 10. What about the units? In this case, metres are being multiplied by metres (m $\times$ m) and, recalling from Box 2.4 the use of superscripts to indicate powers such as squares and cubes, m $\times$ m can be written as m^2. So the units of the answer are m^2, said as 'metres squared' or 'square metres'. In SI units, area is measured in square metres.

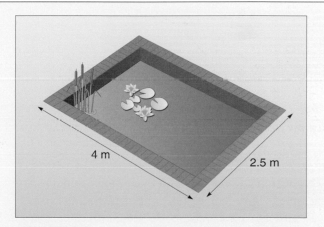

Figure 4.6   A rectangular garden pond 4 m long and 2.5 m wide.

■ What is the area of the room shown in the plan in Figure 4.7?

☐ You could think of the room as being made up of a 3 m $\times$ 2 m rectangle and a 1 m $\times$ 1 m square, as shown in Figure 4.8. The total area is then:

$$(3 \text{ m} \times 2 \text{ m}) + (1 \text{ m} \times 1 \text{ m}) = 6 \text{ m}^2 + 1 \text{ m}^2 = 7 \text{ m}^2$$

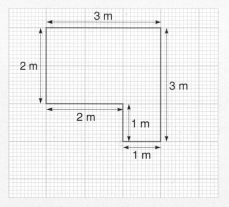

Figure 4.7   Plan of an L-shaped room.

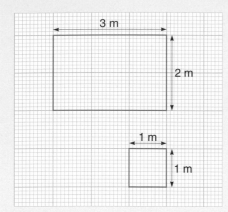

Figure 4.8   Calculating the area of an L-shaped room.

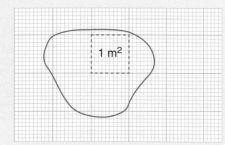

Figure 4.9   An irregularly shaped pond with an area of about 5 m². The dotted square 1 cm × 1 cm has an area of 1 cm² and represents 1 m².

The concept of area is useful even for irregularly shaped objects, such as the pond shown in the plan in Figure 4.9. Each centimetre square on the graph paper represents 1 m², so you can verify that the total area is approximately 5 m² by counting up the number of centimetre squares and part squares: there are one complete square, two nearly complete squares and several additional part squares which could reasonably add together to make another two squares, giving a total of about five squares.

Volume is a measure of the space that a three-dimensional object occupies. The volume of a rectangular block is found by multiplying its length by its width by its height. A simple cube with 1 m long sides (Figure 4.10) has a volume of $1 \, m \times 1 \, m \times 1 \, m = 1 \, m^3$ (said as 'metre cubed' or 'cubic metre'). In SI units, volume is measured in cubic metres.

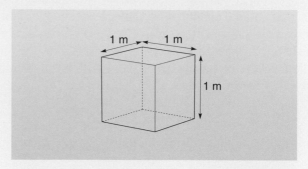

Figure 4.10   A cube with 1 m long sides and a volume of 1 cubic metre ($1 \, m^3$).

The aquarium tank shown in Figure 4.11 has a volume of

$$3 \, m \times 2 \, m \times 1 \, m = 6 \, m^3$$

and six cubes with 1 m sides could, in principle, be neatly stacked in the tank, as the dashed lines on the diagram indicate. For any rectangular block-like structure, such as a brick or a plank of wood, you can use the same method for measuring the volume: just multiply together the length, the width and the height, as you did for the tank in Figure 4.11.

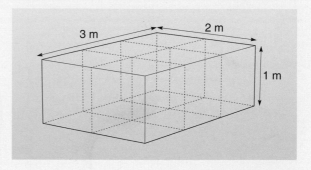

Figure 4.11   An aquarium tank and its dimensions: height 1 m, width 2 m, length 3 m.

■ Suppose you had calculated the volume of a tank using lengths measured in centimetres. What would be the unit of its volume?

☐ The unit would be cm × cm × cm, or cubic centimetres, which is abbreviated to cm³.

However, if you had measured one dimension in mm and the other two dimensions in cm, before calculating the volume you would have to ensure all the dimensions were in the same unit.

■ What is the volume of a carton of fruit juice that is 8 cm long, 45 mm wide, and 12 cm high? Give your answer in cm³.

☐ Since 45 mm = 4.5 cm

volume of carton = 8 cm × 4.5 cm × 12 cm
  = 432 cm³

■ What is the volume of the same carton of fruit juice in units of m³ ?

☐ One way of proceeding is to convert the lengths of each side to m before multiplying them together:

8 cm = 0.08 m, 4.5 cm = 0.045 m and 12 cm = 0.12 m

so,

volume of carton = 0.08 m × 0.045 m × 0.12 m
  = 0.000 432 m³ ✗

Note that the value for the volume of the carton is considerably smaller when measured in m³ than when measured in cm³. This is reasonable – imagine a 1 m³ box and think how much bigger this is than a 1 cm³ box; the fruit juice carton has a bigger volume than the 1 cm³ box but a smaller volume than the 1 m³ box. To convert from cm³ to m³ you need to convert the units of each side from cm to m by dividing by 100, so in total you are dividing by 100 × 100 × 100 = 1000 000. Similar principles apply whenever you need to convert the units of area or volume so, for example, to convert the area of 0.0036 m² to mm², you need to start by recognising that 1 m = 1000 mm, then remember that the area of the square represents two lengths multiplied together, so to covert the units you need to multiply too:

1 m² = 1000 mm × 1000 mm = 1000 000 mm²

so

0.0036 m² = 0.0036 × 1000 000 mm² = 3600 mm²

Although you will need to be able to calculate volumes in m³, cm³ and mm³, a unit that is much more commonly used for measuring volumes of liquids is the litre. This is the unit you used in Chapter 2 when considering water use, and is the unit used in the UK for selling a range of liquids –

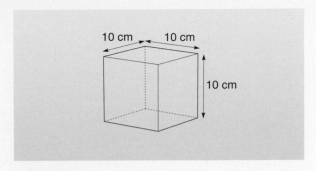

Figure 4.12 A litre is the volume of a cube with sides each 1 dm (10 cm) long.

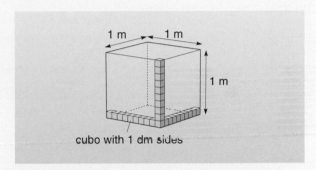

cube with 1 dm sides

Figure 4.13 How many of the yellow 1 dm³ cubes could be stacked in 1 m³ ?

from fruit juice to paint. 'Litre' or 'litres' can be abbreviated by the letter l, but take care when using this symbol as it looks very much like the number one (1). A **litre** is the volume of a cube that has sides each 1 decimetre long, where 1 decimetre (abbreviated to dm) is equal to one-tenth of a metre, i.e. 10 centimetres, so 1 dm = 10 cm (Figure 4.12).

If you think about stacking cubes with 1 dm (10 cm) long sides in a 1 m³ cube (Figure 4.13), you can see that you would need 10 × 10 × 10 = 1000 of the smaller 1 dm³ cubes to fill a cubic metre (1 m³), so:

1 m³ = 1000 dm³ = 1000 litres

■ How many cubic centimetres (cm³) are there in 1 litre?

☐ A cube with 10 cm sides has a volume of 1 litre. If you think about stacking 1 cm³ cubes in a cube with sides each 10 cm long, you can see that there are 10 × 10 × 10 = 1000 of the 1 cm³ cubes in 1 litre, so 1000 cm³ = 1 litre.

Question 4.8

(a) What is the area of the top surface of the box shown in Figure 4.14? Give your answer in both m² and cm².

(b) What is the volume of the box? Give your answer in both m³ and cm³.

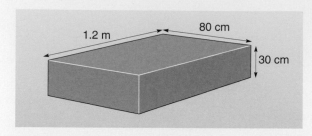

Figure 4.14 A box with dimensions length 1.2 m, width 80 cm and height 30 cm.

Question 4.9

A reservoir has the capacity to store 2.5 million litres of water. How many cubic metres is this?

4.2.1 Density

Now you can return to the original question, 'How can you tell whether a solid will float on a liquid?' To answer this, you need to compare the mass of a particular volume of the solid, such as steel, with the mass of the same volume of water. Table 4.1 lists the masses of one cubic metre (1 m³) of several solids and liquids. Clearly, all these materials have different masses for the same 1 m³ volume. The table shows that one cubic metre of steel has a mass of 7800 kg, and that one cubic metre of water has a mass of 1000 kg. The ratio of these masses is 7800 kg : 1000 kg, which is the same as 78 : 10 or 7.8 : 1; by using a ratio in which the smallest number is 1, you can see that the mass of the steel is 7.8 times greater than the mass of the water. So, since the mass of one cubic metre of steel is greater than the mass of one cubic metre of water, the steel will sink in the water. Conversely, most types of wood will float in water because the mass of one cubic metre of the wood is less than that of one cubic metre of water.

Fortunately, if you want to know whether a 2 m³ steel block floats or sinks in water, you don't need to work out the mass of that block and compare it with the mass of 2 m³ of water. This is because if 1 m³ of steel has 7.8 times the mass of 1 m³ of water, 2 m³ of steel will have 7.8 times the mass of 2 m³ of water. Similarly, 10 m³ of steel will also have 7.8 times the mass of 10 m³ of water. This is because, for any solid or liquid, if you double the volume, you will double the mass, and if you increase the volume 10-fold, the mass also increases 10-fold. The mass and the volume of objects made from the same material increase and decrease in step with each other.

This close link between the masses and volumes of objects leads to the concept of 'density'. You may already be familiar with this concept. It is quite easy to lift a cubic metre of expanded polystyrene (the white synthetic material used for insulation and packaging), but you would need a crane to lift a cubic metre of steel. This is because there is far less mass for a cubic metre of polystyrene than for the same volume of steel. This concept of the amount of mass for a given volume is **density**.

To be more precise, the density of any object, such as a steel screw, is defined as its mass divided by its volume, so:

density *equals* mass *divided by* volume

or

$$\text{density} = \frac{\text{mass}}{\text{volume}}$$

This is a **word equation**, which is a way of working out the density of any object, as long as you know the mass of the object and its volume. You simply replace the word 'mass' in the equation by the actual value of the mass of the object, and replace the word 'volume' by the actual volume.

Consider a one cubic metre block of steel as an example. From Table 4.1 you know that the mass of this block is 7800 kg, and the volume is 1 m³. So

$$\text{density} = \frac{\text{mass}}{\text{volume}} = \frac{7800 \text{ kg}}{1 \text{ m}^3} = 7800 \, \frac{\text{kg}}{\text{m}^3}$$

Note that the unit of mass and the unit of volume are included next to the values in the equation – this is good practice and you should get used to doing this. The resulting units are kg divided by m³, kilograms per cubic metre, more commonly written as kg/m³. This is the SI unit for density. It may look complicated, but it specifies clearly what density is measuring – the amount of mass (kg) in a certain volume (1 m³). Later in the course (in Chapter 9) you will learn about another way of writing kg/m³, the unit of density.

The reason that this concept of density is so important is that *the density of any material doesn't depend on the size or shape of the object made from the material.*

This means that the density of a steel bar is the same as the density of a 1 m³ steel block, as you can confirm by answering the following question. (*Note*: the bar and block are assumed to be made from the same type of steel. There is a range of different types of steel (e.g. mild, stainless) that are manufactured from different proportions of various constituents, and the densities of the different steels vary slightly.)

■ A steel bar has a mass of 234 kg and a volume of 0.030 m³. What is the density of this bar?

☐ $$\text{density} = \frac{\text{mass}}{\text{volume}} = \frac{234 \text{ kg}}{0.030 \text{ m}^3} = 7800 \text{ kg/m}^3$$

Table 4.1 Mass of one cubic metre of various materials. To be completed as part of Section 4.2.2.

Material	Mass/kg
gold	19 280
silver	10 500
steel	7 800
rock (granite)	2 700
bone	1 800
water	1 000
olive oil	920
petrol	800
wood (oak)	*650
expanded polystyrene	20
ice	460
aluminium	
lead	

* This value is typical for most types of wood. However, values for the mass of 1 m³ varies from 170 kg for balsa wood to around 1300 kg for *Lignum vitae*, a tropical hardwood used in the manufacture of police truncheons and croquet mallets (given its combined properties of strength, hardness and heaviness).

So, although the mass of the bar is about 30 times smaller than the mass of the steel block, its density is exactly the same as the value you calculated above for the block. What is more, a steel screw or any other object made from the same steel would also have the same density, 7800 kg/m³. So once the density of the steel, or any other material, has been measured, you don't have to measure it again for every object that you make. You simply look up the value of the density of the material in reference tables.

Now, Table 4.1 lists the masses in kilograms of one cubic metre of various materials, so these numbers are in fact the same as the densities of the materials in units of kg/m³. You could, therefore, write in an alternative title for the table – 'Density of various materials' – and an alternative heading for the second column – 'Density/kg per m³', or for clarity, 'Density/(kg/m³)'. (*Note*: the brackets show that density is divided by the units 'kg/m³'.)

4.2.2   Sink or float?

As pointed out earlier, you can tell whether a piece of steel would sink or float by comparing the mass of that piece of steel with the mass of an amount of water that has the same volume as the steel. That experimental approach to deciding whether something sinks or floats is no longer necessary if tables of density values are available, such as Table 4.1.

If you want to know whether a material sinks or floats in a liquid, all you need to do is compare the density of the material with the density of the liquid. If the material has a higher density than the liquid, it will sink. So, for example, steel will sink in water because its density (7800 kg/m³) is greater than that of water (1000 kg/m³). Similarly, you can see from Table 4.1 that the densities of gold, silver, granite and bone are very much greater than that of water; these materials will also sink in water. However, materials that have a density lower than that of water will float.

■   Which of the materials listed in Table 4.1 will float on water?

☐   Olive oil, petrol, oak wood and expanded polystyrene will float on water because their densities are less than that of water.

The idea that a material floats or sinks in a liquid depending on whether its density is less than or greater than the density of the surrounding liquid provides the answer to the question of why ice floats on water.

■ A rectangular sheet of ice on a pond has dimensions 2.5 m × 2.0 m × 0.10 m and its mass is 460 kg. What is the density of the ice?

□ The volume of the ice is 2.5 m × 2.0 m × 0.10 m = 0.50 m³, so the density of ice is

$$\text{density} = \frac{\text{mass}}{\text{volume}} = \frac{460 \text{ kg}}{0.50 \text{ m}^3} = 920 \text{ kg/m}^3$$

Thus the density of ice is lower than that of water (1000 kg/m³), so ice will float on top of water; hence the top of a pond or lake will ice over. (You should record this value on Table 4.1.)

This capacity of ice to float on water is very important for life in ponds and lakes. To understand its significance, consider what would happen if ice sank to the bottom of water. Think about a pond or lake in winter, with the air temperature below 0 °C. The surface of the water will cool down, and eventually ice will form. If this ice sank to the bottom, more ice would form at the surface and sink, and more ice would form and sink. This would be a very efficient way of cooling down the pond and freezing it solid, with fatal consequences for the fish and other aquatic life. However, because ice floats on water, it forms an insulating blanket on the top, which is then often covered with a further insulating blanket of snow. Conditions have to be very much more severe before the pond will freeze completely. If ice did not float, aquatic life would be restricted to parts of the world where temperatures do not fall below freezing.

Figure 4.15   Two blocks of metal and their dimensions.

Question 4.10

What are the densities of the blocks shown in Figure 4.15? Will either of the two blocks float in water? Record your values in Table 4.1.

4.3   Sweating to keep cool

In Section 4.2 you considered what happens to water when its temperature drops to 0 °C and below, causing the water to change from the liquid state to the solid state. In this section you will look at some of the consequences of water changing from the liquid state to the gaseous state.

When the air temperature reaches 25 °C or more, you feel hot and begin to sweat. You learned in Section 3.3 that one way in which animals, including humans, lose water is through sweating. The real purpose of sweating, however, is not to lose water but to cool the body, although sweating itself doesn't produce cooling. If you wrap up in tight clothes in a hot place, sweating doesn't cool you down.

Sweat needs to be able to evaporate, and it is the evaporation of the water – the change from a liquid to a vapour – that produces the cooling effect.

In order to understand this cooling effect, first think about what happens when you heat water. You can do this in all kinds of ways: in an electric kettle or burning various fuels – for example, gas, paraffin or wood. These all provide energy, in one form or another, and the energy they supply will raise the temperature of a kettle of water. Now focus on an electric kettle: the temperature of the water rises steadily as the heating element in the kettle provides energy to the water. When the water reaches its normal boiling temperature, 100 °C, the temperature stops rising; it stays at 100 °C while the water boils away. Energy is still being supplied to the water – your electricity meter shows this – but now, rather than raising the temperature of the water, the energy supplied is being used to convert the water to vapour, that is to evaporate it (Section 4.1). This demonstrates that it takes energy to raise the temperature of a liquid (or a solid) and it also takes energy to evaporate a liquid and, if you're using an electric kettle, the energy comes from the electricity supply.

So what is the connection between an electric kettle of boiling water and the process of sweating? Sweat on the skin will evaporate into the air. Unlike the boiling water in the kettle, the skin isn't at 100 °C, but energy is still required for the water to evaporate. The energy to evaporate the sweat comes from the body. The energy that is supplied in this way is usually called heat, so the body has to provide heat to evaporate the sweat from the skin. The loss of heat from the surface of the body to the water vapour means that the skin cools down. This cooling effect is even more noticeable when you put perfume or aftershave on your skin; it immediately feels cool because the skin area where you applied it supplies heat to evaporate the liquid.

You are probably aware of some applications of the principle that evaporation of water produces a cooling effect. Suppose you don't have a refrigerator and want to keep a carton of milk cool. A very effective way is to wrap a wet cloth around the carton. The water evaporates from the cloth, and the heat required to evaporate the water comes from the carton, which in turn cools the milk. So the evaporation of the water from the cloth cools the milk in the same way that evaporation of your sweat cools you down on a hot day.

Question 4.11

Does the process of evaporation of water occur only at its boiling temperature? Give examples to support your answer, some of which might be from earlier sections of Chapter 4.

4.4   Dissolving

So far in Chapter 4 you have considered some of the consequences for life, both when liquid water forms ice and when it forms water vapour. You will now consider a third property of water – this time when it is in the liquid state: the fact that substances **dissolve** in water.

If you put a teaspoonful of table salt in a pan of boiling water, it disappears – i.e. it dissolves. However, although the salt seems to have disappeared, in fact it is still present in the water. You can convince yourself by cooling a teaspoon of this water and tasting it. The liquid is now a **solution** of salt in water. The salt can no longer be seen because it has separated into very small particles that are dispersed in the water. If you poured the salty water onto a dinner plate and left it overnight in a warm place, the water would evaporate and the solid salt crystals would reappear, coating the bottom of the plate, and thus providing evidence that the salt was there all the time. This observation also reveals that dissolving is a reversible process.

Any substance that dissolves in water is said to be **soluble** in water.

■ What other examples of solid substances that dissolve in water are you familiar with?

□ You may have thought of some of the following examples: sugar, bicarbonate of soda, soluble aspirin, soda crystals, washing powder, instant coffee. There are many others.

The first living organisms on Earth evolved in liquid water, one important reason for this being that many substances needed to sustain life are soluble in water. The water-based fluids found in living organisms, such as blood, urine and sweat (Section 2.5), all contain different dissolved substances. Equally significant for life is the fact that some substances do not dissolve in water, i.e. they are **insoluble** in water. Among the important insoluble substances are those that form the surface layer of organisms, such as human skin. Hence you won't dissolve if you go for a swim.

■ Make a list of substances you put in water that are insoluble.

□ Examples include china and pottery (crockery), metal (cutlery), wood and plastic (utensils), cotton and wool (clothes), leather (shoes), sand, cooking oil and flowers, to name but a few.

A liquid that dissolves another substance is called a **solvent**. Water is only one kind of solvent. Oil, grease and gloss paints (which are oil-based), for example, do not dissolve in water but do dissolve in white spirit. Even white spirit will not dissolve the spray paint used on cars. It needs another kind of solvent. However, no other liquid dissolves such a large variety of substances as water, which is why water is an ideal solvent for scientists, industrialists and cooks to use.

To help you appreciate the importance of the capacity of water to dissolve substances, the quality of drinking water, and the fate of a glass of water when you drink it, will now be considered.

4.4.1   Purity of drinking water

No natural water found on Earth is pure; any sample of water contains more than just water. As you know, some solid materials, such as table salt, are very soluble and large quantities will dissolve in water, whereas other materials are less soluble. The largest natural water reservoirs on Earth are the oceans, which comprise salty water containing many valuable dissolved substances, such as sodium, calcium and magnesium. Rivers, lakes and artificial water reservoirs usually contain much less of these substances.

Not only solid substances dissolve in water; gases do too. For example, rainwater is almost pure water containing only dissolved gases from the atmosphere; it is a solution of liquid water and gases. One of the most important of these gases is oxygen, which is found dissolved in seawater, particularly near the surface, and in fresh river water. This dissolved oxygen is extracted from water by many aquatic organisms, some of which have special structures for this purpose; for example, fish have gills.

Ideally, all drinking water should be of a certain quality to be acceptable for human consumption, that is, to be **potable**. This water need not be absolutely pure, but it is essential that it does not contain harmful materials, such as dissolved poisons, or harmful bacteria which could cause illness. The World Health Organization (WHO) has set international drinking water standards for the maximum amounts of impurities in potable water.

Unfortunately, much potentially harmful waste from farming and industry is soluble, and can enter water supplies. An example of the former is the nitrogen-containing fertilisers that are required to support plant growth in areas of intensive farming. Rain washes some of the fertiliser from the fields into streams, rivers and underground water sources and problems arise when these fertilisers contaminate drinking water. When drunk, such contaminated water can interfere with the transport of oxygen in the blood. In the East Anglia region of England, where extensive areas are devoted to agriculture, some of the underground water sources on which the region relies have nitrogen (in the form of nitrate) levels higher than that recommended by the WHO. This water has to be mixed with water from other sources that has a very low level of nitrate before it is piped to homes.

It would be a difficult task to make water absolutely pure on a large scale but, fortunately, it isn't desirable to do this because many of the substances water contains are required in the human diet. An example of one such ingredient is calcium, which is required for healthy bones and teeth. Even bottled drinking waters are not 100% water. Look at the label the next time you see a bottle of water, and note the amounts of calcium and other substances that it contains. The amounts of dissolved substances in two samples of bottled water are shown in Figure 4.16 for comparison. You will learn about these substances during your study of this course.

Question 4.12

Look at Figure 4.16. How many times more calcium does water (a) contain per litre than water (b)? What is the ratio of these two quantities of calcium?

Typical analysis mg/l
calcium 117 • magnesium 19 • sodium 13 • potassium 2 • sulfate 16 • bicarbonate 405 • chloride 28 • nitrate 20

(a)

Typical analysis mg/l	
calcium	30
magnesium	19
sodium	24
potassium	1
bicarbonate	248
chloride	42
sulfate	23
nitrate	<0.1

(b)

Figure 4.16 The amounts of dissolved substances in bottled water from two different areas (a) and (b) of the UK. The units used are mg/l, which means milligrams of dissolved substance per litre of bottled water. The symbol < means 'less than'.

Bacteria, of which there are many different types, can also contaminate water supplies. They are very small organisms, too small to be seen without the magnification of a microscope. They are found nearly everywhere, including inside your intestine, in soil and in water. Many of them are harmless and indeed can be beneficial; for example, bacteria in the soil break down dead organic material and thus stop it accumulating. However, other bacteria can cause disease in a variety of organisms, including humans. For example, drinking water contaminated with typhoid bacteria can lead to the development of typhoid fever in people who drink the water (Figure 4.17).

Figure 4.17 'Monster soup': a cartoon from about 1830 mocking the quality of water from the River Thames being supplied as drinking water by the London Water Companies. Harmful bacteria in the water caused regular outbreaks of illness in London at this time.

4.4.2   Water in the human body

It is important to realise that ingested water (taken in by mouth) doesn't simply travel directly to the bladder, ready to be expelled. Water permeates the whole of the human body and it can move from one location to another by a variety of routes.

As you learned in Section 3.2, about 65% of the human body is water. Water is a major component of all fluids in the body, and only a surprisingly small amount – about 8% of the total amount of water in the body – is found in the blood. You may recall from Section 2.5 some other essential water-based fluids in the human body. These include mucus in the lining of the lungs and nose, tears which continually bathe the eyes, saliva secreted in the mouth, and various digestive juices secreted in the intestines. These fluids are localised in particular parts of the body. However, there is another important fluid in the body – tissue fluid. This fluid surrounds organs such as the brain, kidney, heart and lungs, and is within the tissues that make up these organs.

All living organisms are composed of small cells; indeed, the cell is often referred to as the 'unit of life'. You, for example, consist of many millions of cells. Cells are too small to be seen with the naked eye but, if you took a thin scraping from the inside of your cheek and looked at it under a microscope, you would see some cells, like those in Figure 4.18. The important point about cells for the theme of 'water for life' is that every cell contains water (in most cases as much as 70%) and the cell surface is also bathed by tissue fluid. Clearly, water is a crucial component of all living organisms.

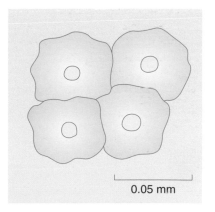

0.05 mm

Figure 4.18 Schematic diagram of four cells from the inside of a human cheek. The scale bar shows the length on the figure that the bar represents. In this case, the length of the bar is much larger than the length it represents (only 0.05 mm), which shows that the drawing is greatly magnified. The size of a cheek cell is roughly the same size as the bar, so each cell is about 0.05 mm wide.

4.4.3 A drink of water

In this section you will follow the journey of a glass of water through the body. You will also be helped to develop your study skills, first by studying Box 4.4.

Box 4.4 Active reading: making notes

Chapter 3 introduced the idea of thinking actively about the text as you read it. It was also suggested that you keep asking yourself 'what are the key points of this section?' and that you highlight (or underline) the important ideas in the book as you are studying. Another activity that most students find helpful is making notes as they read. These notes might include examples that illustrate what is being discussed in the text, thoughts that you have as you read that help you understand the arguments presented, connections with other topics that you have studied, or something that helps jog your memory. It is also very useful to make a note of parts of the text that you don't understand, so that you can come back to them later, or discuss them with other students or your tutor. Of course, the 'notes' that you make don't just have to be words; your own sketches and diagrams are equally valuable ways of recording your thoughts and responses to the text. You will find that your notes are extremely valuable when you return to a section later in the course, particularly when you need to answer assignment questions.

The margins of this book are generally the best place for most notes; if you make them in pencil you can erase any of them that are no longer appropriate. For example, when the meaning of a paragraph that initially puzzled you eventually becomes clear, you can erase your note that indicated you didn't understand it. There will be places in the book where there isn't enough space for the notes you want to make, so you can then use sheets of paper that you file in your study folder with your responses to questions and activities. To remind yourself that you've made such notes, you could write 'see S154 folder' at the appropriate place in the book.

Activity 4.2 Annotating text: fluids in the body

You should allow about 15 minutes for this part of the activity in addition to the reading time for Section 4.4.3.

As you read this section you should highlight and make notes in your study folder on the *roles* of water-based fluids in the body – the details of the movement of water through the body are not so important. At the end of the section, in the continuation of this activity, you will be asked to produce a list of these fluids and their functions. You can't assume that the name of each fluid is immediately followed in the text by its role. Therefore, in addition to highlighting appropriate words and phrases, you need a system for identifying which role is linked to which fluid. For example, you may choose to number each fluid and number its role.

Starting in the mouth, the water is mixed with a little saliva, the role of which is to moisten and soften food and to start the digestive process. It is then swallowed to begin a journey to the stomach (Figures 4.19a and b). In the stomach the water is one of many substances, eaten or drunk, that are churned and mixed together. A big muscular wave of the stomach propels the water with part-digested food through the small opening to the first section of the small intestine, called the duodenum. Here it is joined by secretions of digestive juices with which it is mixed and is thrown from one end of the duodenum to the other as if in a cocktail shaker. As it continues its journey through the intestine, for ever being propelled forward, it is mixed with more digestive juices. These break down the food into smaller and smaller pieces, releasing the water content of the food into the intestine. Eventually, the mixture of water and broken-down food becomes a soft milky suspension. The soluble bits of digested food (nutrients) are taken up into fine blood vessels. The blood carries the nutrients taken up from the small intestine to the liver for storage and redistribution to other parts of the body that need them. The remaining food eventually passes into the large intestine in a watery condition. The large intestine takes up water from the liquid matter, leaving a semi-solid mixture, which is carried to the rectum to be expelled as faeces.

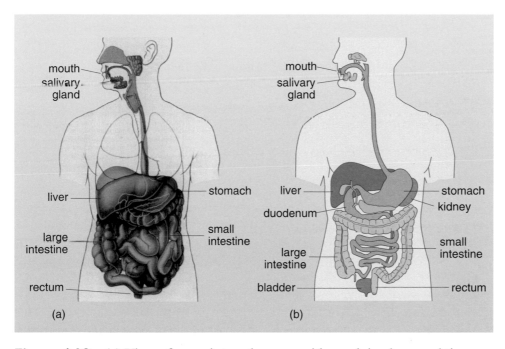

Figure 4.19 (a) View of some internal organs with overlying bone and tissue removed. (b) Simplified diagram of certain internal organs.

The water absorbed by the intestine becomes part of the rapidly circulating blood fluid. (If this take-up of water is interrupted, for example by the consumption of excessive amounts of alcohol, the body rapidly dehydrates.) The increased blood volume that follows the uptake of water results in dilution of the blood. When this occurs, water filters out of the blood into the tissues, which helps to keep the blood volume constant. Some of the water transported in very fine blood vessels may reach the skin to be excreted from one of the numerous pores as sweat, carrying some waste salts with it, and cooling the body. As described in Section 3.3, the blood becomes more concentrated as a consequence of sweating, so water is then taken up from the tissues into the blood to replace the lost fluid. Hence one important function of the movement of water is the regulation of blood volume.

Some of the water leaves the blood vessels to become part of the tissue fluid, which drains into a network of fine tubes (called the lymphatic system). These tubes collect tissue fluid from around the body and return it to the bloodstream, completing the circuit. Water in tissue fluid can move into and out of cells, so when it re-enters the bloodstream it brings with it dissolved waste materials, including gases, such as carbon dioxide. Some of the water passes to the lining of the lungs where it may be lost to the outside in the moist air that is exhaled. Breathe on a mirror and tiny droplets of water condense on it, showing that exhaled air contains water vapour.

Blood circulates to the kidneys (Figure 4.19b), where it passes through a filtering system. The kidneys not only regulate water balance but also clean and filter the blood. Each day human kidneys filter about 1900 litres of recycling blood. Excess water, along with large amounts of waste products, including salts and toxic substances, form urine. The urine enters the bladder (Figure 4.19b) where it is stored until it is expelled.

Over a period of time, the total amount of water in the body stays about the same; that is, the amount taken in equals the amount expelled:

amount of water taken in by the body = amount of water expelled by the body

Question 4.13

Write down the substances that contribute to each side of this word equation, that is, the various substances in which water enters and leaves the body.

During a day the amount of water in the human body fluctuates but, overall, there is a balance between the amount of water consumed in a day and the amount of water lost. This is illustrated by the data in Table 4.2. The body has control mechanisms that maintain this water balance. So, for example, when the water content of your body is too low, you feel thirsty and will find something to drink. Similarly, when the water content of your body is too high, after drinking large quantities, your body will increase production of urine to remove the excess. The data in Table 4.2 show very clearly that, on average, there is no net gain, or loss, in water content over 24 hours; the amount of water taken in equals the amount lost.

Table 4.2 Approximate figures for the water balance in a human over 24 hours.

Source of water	Gain/litres	Form of water loss	Loss/litres
food	1.5	faeces	0.1
drink	1.0	urine	1.5
		evaporation (from sweat and breathing)	0.9
total gain	2.5	total loss	2.5

Activity 4.2   Annotating text: fluids in the body (continued)

You should allow about 10 minutes for this activity.

Section 4.4.3 contains information about the water-based fluids in the human body and the functions that each performs. Use your notes and/or highlighting of the text to make a list of these fluids and their roles.

Activity 4.3   Uses of illustrations

You should allow about 10 minutes for this activity.

Box 2.2 described two ways in which illustrations are used in scientific writing and the notion of 'reading' illustrations. This activity involves you in looking a little more closely at the information illustrations contain, and how different types of illustration are used for different purposes. Note down your answers to the following questions.

(a) In Figure 4.19 is (a) or (b) the most useful in clarifying the journey of a glass of water and why?

(b) Why are only the torso and part of the head shown in Figure 4.19, rather than the whole human body?

(c) Why are other internal organs, such as the gall bladder, pancreas and appendix, not labelled, although drawn, in Figure 4.19b?

(d) Why is only one kidney shown, instead of two, in Figure 4.19b?

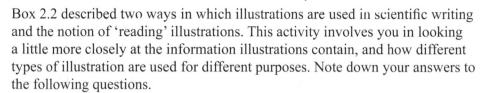

4.5   The water cycle

Most living organisms depend on rainfall for the water that they need to survive, but where does the rain come from, and where does it go to once it has fallen on the ground?

On the Earth, water is constantly moving around in what is called the **water cycle**. The cycle describes the ways in which water is transported and stored on the Earth, and illustrates the dependence of this natural cycle on the interconversion between gaseous, liquid and solid states of water (see Section 4.1). An important feature of this cycle is that it involves living organisms.

The movement of water through the water cycle is considered now, beginning in one of the salty oceans where most of the Earth's water is found. This water travels thousands of kilometres in ocean currents. It may pass through the mouths and gills of fishes, or be blown out of the blowholes of whales, or drawn in and expelled through the 'mouth' of a jellyfish. Water at the ocean's surface is heated by the Sun, and evaporates into the air. The process of evaporation is important, not only for the water cycle but also because the water evaporated from the oceans is pure water. The evaporation process separates the water from all the dissolved and solid substances the oceans contain. Once in the air, the water vapour becomes part of an air stream and is carried by the wind.

Figure 4.20 shows that some water vapour rises over the oceans and that some is blown inland and moves upwards over land masses. As the air and the water vapour it contains rises, it cools down. You may have experienced this decrease in temperature when climbing a hill or mountain. You may know that even in summer there is ice near the summit of high mountains even in countries with hot climates (Figure 4.21).

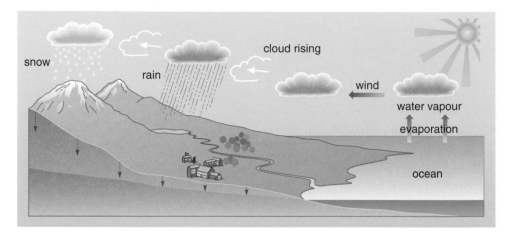

Figure 4.20 Schematic diagram of the water cycle.

Figure 4.21 Snow-covered summit of Mount Kilimanjaro in Tanzania. Note that the effects of climate change reduced snow cover to a mere 2 km^2 in 2006 with predictions that the snow might disappear altogether in 10–15 years.

Another example is Mount Everest where there is subtropical vegetation at its base but the summit is decidedly less hospitable! As the air becomes colder, some of the water vapour condenses into water droplets, which form a cloud. The process is just like the 'clouds' of condensation that form when you exhale warm air from your lungs into a cold atmosphere, an effect that is particularly noticeable on cold winter days and nights. In a cloud, the small droplets join together to make larger droplets and eventually the droplets grow too large to be held in the air any longer and start to fall to Earth. You are, of course, familiar with the end product of this process: rain (or snow over mountain peaks at higher altitudes).

■ What happens to water droplets if they pass through air that is at a temperature of less than 0 °C?

☐ They freeze and become hailstones.

However, if the air temperature is below 0 °C in the region where water vapour condenses, then the vapour changes directly to ice without passing through the liquid state. The ice crystals formed in this process are snow, and they are much less dense than hail. Once on the ground, a water droplet, or a thawed snowflake or hailstone, may be subject to any one of several different fates. Some water will soak into the soil and percolate down to the level below where the rocks are permanently wet, where it may remain for hundreds of years as underground water. Other water falling on the soil might be taken up by the roots of a tree and eventually return to the atmosphere by evaporation from the leaves, or it might run off directly into a stream or river. From a stream the water might be drunk by a cow or join other streams or lakes, and from a river the water might possibly be collected into a reservoir. Water that falls on pavements and roads in towns is likely to be transported down gutters into drains, where it might be mixed with domestic waste and taken to a sewage works. Eventually, the water joins a river, and returns to the oceans, the Earth's largest reservoirs, and so the cycle continues.

Activity 4.4 Learning from illustrations

You should allow about 10 minutes for this activity.

Diagrams are a useful way of summarising complex relationships and Figure 4.20 is designed to summarise aspects of the water cycle described in the text. Look carefully at it and write down what it is telling you about the water cycle.

4.6   Summary of Chapter 4

Water has three states: solid ice of fixed volume and shape; highly mobile liquid water of fixed volume which flows and adapts to the shape of the container; and water vapour (a gas) with no fixed volume or shape.

On the Celsius scale, the normal freezing temperature of pure water is 0 °C and its normal boiling temperature is 100 °C.

Density is mass divided by volume and the SI unit is kg/m³. Objects with a higher density than water will sink in water; objects with a lower density than water will float on water.

Sweat must evaporate in order to cool the body. It takes energy to convert liquid sweat into water vapour and this energy comes from the body in the form of heat. The loss of this heat cools the body.

Water is a powerful solvent; a huge variety of substances dissolve in it (including solids and gases).

Water permeates the whole body of a living organism, such as a human; there is an overall balance between the amount of water taken in by an organism and the amount lost.

Water on Earth is constantly being cycled.

The area of a square or rectangle is length × width and the SI unit is m². The volume of a rectangular block is length × width × height and the SI unit is m³.

One approach to studying is to scan the text first, before studying it carefully and completing all the questions and activities.

Illustrations convey important information by making paragraphs of text easier to understand or by summarising what is in the text.

Learning outcomes for Chapter 4

When you have completed Chapter 4 you should be able to:

- Scan written material to gain the gist of its contents.
- Do calculations with negative numbers.
- Calculate areas and volumes and assign the correct units of measurement.
- Calculate the density of a solid and predict whether it will float or sink in a liquid of known density.
- Make notes as part of active reading.
- Read and interpret illustrations.

Activity 4.5   Reviewing your study methods and planning future study

You should allow about 30 minutes for this activity.

This activity is designed to make you think about the way you have studied Chapter 4 before you move on to Chapter 5. In the introduction to this chapter you were introduced to a new approach to studying text and to the activity of making notes as you study. You are now asked to compare your study of Chapter 4 with that of earlier chapters. To do this you should review your earlier comments in your learning journal and add your reflections.

Read through your own comments on your study of the earlier chapters and then consider the following questions.

(a) Scanning text

In Activity 4.1 you tried an approach to study that involved scanning the text before studying it carefully and completing the questions and activities. Think about the benefits of approaching the text in this way; what did you gain from it? Did scanning the text give you a broad overview of what you would be studying? Were you able to identify, from your scanning, sections that would be straightforward or would need extra attention? Do you think that this approach made your study of the text longer or shorter overall? Decide whether you are going to use this approach, of scanning a section before studying it in detail, in subsequent sections.

(b) Making notes and annotating text

In Activity 4.2 you practised making notes and annotating the text. Did doing this and carrying out the related activities help you understand more clearly what the text was about?

Record your comments in your learning journal before reading the comments on this, and other activities in this chapter, on the course website.

Chapter 5
Communicating science

Communication is an important aspect of studying science. All scientists need to be able to communicate their findings to others, and the authors of this book had to use their communication skills to produce the course materials. During your study of this course you will need to be able to communicate with others, for example, by writing answers to assessments and discussing course topics by email. This is why Chapter 5 is devoted to the skills you need not only to communicate your understanding of science in writing to other people in a way that they will understand but also to understand what they want to communicate to you. It begins by going back to the basics of good writing, such as sentence construction and the use of punctuation, and moves on to discuss how to put scientific content together to produce a clearly structured piece of writing. To help you decide which sections of this chapter you should study in more detail, to estimate how long this is likely to take, and then to plan your study of the rest of S154, first complete Activity 5.1.

Activity 5.1   Planning your study

You should allow about 30 minutes for this activity.

In Activities 2.1 and 3.1 you kept a log of the time spent on study, and then reviewed your plans for finding the time for study. Before you begin to study this chapter you need to plan when and how you are going to study the remainder of this course. Again, you should remember to keep a log of the time you actually spend on studying.

To plan your time you need to know the following information and use this to help you estimate how much time you need:

- the course team's estimates of study time for the 'average' student

- how your study time has, so far, compared with those estimates

- whether you are likely to find certain chapters easier or harder than the 'average' student.

The course team's original estimates of study time for the whole course are reproduced in Figure 5.1. You should also have kept a record of time spent studying so far in your learning journal.

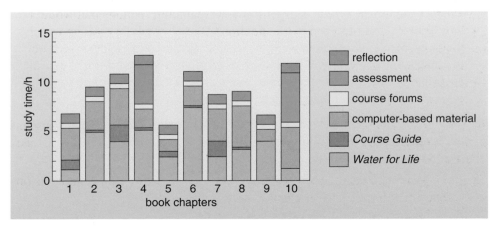

Figure 5.1   A bar chart of the course team's initial estimate of time required to study each chapter of the book and the associated material. When you study S154 these estimates may have been updated in response to feedback, in which case you should use the up-to-date version, which will be on the course website.

First consider the course team's estimates of study time for the 'average' student in Figure 5.1. This shows the time that it is likely to take an 'average' student to study each chapter. The information is presented as a **bar chart**. Note that the horizontal axis gives the chapter number and the vertical axis gives the number of hours estimated as being required for study. Note also that the bars on this (or any other) bar chart do not touch each other; this is because each bar refers to a separate, distinct category, in this case a specific chapter of the course. The study times for Chapters 4 and 10 include time (4 and 5 hours respectively) for completion of the course assessments.

Before you use the bar chart, make sure you can read values from it by answering the following questions about Figure 5.1.

■ How much time does the course team estimate that it will take to study Chapter 5?

☐ The course team's estimate is just under 6 hours.

■ How much time does the course team estimate that it will take to study the rest of the course, i.e. Chapters 5–10 inclusive?

☐ To answer this question, you need to add the times given for Chapters 5–10, which gives a total of about 54 hours.

Now you need to consider how your study time has compared with the estimates so far.

Task 1   Estimating study time

Estimate the approximate time you think you will need to study each of Chapters 5 to 10 (to the nearest hour) and complete Table 5.1. Base this on the following information.

(a) Your experience of studying Chapters 2, 3 and 4, compared with the estimates in Figure 5.1. For example, if Chapter 3 took you 13 hours (instead of the suggested 11 hours), you may need to add about 2 hours to each estimate for later chapters.

(b) The reason why some chapters took you more or less than the estimated time. If you have already scanned through the rest of the book you'll see that the content of each chapter is quite different: Chapters 5 and 7 are about communicating science; Chapter 6 includes an introduction to chemistry; Chapter 8 requires you to view an experiment, record the changes in volume you observe over time and to plot a graph of these values; and Chapter 9 includes quite a lot of maths. If, for example, you are already familiar with the maths in Chapter 9 you may want to reduce the estimated time accordingly. Alternatively, if you anticipate needing to spend extra time on maths then it's advisable to increase the estimated time for this chapter.

(c) Note where there are activities of a particular length and whether you need access to a computer or other equipment.

Table 5.1 My estimated time for studying Chapters 5–10.

Chapter	Course team's original estimate/hours	My estimate/hours
5	6	
6	11	
7	9	
8	9	
9	7	
10	12	
Total	54	
Hours needed each week*	9	

* Divide the total by the number of weeks, i.e. 6.

Decide how much time you should set aside each week by dividing the total number of hours needed by the number of study weeks remaining. If you have kept up to date with the course so far, you will have 6 weeks left (as assumed in bottom entry of the second column in Table 5.1). This calculation should give you an indication whether the total 'free' time you have each week is sufficient for your estimated study time. Although as a general rule you should allow about one week per chapter, you will see from Figure 5.1 that some chapters are expected to take a little more time than others, so you should allow for this and expect to spend more than a week on some but less than a week on others.

Task 2   Planning the rest of your studies

Continue to keep a log of the time you *actually* spend on studying each chapter. You might want to plot them on the bar chart to give you a quick visual comparison with the suggested times. This will help you to see how your plans match reality and enable you to adjust them as you progress.

You are now ready to complete this activity by planning your work for this week and the remainder of this course. To do this you will need to access the weekly planners that you saved in Activity 1.2, your log of time spent studying, your learning journal and the course team's estimates of study time.

Now that you have planned your study timetable, you are ready to develop your skills for communicating science effectively.

5.1   Thinking about writing

The skill of writing clearly and effectively is important, not least because it is useful in many work and day-to-day activities. Pause for a moment and think about when you last had to write something in order to pass on some information to someone else. Who were you communicating with? What was the information about?

You may have thought about a text message sent from your mobile phone to a friend's phone. It may have read something like 'cul8r my place 8pm?' ('see you later my place 8pm?'). It would be safe to assume that your friend would realise you were suggesting they could call round later that evening and that they know where you live. Your abbreviated text would have been intelligible to them because the background to what you were saying would be fully understood.

When it comes to writing more formal letters, the same shorthand won't do. If you wanted some information from your bank about your account, the bank would require full details of your account number and the nature of your query before releasing information. Your letter must be clear, and contain the appropriate information.

The sort of shorthand notes you might make as reminders in the margins of this book, or in your study folder, are likely to be meaningful only to yourself. When you make entries in your learning journal you will have to make your meaning absolutely clear so that your tutor can understand what you are saying; even more importantly, when you write your course assessments your answers must be clear so that your tutor knows you have *understood* what you have been studying.

From this brief discussion you will have recognised the importance of knowing your audience, i.e. *to whom* you are writing, and your *reasons* for writing, before you begin to write. Both your style of writing and the content will vary according to your intended reader and what you are trying to say. Most of the formal writing you will be expected to do for the course assessments will require the use of properly formed sentences rather than abbreviated notes.

You may be confident about your ability to write in complete, well punctuated and grammatical sentences. To check whether you need to study Box 5.1 in detail, try the following question.

Question 5.1

(a) How does punctuation signal the start and end of a sentence?

(b) Where are capital letters used?

(c) What two parts of speech are essential to form a complete sentence?

(d) Which of the following are sentences and which are phrases, i.e. not complete sentences?

(handwritten note: A sentence must have a verb + a subject)

   (i) A beaker of hot water. *(handwritten: ✗ No subject.)*
   (ii) He finished his assessment.
   (iii) Dissolved the solid. *(handwritten: ✗ Phrase)*
   (iv) A better text book than that one. *(handwritten: ✗ Phrase. No subject)*

(e) In the following sentence, which word or phrase is the subject, which the verb, and which the object?

   The student reads the course textbook.
   (handwritten: S   V   object)

(f) Give two different examples of the ways in which commas are used.

Box 5.1 Making sense in sentences

The first stage in turning notes into intelligible text is turning notes into proper sentences. Below is a passage of 'intelligible text' that you have already read in this book. Read through it again, at your normal reading speed.

figure 4.20 shows that some water vapour rises over the oceans and that some is blown inland and moves upwards over land masses as the air and the water vapour it contains rises it cools down you may have experienced this decrease in temperature when climbing a hill or mountain you may know that even in summer there is ice near the summit of high mountains even in countries with hot climates another example is mount everest where there is subtropical vegetation at its base but the summit is decidedly less hospitable as the air becomes colder some of the water vapour condenses into water droplets which form a cloud

■ What is wrong with this passage about the formation of clouds and rain, as reproduced above?

☐ There is no indication of where one sentence ends and the next begins, because there are no full stops and no capital letters. There are no other forms of punctuation either.

When you read this passage at your normal speed, how easy was it to make sense of it? You probably found it quite hard, even though the content should have been familiar to you. This example illustrates the importance of using properly punctuated sentences.

Question 5.2

Without looking back at the original in Chapter 4, attempt to make sense of the unpunctuated passage reproduced above by breaking it up into sentences. Add capital letters wherever else you think they are appropriate, together with any other appropriate punctuation.

Note that, as well as being used to signal the start of sentences, capital letters are used for the names of people and places, and anything else that has a unique identity. As you work through this course, it is important to note which scientific terms begin with capital letters and which don't.

Question 5.3

Which of the following words you have met so far in this course should begin with a capital letter, and why?

barrel cactus; desert; celsius scale; sahara desert; oxygen; arctic circle; earth

Words into sentences

The preceding discussion assumes that you understand how a sentence is constructed, apart from it being a sequence of words beginning with a capital letter and ending with a full stop.

To make sense, a sentence must contain at least one verb, which is a word describing some sort of action (a word of 'doing'), and something or someone to carry out the action (the *subject* of the verb). Within the context of the water cycle, the simplest possible sentence consists of just two words, a verb and its subject, for example: 'Rain falls.'

■ What is the verb in the sentence 'Rain falls', and what is the subject?

☐ 'Falls' is the verb because it describes an action, and 'rain' is the subject because it is the rain that is falling.

The statement constitutes a sentence because it not only contains a subject and a verb but also it is self-contained. It makes complete sense as it stands without adding any other words.

■ Suppose 'falling' is substituted for 'falls'. Would the sentence still be self-contained?

☐ No, it wouldn't. If you say it aloud, it sounds incomplete.

A verb that ends in '-ing' is incomplete (the technical term for this form of the verb is the *present participle*, but you do not need to remember this). To complete the sentence you would need to add something else, such as 'is' to make 'Rain *is* falling.' and this now contains the verb 'is falling'.

■ Consider another very simple sentence, containing a subject 'heat' and a verb 'evaporates': 'The Sun's heat evaporates.' Is this a self-contained sentence?

☐ 'The Sun's heat evaporates' is not a self-contained sentence since it is not the Sun's heat *itself* that is evaporating. You know that this heat can cause evaporation, but you need to say *what it is* that the heat is evaporating.

For this sentence to be complete and make sense, the verb must be followed by an *object* indicating someone or something that is having whatever it is done to them. This may be a single word, for example 'water': 'The Sun's heat evaporates *water*.' Or it may consist of a group of words, such as those shown in italics in this example: 'The Sun's heat evaporates *what is left behind* once the flood waters have drained away.' Any group of words, such as 'the Sun's heat evaporates' or 'rain falling', that does not form a complete sentence is called a *phrase*.

Question 5.4

(a) Examine sentences 1 and 2 below. In each case, identify the verb, or verbs, and state what the subject of the verb is. Where relevant, state what the object of the verb is.

1 Switzerland has heavy snowfall in winter.
2 As the snow thaws, it forms gushing torrents of water.

(b) Rewrite the following passage completing any incomplete sentences.

> From a stream the water might be drunk by a cow or join other streams or lakes. The water eventually joining the rivers and returning back to the sea. From here the droplet moves back to the oceans, the Earth's reservoirs. The cycle continuing indefinitely.

Use of commas

Most writing contains forms of punctuation other than full stops, most commonly the comma. When you read a sentence aloud, the effect of a comma is to add a slight pause. This pause helps to break up the sentence so that you can make sense of it more easily. Look at the short passage of text below, and note where the commas are placed.

Some countries, such as Switzerland, have heavy snowfall which, as it thaws, forms vast, raging, gushing torrents of water that tumble down the steep mountain streams, and which are used to generate hydroelectric power. A water droplet or thawed snowflake might soak into the soil, or fall on pavements and roads, or it may run off directly into a stream or river.

Commas are used in three different ways in this passage.

1 They are used in between lists of two or more *adjectives* (descriptive words): 'vast, raging, gushing'. Note, however, that there is no comma in between the last adjective, 'gushing', and the word that all the adjectives describe, 'torrents'.

2 They occur *in pairs* around phrases 'such as Switzerland' and 'as it thaws'. In each example, the phrases not only separate a subject from its verb ('countries … have', 'snowfall … forms'), they also describe the subject in some way. 'Such as Switzerland' is an example of 'some countries', and 'as it thaws' describes what happens to 'snowfall'.

3 They are used to break up long lists of items, as in the second sentence where several possible alternative fates for a raindrop or thawed snowflake are described.

Question 5.5

Some students were asked to write accounts of the same potato experiment that you carried out in Activity 3.2. This question requires you to add commas to an extract from one of their accounts to make it easier to follow.

'In order to carry out the experiment I used some kitchen scales a sponge tin kitchen foil a sharp knife a chopping board around 500 grams of potatoes an oven glove and a gas oven. To begin with I cut the potatoes which were quite large into thin slices using the knife. Next I placed the slices making sure that they were lying flat and spread out so that they were separated on kitchen foil on top of a metal sponge tin which had a raised patterned rough base to help evaporate the water given off.'

5.2   The three Cs

Of all the skills involved in studying and learning, writing is, perhaps, the most daunting. Even very experienced scientists or authors may find it difficult to put pen to paper (or fingers to keyboard) when they are ready to publish their findings or to write teaching texts, such as this book. Why should this be so? To answer this question, consider a mathematics problem of the sort you have already encountered. When you are dealing with this sort of calculation there is usually only a single correct answer. By contrast, there are many ways of putting across what you want to say in writing, and some will be more effective than others. Deciding which way is best can be a source of anxiety. Moreover, writing tests your understanding of a subject; if you haven't understood something properly, it will show up in what you write and no one wants to display ignorance. Fortunately, the challenge of writing also involves thinking fairly deeply about what it is you have to write and this, in turn, helps you to develop a better understanding of the subject. This is why writing an answer to a course assessment is such a valuable aid to learning.

So what makes good scientific writing that is effective in communicating your ideas? Broadly speaking, the answer lies in 'the three Cs': conciseness, coherence and clarity.

Conciseness means saying what you want to say in as few words as are feasible. **Coherence** involves making sure that your piece of writing has a logical flow, and hangs together properly; in other words, that you are saying things in an order that will make sense to someone else trying to follow your argument. Conciseness and coherence will both help to ensure **clarity**, but there are other factors, as well, that are equally crucial if you want your writing to be totally clear to the people who read it. You will explore these other factors later in this section.

Conciseness, coherence and clarity are the key to good scientific writing.

5.2.1   Conciseness

Most of the writing you encounter, or for which you are responsible, will consist of sentences that are far more complex than those used as examples in Box 5.1. However, the longer and more complex your sentence is, the more chance there is that it will be difficult for others to understand. Being concise means saying what you want to say in as few words as possible, without loss of meaning. Consider the following two sentences, which are attempting to say the same thing about the process of evaporation.

1   The process of evaporation, when it occurs, is important because not only does it result in water being evaporated into the air where it may condense into water droplets to form clouds which may lead eventually to rain which will fall onto the land surface, but also because it leads to the water evaporated, if it is evaporated from the oceans, being separated from all the dissolved and solid substances.

2   The process of evaporation is important, not only for the cycling of water, but also because the water evaporated from the oceans is separated from all the dissolved and solid substances they contain.

■   Which of the two sentences about evaporation is easier to understand?

☐   You probably had no difficulty answering this. The second sentence, which is a shorter and more direct statement, is easier to understand.

Both statements give two reasons why the process of evaporation is important. The first reason is signalled by 'not only', and the second by 'but also'. In the first sentence various aspects of the water cycle are described. These are summarised by the phrase 'the cycling of water' in the second sentence. Due to the length of the explanation in the first sentence, by the time you reached 'but also', you had probably forgotten what the first reason was, if not what the whole statement was about. This rambling style also obscures the main point of the sentence, which is to explain how water becomes separated from dissolved and solid substances during evaporation. There are also many other redundant (unnecessary) words in the first sentence.

Question 5.6

This question requires you to identify the redundant words and phrases in sentence (1) above, so that the amended sentence is easier to understand. The sentence is reprinted below. Study it again, carefully, and pencil across the words or phrases that are redundant. Make a note of why you think they are unnecessary.

> The process of evaporation, when it occurs, is important because not only does it result in water being evaporated into the air where it may condense into water droplets to form clouds which may lead eventually to rain which will fall onto the land surface, but also because it leads to the water evaporated, if it is evaporated from the oceans, being separated from all the dissolved and solid substances.

5.2.2   Coherence

For a piece of writing to be coherent, it must have a logical flow. Imagine that you are following a recipe to make a cake or following a set of instructions to construct a piece of furniture from a DIY store 'flat pack'. The instructions need to be given in the most logical order, otherwise you may end up with a cake tin full of something inedible when you take it out of the oven or with a rather strange-looking piece of furniture!

Question 5.7

Section 4.4.3 described the journey of a glass of water through the human body in a logical order. The sentences below summarise some of the stages in the journey of a glass of water, but they are no longer ordered logically. Without looking back to the original version, reorganise the list to make the order coherent.

1   The water enters the stomach.

2   Food, not taken up by blood vessels in the small intestine, passes with the water into the large intestine.

3   In the small intestine, the mixture of water and broken-down food becomes a soft, milky suspension.

4   Removal of water in the large intestine converts the waste to a semi-solid mixture, which is carried to the rectum and expelled as faeces.

5   Within the small intestine the water is mixed with digestive juices which break down food.

6   The water enters the mouth.

7   Water is propelled from the stomach into the small intestine.

5.2.3 Clarity

Sections 5.2.1 and 5.2.2 show how conciseness and coherence both lead to clarity in your writing. A factor that diminishes clarity is ambiguity, which arises when a phrase or sentence has more than one meaning. In Box 5.1 you saw how the lack of proper sentence construction is one source of ambiguity. Sometimes the way in which words are ordered in a sentence leads to ambiguity. Consider this sentence: 'The carton of milk in the freezer in my kitchen which is mostly composed of water expands when it freezes.'

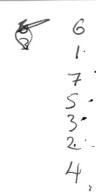

■ According to this sentence, what is mostly composed of water?

☐ Common sense tells you it must be the milk. However, the way the sentence is written implies that it could be the freezer or the kitchen, instead.

■ How could the words be reordered so that the sentence is not ambiguous?

☐ You could place the phrase 'which is mostly composed of water' directly after the word it describes so that the sentence reads: 'The carton of milk, which is mostly composed of water, in the freezer in my kitchen expands when it freezes.'

The sentence is now rather clumsy and it is still ambiguous because it is the frozen milk that expands, not the carton. To make it easier to follow, a little more shuffling around is required and a slight change in wording: 'Milk, which is mostly composed of water, expands when it freezes in the carton in the freezer in my kitchen.' The milk is now followed by the phrase which describes it, and the verbs 'expands' and 'freezes', which are related processes, are almost next to each other. It is also clear, now, that it is the milk, and not the carton, which expands.

> The golden rule when writing is: *place the words most closely related to each other as near to each other as possible.* If you observe this simple rule, you will avoid at least some sources of ambiguity.

Box 5.2   Sentences into paragraphs

You will have noticed when reading this book, or any book, magazine or newspaper article, that the printed text is not continuous down the page. It is broken up into discrete chunks called *paragraphs*. Sometimes one paragraph is separated from the next by a gap, a line where no text is printed. An alternative format involves beginning each new paragraph by indenting the first line a little way.

Question 5.8

The text at the beginning of Section 5.1 (up to Question 5.1) is divided into six paragraphs which vary in length.

(a) Skim-read the first five paragraphs, and write down, in a few words for each paragraph, what each of them is about.

(b) On the basis of your answer to (a), decide what determines where a new paragraph begins.

The answers to Question 5.8 show the importance of paragraphs as signals, or visual cues, to the reader that there is about to be a change in the discussion. A typical paragraph has three parts to it:

- a first or 'lead' sentence which introduces or signposts the topic being covered.
- the body of the paragraph where the material is developed
- an end sentence which sums up or rounds off the paragraph, and can also provide a link to the next paragraph.

Paragraphs also make the printed page much easier to read. You can imagine how daunting it would be if you were faced with whole sections of this book as continuous text. Your tutor will feel equally daunted by your assessments if they are not properly structured in paragraphs to break up the subject matter of your answers. When you begin your final assessment for this course, you will probably be more concerned to 'get it all down' than to worry about your writing style. This doesn't matter, provided you are prepared to go back over what you have written with a critical eye, to make sure it is structured correctly and contains no unnecessary words and phrases.

Activity 5.2   Turning key points into sentences and paragraphs

You should allow about 20 minutes for this activity.

In this activity you will write some sentences and paragraphs about cacti and camels based on key points identified from the text.

Look at the highlighted words about cacti in the comments on Activity 3.5 (reproduced below for convenience). Imagine that the comments represent the notes you made on this section and included in your study folder. Similar highlighted words about camels have been added.

(a) *Without referring to Section 3.3*, turn the words and phrases into properly formed sentences that make sense by adding words in the places where there are dots. Don't worry if you have to change some of the words slightly, or their order. Underline the original highlighted words and phrases that formed part of the comments, for identification.

(b) Suppose that these sentences are to form part of an account of how cacti and camels obtain, store and conserve water in hot deserts. How might you structure them into paragraphs, and why?

Comments on Activity 3.5 and comments about camels:

> *cacti* … efficient at storing water in their thick, fleshy stems … extensive system of shallow roots … take up water very rapidly … surface layer is exceptionally waterproof … leaves are reduced to spines … *camels* do not sweat very much … body temperature can rise by about 2 degrees … water lost … comes from throughout the body tissue … urine … very concentrated … faeces … very dry … drinking enormous quantities … water intake from their food … breaks down fat from its hump … water is produced.

5.3   Summary of Chapter 5

Good writing in science requires you to:

Remember to whom you are writing, and why, before you begin to write.

Use complete sentences that contain a verb with a subject and, where appropriate, an object.

Use commas between adjectives (in lists of two or more), to separate items in a list and around phrases that separate a verb from its subject or object.

Keep your writing concise by avoiding unnecessary repetition and redundant words.

Make sure that what you write has a logical flow so that it is coherent.

Maintain clarity in your writing, avoiding ambiguities by placing the words most closely related to each other as near to each other as possible.

Use a new paragraph for each new subject and to break up the text.

Learning outcomes for Chapter 5

When you have completed Chapter 5 you should be able to:

- Estimate the time you need to study a section of the course and be able to plan your time accordingly.
- Read and interpret information from bar charts.
- Write competently about science.
- Write appropriately for your target audience.
- Write in grammatically complete sentences, with appropriate punctuation and paragraphing.
- Write concisely, coherently with a logical flow, and clearly, avoiding ambiguities.

Activity 5.3   Reflection on time planning and communication

You should allow about 20 minutes for this activity.

In Activity 5.1 you planned your study time not only for this chapter but also for the remainder of the course. While you studied this chapter you should have been keeping a log of how much time you spent. Before leaving Chapter 5, you should check your log of study time and compare it with your work plan. This would be a good time to adjust your plans for studying Chapters 6 to 10 if necessary.

Task 1

Compare your log of study time with your plan and make any necessary adjustments to your plan for Chapters 6 to 10.

Task 2

Post a message to your tutor group forum about your study this week. This could be about something that either went well or not so well, and any strategy you used that was particularly helpful. Aim to make your message, clear, coherent and concise.

Task 3

Read any messages that your fellow students have posted. Do they conform to the three Cs? If not can you identify why?

Task 4

Complete your learning journal for this week, including any thoughts on tasks 2 and 3 of this activity.

Chapter 6
'Water, water, everywhere …'

The ways in which human activities interact with the water cycle can have devastating consequences for all forms of life. These range from the very large scale – for example, the effects of the movement of large volumes of water in a tsunami – to the molecular scale and the ability of water to dissolve solids, such as agricultural fertilisers (Figure 6.1).

(a)

(b)

(c)

Figure 6.1 (a) A tsunami wave; (b) a bag of agricultural fertiliser; (c) white crystals of the fertiliser sodium nitrate dissolving in a beaker of water. The image in (b) is a still taken from the video sequence *Elements and Compounds* which you will watch in Activity 6.1. It shows a bag of Chilean nitrate of soda which is sodium nitrate.

Much of this chapter is devoted to exploring the smallest water particle – a water molecule – what it is and how it gives rise to the particular properties of water you are already familiar with from Chapter 4. You will be introduced to the use of powers of ten and scientific notation, which give a convenient way of expressing both very large and very small numbers. As you study this chapter you will draw on facts and concepts that you have met in earlier chapters. There is a video sequence to watch during your study of this chapter, and an interactive activity.

6.1 Earth's store of water

Figure 6.2 A view of the Earth from space. The brown areas are Africa and Arabia, the larger blue areas are the oceans, and the white areas are cloud.

When astronauts first ventured to the Moon in the late 1960s, they were captivated by a vision of the Earth in colour as it had never been seen before (Figure 6.2). It is not surprising that, after pictures like this were published, the Earth became known as the 'blue planet'.

It is astonishing how much of the Earth's surface is covered by water. The oceans occupy about 71% of the Earth's surface. Altogether, the total volume of water on Earth, including the oceans, lakes, rivers and what is stored in rocks underground, is estimated to be roughly 1460 000 000 000 000 000 000 (1460 billion billion) litres.

■ What is the average daily intake of water for a person in the UK (from food as well as drinks)? (You may recall this from Chapter 4.)

☐ It's about 2.5 litres (see Table 4.2 in Section 4.4.3).

Even allowing 5 litres per person to ensure the most basic standard of domestic use (i.e. the minimum for cooking and washing), in addition to what humans take into their bodies, it would be reasonable to imagine that there is enough water around to sustain not only the Earth's 6000 000 000 (6 billion) human inhabitants, but all the other species of animals and plants as well – with an awful lot to spare.

However, there are frequent news bulletins that illustrate the appalling consequences of droughts in some parts of the world. Even countries such as the UK suffer water shortages: for example, in southeast England during the summer of 2006. It seems that the planet is well endowed with life-giving water but, from a human perspective, it is often in the wrong place, in the wrong form (for example, seawater is plentiful in coastal towns but fresh drinking water could be in short supply), or available at the wrong time.

To find out why there are water shortages and droughts on a planet endowed with 1460 billion billion litres of water, it is necessary to look at where the water occurs. First, the numbers need to be made more manageable by introducing a larger unit to measure the volumes. The unit most commonly used for this purpose is the **cubic kilometre**, abbreviated to km³, which is the volume of a cube with sides 1 km long. One cubic kilometre is equivalent to 1000 000 000 000 litres, or one million million litres, which can be demonstrated as follows.

To discover how many litres (each of which is equivalent to a 10 cm cube – see Box 4.3) can be stacked up in a 1 km cube: there are 10 lots of 10 centimetres in one metre (since 10×10 cm $= 100$ cm $= 1$ m), and there are 1000 metres in 1 kilometre, and so there are 10×1000 lots, or 10 000 lots, of 10 centimetres in

1 kilometre. This means that 10 000 one-litre cubes could be placed side-by-side along one edge of a one-kilometre cube. So the total number of one litre cubes that could be stacked within a one-kilometre cube is $10\,000 \times 10\,000 \times 10\,000$, which is 1000 000 000 000. The relationship between litres and km^3, m^3 and cm^3 is summarised in the margin.

A cubic kilometre is 1000 000 000 000 times *larger* than a litre, so the number of cubic kilometres of water on the Earth is 1000 000 000 000 times *smaller* than the number of litres. This means that the number of cubic kilometres of water on Earth is:

$$\frac{1460\,000\,000\,\cancel{000}\,\cancel{000}\,\cancel{000}\,\cancel{000}}{1\cancel{000}\,\cancel{000}\,\cancel{000}\,\cancel{000}} = 1460\,000\,000$$

Note how 12 zeros have been cancelled out. (Look back to Box 2.5 'Fractions, percentages and ratios' if you need reminding how to do this.) This makes the number representing the total water volume a little more manageable, and this volume is shown as the bottom line in Table 6.1, together with the volumes (in km^3) stored in each of the Earth's various natural reservoirs. (Don't confuse this use of the term 'reservoir' with the reservoirs that are built to store water for human use.) The volumes listed in Table 6.1 for ice and snow and for the atmosphere are the volumes of liquid water that would be produced by melting the solid ice and snow and by condensing the water vapour from the atmosphere. It is important to note that all of the volumes shown in Table 6.1 are estimates; clearly, no one has been able to measure the volume of water in the oceans accurately.

Units of volume

$1\ km^3 = 1000\,000\,000\,000$ litres
$1\ m^3 = 1000$ litres
$1\ cm^3 = 1/1000$ litre so
$1000\ cm^3 = 1$ litre

Table 6.1 Estimated volumes of water stored in the Earth's natural reservoirs. To be completed as part of Question 6.1.

Reservoir	Volume/km^3	Volume/% total water
oceans	1400 000 000	96
ice and snow	43 000 000	
underground water	15 000 000	1.0
lakes and rivers	360 000	0.025
atmosphere	15 000	0.001
plants and animals	2 000	0.000 14
total	1460 000 000*	100*

*The numbers in the middle column add up to 1458 377 000, but they have been rounded to 1460 000 000 to reflect the limited accuracy of the larger numbers. Similarly, when you have filled in the gap in the third column (Question 6.1), you will find that the numbers do not add up to exactly 100.

Even though the 12 zeros have been removed by expressing the volumes in km^3 rather than litres, the numbers in the middle column of Table 6.1 are still too large to be handled easily. They still have too many zeros. It is much easier to work with percentages of the total water volume in the Earth's natural reservoirs, which are displayed in the right-hand column of the table. You can see that about 96% of the water is stored in the oceans, which means that there is only a small percentage available for human use on the land. To put it another way, if all the

Earth's water was represented by the contents of a 4.5 litre (1 gallon) can, all but the contents of a tea cup would be seawater.

Question 6.1

There is a gap in the right-hand column of Table 6.1. Calculate the proportion of water that is stored in ice and snow as a percentage of the total volume of water stored on Earth, and enter your answer in the table.

(*Hint*: to do this, first write down the proportion as a fraction. If the numbers involved are too large to enter on your calculator, you will need to reduce the fraction to an equivalent fraction with smaller numbers on the top and the bottom by cancelling out some zeros. Then use your calculator to work out the required percentage.)

Percentages are one way to avoid having to work with cumbersome numbers such as those in Table 6.1, but an alternative is to use a mathematical notation for expressing the numbers in a more convenient form. This notation is called scientific notation and it is based on the observation that every time a number is multiplied by 10, a zero is added to the end of the number. The use of powers of ten and scientific notation is explained in Box 6.1.

Box 6.1 Going up: using scientific notation for large numbers

Think again about the value for the total volume of water stored on Earth: 1460 000 000 km^3.

When dealing with large numbers such as one thousand four hundred and sixty million (1460 000 000), it is tedious to write the number in words or to keep writing all of those zeros. Worse still, it is very easy to lose some of the zeros or add extra ones by mistake. Fortunately, large numbers can be referred to without having to write out all of the zeros. The **powers of ten** notation is less prone to errors and tedium because it removes the zeros. However, the powers of ten notation will be introduced with some numbers more manageable than 1460 000 000.

One thousand is ten times ten times ten, i.e.:

$$10 \times 10 \times 10 = 1000$$

Powers notation can be used (see Box 2.4) to write $1000 = 10^3$.

Two tens are multiplied together to give one hundred ($10 \times 10 = 100$) so the superscript after the 10 must be 2, i.e. 10^2.

When expressing 100 and 1000 in powers of ten, there are no great savings on writing zeros, but what about one million (1000 000)? One million is the product of multiplying together six tens:

$$10 \times 10 \times 10 \times 10 \times 10 \times 10 = 1000 000$$

so it is written as 10^6. Now you can begin to see the benefit of the powers of ten notation.

One thousand is often written not just as 10^3 but as 1×10^3. Spoken aloud, this is 'one times ten to the power three' or just 'one times ten to the three'. Likewise, one million is either 1×10^6 or simply 10^6. Now two alternative explanations can be given that may help you to grasp powers of ten. The power of ten shows how many times 1 has been multiplied by 10. Taking 1×10^3 as an example, 1000 is seen to be $1 \times 10 \times 10 \times 10$. In a second view, the power of ten shows how many places the decimal point has to move to the right to give the actual number. If 1 is written as 1.0 to remind you where the decimal point is, one move to the right would turn 1.0 into 10.0, a second move would give 100.0 and a third move would give 1000.0, i.e. one thousand.

$$1.\overset{\frown}{0}\overset{\frown}{0}\overset{\frown}{0}0$$

You do not have to recall both of these ways of understanding powers of ten; just use the one that suits you best, or develop your own way of fixing the idea in your armoury of mathematical techniques.

Using the powers of ten notation, the total amount of water on Earth – 1460 000 000 cubic kilometres – could be written as 1.46×10^9 km^3. A significant saving on zeros! The complete number would be spoken as 'one point four six times ten to the power nine' or just 'one point four six times ten to the nine'. The '9' in 10^9 tells you how many times 1.46 has been multiplied by 10 to give the final number of 1460 000 000. It is nine times, i.e. the number comprises:

$$1.46 \times 10 \times 10 \times 10 \times 10 \times 10 \times 10 \times 10 \times 10 \times 10$$

To see clearly that this expression is still one thousand four hundred and sixty million, it helps to begin with 1.46 and to then multiply each time by ten to get the number you want:

1.46

1.46×10	=	14.6	=	1.46×10^1
$1.46 \times 10 \times 10$	=	146	=	1.46×10^2
$1.46 \times 10 \times 10 \times 10$	=	1460	=	1.46×10^3

If you carry on doing this, you will end up with:

$$1.46 \times 10 \times 10 \times 10 \times 10 \times 10 \times 10 \times 10 \times 10 \times 10$$

$$= 1460\ 000\ 000$$

$$= 1.46 \times 10^9$$

Alternatively, you can think of each increase by one in the power of ten as moving the decimal point one place to the right. That is, if you multiply 1.46 by 10 the decimal point moves one place to the right, giving 14.6.

$$1.\overset{\frown}{4}6$$

Likewise, to multiply 1.46 by one thousand, the decimal point moves three places to the right, giving 1460.0. In the powers of ten notation, this is written as 1.46×10^3.

$$1.\overset{\frown}{4}\overset{\frown}{6}\overset{\frown}{0}0$$

The convention called **scientific notation** is used when writing a number with a power of ten. Scientific notation requires the number accompanying the power of ten to be less than 10 but equal to or greater than 1. Take the example of one million. It could be correctly expressed as 1×10^6, 10×10^5, 100×10^4, 1000×10^3, and so on, or even as 0.1×10^7 but only the first of these obeys the convention of scientific notation and this is the one that should be used. As a second example, it is mathematically correct to write 85 000 as 85×10^3 or 0.85×10^5 but correct scientific notation would demand 8.5×10^4.

Scientific notation requires the number accompanying the power of ten to be less than 10 but equal to or greater than 1.

Question 6.2

Express the following numbers in scientific notation.

(a) 100 000 000

(b) 35 000

(c) 95×10^5

(d) 0.51×10^3

Question 6.3

Write out in full the numbers corresponding to:

(a) 7.3×10^4

(b) 4.44×10^5

(c) 6.05×10^3

Using a calculator for scientific notation

You are likely to be doing many calculations with numbers in scientific notation, so it is important that you know how to input them on your calculator efficiently and how to interpret the results.

First, make sure that you can input numbers in scientific notation on your calculator. You could do this using the button you used to input powers in Box 2.4, but it is more straightforward to use the special button provided for entering scientific notation. This might be labelled as EXP, EE, E or EX, but there is considerable variation between calculators. Make sure that you can find the appropriate button on your calculator. Using this sort of button is equivalent to typing the whole of '× 10 to the power'. So, on a particular calculator, keying 2.5 EXP 12 enters all of 2.5×10^{12}.

To enter a number such as 10^9 on your calculator using the scientific notation button, it is helpful to remember that 10^9 is written as 1×10^9 in scientific notation, so you will need to key in for example 1 EXP 9.

In addition to being able to enter numbers in scientific notation on your calculator, it is important that you can understand your calculator display when it gives an answer in scientific notation. Enter the number 2.5×10^{12} on your calculator and look at the display. Again there is considerable variation among calculators, but the display will probably be similar to one of those shown in Figure 6.3. The 12 at the right of the display is the power of ten, but note that *the ten itself is frequently not displayed*. If your calculator displays 2.5×10^{12} as shown in Figure 6.3e, you will need to take particular care; this *does not* mean 2.5^{12} on this occasion. You should be careful not to copy down a number displayed in this way on your calculator as an answer to a question; this could cause confusion at a later stage. No matter how scientific notation is entered and displayed on your calculator or computer, when writing it on paper you should always use the form exemplified by 2.5×10^{12}.

Question 6.4

To check that you can use your calculator for scientific notation, do the following calculations.

(a) $(4.5 \times 10^4) \times (4.0 \times 10^{11})$

(b) $10^{12} - (5.66 \times 10^{11})$

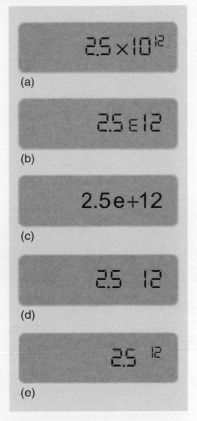

Figure 6.3 Examples of how various calculators display the number 2.5×10^{12}.

The numbers in Table 6.1 can be presented in a different way. In Figure 6.4 they are given more visual interest by being displayed in a diagram that shows the locations of the reservoirs as well. The amounts of water stored in the various natural reservoirs are shown in the boxes.

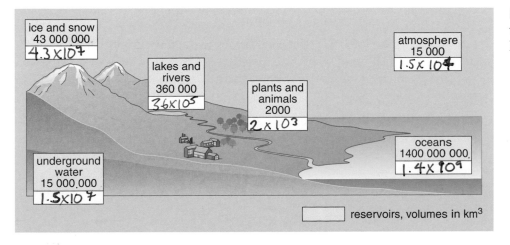

Figure 6.4 The amounts of water (in km^3) stored within the Earth's natural reservoirs.

Question 6.5

Under each number on Figure 6.4 there is a space. Convert each number into correct scientific notation, and write your answers in the appropriate spaces.

6.1.1 The study of a raindrop

Figure 6.5 A water droplet.

Most of the usable water is derived from the 1.1×10^5 km^3 that falls over the land surface each year as rain, snow, sleet or hail. The collective term for all of these sources of water is **precipitation**. You have already discovered how rain is formed as part of the water cycle (Section 4.5). At this point, you will consider in more detail the size of the drops of water that make up clouds or rain (Figure 6.5).

The typical distance across a water droplet in a cloud is one hundred-thousandth of a metre, that is, $\frac{1}{100\,000}$ m or 0.000 01 m. This corresponds to $\frac{1}{100}$ mm or 0.01 mm, which is very small. Imagine dividing the gap between adjacent millimetre marks on a ruler into 100 parts! Many of these droplets coalesce to give a raindrop that is about two-thousandths of a metre wide ($\frac{2}{1000}$ m, 0.002 m or 2 mm). Even these drops are small, but clearly they are water.

It is interesting to contemplate whether there is such a thing as a smallest particle that is still recognisably water and from which all larger volumes of water are made. In other words, if you start with a raindrop and keep halving its volume, is there a point when a further reduction gives something that stops being water? It is often useful in science, when dealing with complex ideas, to think of an *analogy*. One analogy for this 'halving' of a drop of water is to define a single living cow starting from a small herd of eight cows. If you halve the herd, you get four cows. Repeating the process gives two cows and repeating it again leaves one living cow. If this remaining cow were halved, you would agree that what remains is certainly not a living, whole cow. The cow would have been destroyed. You can conclude that one whole living cow is the smallest item from which herds of any size can be composed. Unfortunately, once a drop of water is halved several times, it becomes extremely small. It is a process that cannot be studied with the naked eye – or even with a conventional microscope.

In principle, a typical raindrop – say, 2 mm across – could be halved in volume 67 times before a single particle that is still recognisably water emerges. The 68th division by two, like the halving of a single cow, would destroy the water. This smallest particle that is still water is called a water **molecule** and its dimensions are almost inconceivably small. Molecules are the basic particles of many solids, liquids and gases.

It is not easy to describe the size of a water molecule because its shape is not regular. However, if its shape were likened to a tiny sphere, it would be about 0.000 000 0002 m across. It is difficult to comprehend a number this small, but you can probably imagine why it is impossible to do the halving experiment with a molecule. Roughly 10^{20} of these molecules would be needed to make a single raindrop.

As when writing very large numbers, there is an inherent danger in writing very small numbers such as 0.000 000 0002. Once again, the zeros are the problem. There are just too many of them! However, there is a notation that minimises the risk of making mistakes when working with such numbers. As before, it relies on the powers of ten idea to reduce many of the zeros. It is explained in Box 6.2.

Box 6.2 Going down: using scientific notation for small numbers

You saw in Box 6.1 how the powers of ten notation provides a concise method of expressing very large numbers and reduces the chances of errors when, otherwise, many zeros would have to be written out. You will now see how the powers of ten notation can be extended to cover small numbers, such as 0.000 000 0002 m.

Write down the next two numbers in each of the following two sequences.

10 000	1000	100	...10...	...1...
1×10^4	1×10^3	1×10^2	1×10^1	1×10^0

In the first sequence, each successive number is *divided* by 10 (i.e. one zero is taken off the end) so the number that follows 100 is $\frac{100}{10} = 10$. The next number in that sequence must result from another division by 10. That is, you must divide 10 by 10 and $\frac{10}{10} = 1$. Therefore, the second answer is 1. In the second sequence of numbers, each successive number has 1 *subtracted* from its power, so the first answer is 1×10^1 because $2 - 1 = 1$. For the second answer, you must subtract 1 from the power 1. Because $1 - 1 = 0$, the next answer is 1×10^0.

In fact, both sequences are the same because 10 000 is 1×10^4, 1000 is 1×10^3, 100 is 1×10^2, and 10 is 1×10^1. The implication is that $1 = 1 \times 10^0$ and hence $10^0 = 1$. This makes perfectly good sense if you recall that, in the second sequence given above, the power is the number of times that 1 is multiplied by 10 (e.g. $10^2 = 1 \times 10 \times 10$). For 1×10^0, 1 is multiplied by 10 no times at all, leaving it as 1.

Why stop at 1 or 10^0? Using the same rules, write down the next number in each of the following sequences.

100	10	1	0...1...
1×10^2	1×10^1	1×10^0	1×10^{-1}

In the first sequence, dividing 1 by 10 gives $\frac{1}{10}$ or 0.1 as the next number. Here, decimals are being used, so the answer you want is 0.1. But what about the second sequence? The answer is more straightforward than it may seem. You continue to subtract 1 from the powers of ten so that the next number in the sequence has a negative power of ten (1×10^{-1}) because $0 - 1 = -1$. Remembering that the two sequences are equivalent, it seems that $1 \times 10^{-1} = 0.1$. This is exactly right! You could equally write $10^{-1} = 0.1$.

Just as a positive power of ten denotes how many times a number is *multiplied* by 10, so a negative power of ten denotes how many times a number is *divided* by 10. For 10^{-1}, you must divide 1 by 10 once and you get 0.1.

■ What is the meaning of 10^{-2}?

□ The power is now −2, so you must divide 1 by 10 *twice*. That is, $1 \div 10 \div 10 = 0.01$.

Another way to think about powers of ten for very small numbers involves shifting the decimal point. A negative power of ten denotes the number of places that the decimal point moves to the left. For example, think of 1×10^{-2}, which is written as 1.0×10^{-2} to remind you of the position of the decimal point. Starting with the number 1.0, the power of −2 requires the decimal point to be moved two places to the left. One place to the left gives 0.1 and two places 0.01.

0 0 1.0

You therefore have $10^{-2} = 0.01$.

Try an example. Suppose a raindrop has a breadth of about 0.002 m. This distance could be given in scientific notation as 2×10^{-3} m. This is clear from the following series.

Start with: 2

Divide by ten: $2 \div 10 = 0.2 = 2 \times 10^{-1}$

Divide by ten again: $2 \div 10 \div 10 = 0.02 = 2 \times 10^{-2}$

And again: $2 \div 10 \div 10 \div 10 = 0.002 = 2 \times 10^{-3}$

Alternatively, in considering the meaning of 'two times ten to the power minus three,' you could start with the number 2.0 and move the decimal point three places to the left to give 0.002.

You know from Box 6.1 that when expressing large numbers in scientific notation, the power of ten (which is positive) denotes the number of places that the decimal point moves to the right. Similarly, when expressing small numbers in scientific notation, a negative power of ten denotes the number of places that the decimal point moves to the *left*.

You have seen that a negative power of ten tells you how many times you need to divide by ten, so that

$$0.001 = 10^{-3} = 1 \div 10 \div 10 \div 10 = \frac{1}{1000}$$

Of course, $1000 = 10^3$, so

$$0.001 = 10^{-3} = \frac{1}{1000} = \frac{1}{10^3}$$

and so

$$10^{-3} = \frac{1}{10^3}$$

This relationship between positive and negative powers of ten is quite general, so

$$10^{-6} = \frac{1}{10^6}, 10^{-8} = \frac{1}{10^8}, 10^{-13} = \frac{1}{10^{13}}, \text{ and so on.}$$

Recall from Box 6.1 that, when writing large numbers in scientific notation, the power of ten should be accompanied by a number that is equal to or greater than 1 but less than 10. The same convention is used when dealing with small numbers and hence negative powers of ten. This is why 0.002 m, the width of the raindrop, is given in scientific notation as 2×10^{-3} m, and not as 0.2×10^{-2} m or 20×10^{-4} m.

To enter a number such as 5×10^{-16} on your calculator, you may need to use the button labelled something like $+/-$ or $\pm$ (as used in Box 4.2) in order to enter the negative power.

Question 6.6

Express the following measurements in scientific notation.

(a) A water molecule, about 0.000 000 0002 m across

(b) An average-sized sand grain (on a gently sloping beach), about 0.000 25 m across

(c) The size of one particle of clay, the main constituent of mud, about $\frac{1}{1000\,000}$ m across

(d) The average size of a hailstone, 0.0035 m across

Question 6.7

Write out in full the decimal numbers corresponding to:

(a) 7.3×10^{-4}

(b) 2.9×10^{-7}

Question 6.8

To check that you can use your calculator for scientific notation, including negative powers of ten, do the following calculations.

(a) $(6.5 \times 10^{-27}) \times (2.0 \times 10^{-14})$

(b) $10^8 \div (2 \times 10^{-17})$

6.1.2   What is water made of?

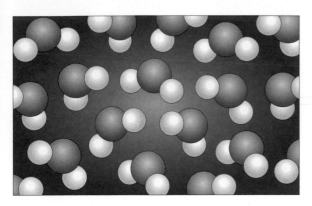

Figure 6.6   The individual atoms in water that could be seen if the drop was magnified 10^9 times. The white spheres represent hydrogen atoms, and the red ones represent oxygen atoms.

The size of a water droplet may seem very small but in terms of the scale of scientific measurement it is relatively large. You already know that water is made up of molecules so now consider a water droplet more closely to see what water molecules are made up of. If you could magnify a water droplet until it no longer has a smooth surface, you would see something similar to that shown in Figure 6.6. The spheres shown in the diagram are about 10^{-10} m in size and are called **atoms**.

One way of trying to visualise the size of an atom within a water droplet is to imagine a droplet magnified to the size of the Earth; an atom would be roughly the size of a tennis ball.

Figure 6.6 illustrates an important aspect of water, namely that it is made of water molecules, and that each molecule is made up of two types of atom: hydrogen atoms (shown as small white spheres) and oxygen atoms (shown as larger red spheres). Atoms are the basic building blocks of *all* material, whether the material is natural, such as rocks, plants and animals, or synthetic, such as plastic.

■ How many hydrogen atoms are there compared with oxygen atoms in Figure 6.6?

☐ There are two hydrogen atoms to every oxygen atom.

■ How many hydrogen atoms and how many oxygen atoms are there in one molecule of water?

☐ Two hydrogen atoms are joined to one oxygen atom to make one molecule of water.

Atoms are extremely small – about 10^{-10} m in diameter. Because they are so small, a *model* is needed to represent them and, moreover, to show how they are linked together to form molecules. Scientists use the term 'model' to mean any method of representing some structure or idea, so you won't be surprised to learn that there is more than one way of representing a water molecule. Figure 6.6 is one version, but there are others. If you are familiar with the children's building blocks called Lego®, you may find that a model based on this is helpful (see Box 6.3).

Box 6.3 Models of a water molecule

(a) Using Lego as a model

In this kind of building set, there are a limited number of types of block and each block has a particular shape. Just as importantly, each one has a particular way in which it can link to other blocks because of the way the studs are arranged.

The blocks can help you see how the atoms link in a molecule of water. Look at Figure 6.7 where the red brick represents an oxygen atom and the white bricks represent hydrogen atoms. There are only two locations where the hydrogen atoms can join the oxygen atom – at the top and bottom – as shown in Figure 6.7.

(b) Using spheres

Chemists have their own convention for representing molecules and their constituent atoms. As in Figure 6.6, they often use circles (or spheres if they make a three-dimensional model) to represent atoms – and they often use *short, straight lines* between the circles to represent the **bonds** that join one atom to another in molecules such as water. For now, think of these bonds as a sort of 'glue' that holds the atoms together (much like the studs on Lego). Thus a chemist's drawing of water might look something like Figure 6.8a. Chemists sometimes make models using specially designed 'ball and stick' kits – an example is shown in

Figure 6.7   A Lego representation of a water molecule where the red brick represents an oxygen atom which is sandwiched between the two white bricks each representing a hydrogen atom.

Figure 6.8b. This enables the relative positions of the centres of the atoms to be seen more easily; water is a bent molecule with an angle of about 104° between the two hydrogen–oxygen bonds in each molecule. Figure 6.8c is a computer-drawn space-filling view. A note on colour: chemists traditionally use white spheres for hydrogen atoms and red ones for oxygen atoms. Later in this chapter you will see that black spheres are used for carbon atoms and blue ones for nitrogen atoms.

Models can be very helpful in showing how atoms fit together to make molecules.

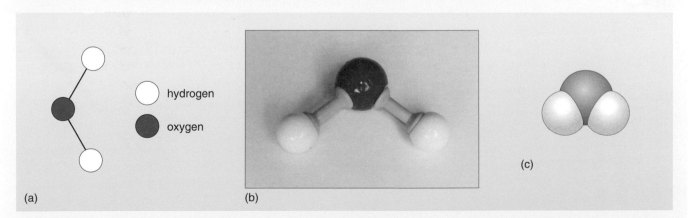

hydrogen

oxygen

(a)

(b)

(c)

Figure 6.8   Models of a water molecule: (a) a chemist's representation of water; (b) a ball-and-stick model; (c) a space-filling model. *Note*: although the hydrogen and oxygen atoms are shown as the same size in (a), in fact they are different sizes as reflected in (b) and (c).

With Lego, an enormous range of structures can be built from a small number of different types of block. It is just the same for atoms: there are only about 100 different types of atom in the entire Universe! Yet everything is built from these atoms.

A substance containing only one type of atom is known as a **chemical element**, or just an **element**.

■ Given that there are about 100 different kinds of atom in the Universe, how many different elements are there?

☐ The same number as for the kinds of atoms – about 100.

Examples of elements* that you might have heard of include hydrogen, which has its own unique hydrogen atoms, oxygen which has its own unique oxygen atoms and, an example of an element that you can see, *gold* which has its own unique gold atoms. A piece of pure gold contains nothing but identical atoms of the element gold.

■ Why is water not classified as a chemical element?

☐ Water contains the elements hydrogen and oxygen combined together.

Table 6.2 The ten most common elements in the human body and their approximate percentages (of the total number of atoms in the body).

Element	%
hydrogen	63.0
oxygen	25.2
carbon	9.5
nitrogen	1.4
calcium	0.31
phosphorus	0.22
potassium	0.06
sulfur	0.05
chlorine	0.03
sodium	0.03
all others	0.20

Table 6.2 lists the ten most common elements in the human body which together make up 99.8% of the total number of atoms present in the body. One important kind of atom in living systems, the third one down in Table 6.2, is the element *carbon*. It is possible to have some of the element itself – that is, some pure carbon containing nothing but carbon atoms – for example, a piece of charcoal of the type used in barbecues.

6.1.3 The 'salt' in seawater

The difficulty with having so much of the Earth's water locked up in the oceans is summed up poetically by Coleridge's 'Ancient Mariner', becalmed on board ship in the doldrums, beneath a blazing Sun.

> Water, water, everywhere,
> And all the boards did shrink;
> Water, water, everywhere,
> Nor any drop to drink.

(Samuel Taylor Coleridge, *The Rime of the Ancient Mariner*, 1797–8)

With so much Pacific Ocean around them, and dying of thirst, why didn't the ship's crew just lower a bucket and bring up some seawater to drink? As you know, there is a very important difference between seawater and fresh water. Seawater contains various salts. The most abundant of these salts is known as

---

* The Ancient Greeks believed that there were four earthly elements – earth, air, fire and water. However, by the 18th century, the idea that these were fundamental substances was discredited. The scientist John Dalton was the first to propose (in 1808) that elements were composed of atoms, and that substances that were not elements were compounds, comprising a combination of atoms. (Compounds are considered in detail in Section 6.2.)

sodium chloride, the most common constituent of table salt. Other salts contain calcium and magnesium. If you were to put 100 g of seawater in a pan and boil it, you would find about 3.5 g of the different salts left behind as a residue after all the water had evaporated. Although some salts are required in the human diet, there is only a certain amount that can be tolerated. The excess is removed by the body.

■ How are these excess salts removed from the body? (Think back to Section 4.4.3.)

☐ Some salts may be lost in sweat, but most of the excess is removed by the kidneys and excreted in urine.

The problem for the kidneys is that in order to remove the salts, they need water. The more salts, the more water they require. So, after drinking seawater, the 'Ancient Mariner' crew would have been even thirstier, because of the need to remove the excess salts. The problem is compounded by the fact that one of the constituents of the salts in seawater irritates the last section of the large intestine called the rectum (see Figure 4.19). This causes diarrhoea, with a further loss of water. The end result would be that the crew members would be thirstier than before.

Seawater can be converted into fresh water by a process called **desalination** (which means, literally, salt removal). The easiest and cheapest way to do this is to use the natural energy of the Sun to evaporate seawater, but this is a slow process. Other methods of desalination use different energy sources – oil, for example. Either way, desalination is a costly business and so is generally used only in those countries wealthy enough to afford it (e.g. in the Arabian Peninsula, Iran and the USA – in Arizona and California), and only where there is no other source of fresh water. The salt residue left over from the evaporation of seawater may be used as a commercial source for the brands of table salt that are sold as 'sea salt' (Figure 6.9). One such brand boasts on its label: 'Obtained from the Mediterranean Sea, naturally evaporated by the hot sun'.

Both water and salts are described as chemical compounds. You will take a closer look at them in the next section.

Figure 6.9 At the Janubio saltpans on the west coast of Lanzarote, salt is produced as seawater evaporates in an extensive area of small, shallow ponds. These old saltpans are not used as much now as in earlier times.

Activity 6.1   Elements and compounds

You should allow about 10 minutes for this activity.

This video sequence *Elements and Compounds* focuses on water and its constituent elements. Ideally, you should view it during your study of Section 6.2.

6.2   What are compounds?

Although there are about only 100 elements, there are many, many more than 100 substances in the world – not just thousands but millions of different substances. You could begin a list starting in your kitchen: water, salt, sugar, vinegar, bicarbonate of soda. None of the substances in this particular list are elements, so what are they? They are substances in which atoms of *different* elements are joined together. The proper chemical term for any such substance is **chemical compound** or just **compound**.

■   Is water a compound or an element?

☐   Water is a compound. It contains more than one element: hydrogen and oxygen atoms are joined together; as illustrated in the video sequence *Elements and Compounds*.

An important feature of compounds is that they are very different from the elements from which they are made. For example, water is made from hydrogen and oxygen, which are both colourless gases, whereas water is the wet liquid you drink that makes up 65% of your body. So, it is important to realise that a water molecule is quite different from the two types of atom from which it is formed. Water is not simply a *mixture* of hydrogen and oxygen; it contains hydrogen and oxygen atoms linked together in an ordered way. (You can make a house from Lego but you would not look at a pile of the separate blocks and say that is a house! In scientific terminology, the house is the molecule and the blocks from which it is built are the atoms.)

■   Look back at Table 6.2. From what you know about the composition of living organisms – picture a cucumber (Figure 3.1b) or recall the experiment using potatoes – why do you think the percentages of hydrogen and of oxygen atoms are so great?

☐   If 65% of human bodies is water, you would expect to have a high percentage of the elements that make up water (hydrogen and oxygen) in your body.

The next most common element in human bodies, after hydrogen and oxygen, is carbon. This, when linked to other atoms, forms most of the compounds of which plants and animals are made (apart, that is, from water). One very important category of compounds found in plants and animals is the **proteins**. Part of a protein molecule is shown in Figure 6.10. This very large molecule (it contains

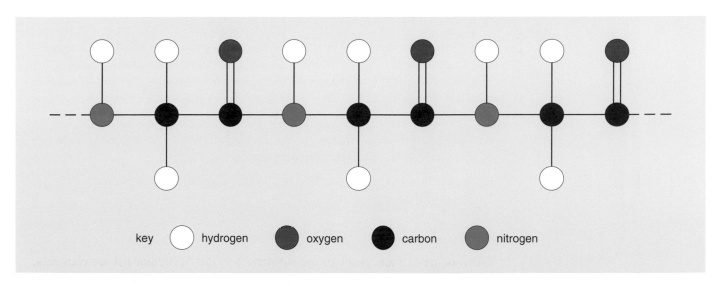

Figure 6.10 Part of the structure of a molecule of a protein. It is composed of four different types of atom.

thousands of atoms!) is made up of *only* four different types of atom; note the complex way in which the atoms are put together.

■ Using the key in Figure 6.10, name the different kinds of atom (hence different kinds of element) found in a protein molecule.

☐ Carbon, nitrogen, oxygen and hydrogen atoms are found in protein molecules.

Therefore, it is possible to have simple molecules such as water where only three atoms are bonded together to make a water molecule, and very complex molecules such as proteins where very large numbers of atoms are bonded.

Practise your understanding of elements and compounds by trying the following questions.

Question 6.9

Using the information about the types of atoms in water and protein (Figures 6.8 and 6.10), which of the following are elements and which are compounds?

hydrogen; water; nitrogen; carbon; protein

Question 6.10

The gas methane is a major constituent of the gas used for cooking and heating. The only kinds of atom present in a molecule of methane are hydrogen and carbon. Use your understanding of the earlier parts of this chapter to fill in the blanks in the following correct statement.

Methane contains the ...element,carbon and ..hydrogen Methane is not an element. It is a chemical ...compound.

Question 6.11

The atmosphere contains several different kinds of gas: about 80% is nitrogen and about 20% is oxygen. There is a small amount of other gases, one of which is carbon dioxide. From the information given in statements (a) and (b), decide whether the gas named in each statement is an element or a compound.

(a) The bubbles of gas produced in beer and wine making are pure carbon dioxide. Analysis shows that the bubbles contain molecules in which there are two kinds of atom bonded together, namely carbon and oxygen.

(b) In nitrogen gas, nitrogen atoms are bonded together in pairs.

6.3   Inside the atom

Before going on to see how atoms can link (bond) with each other, you need to look at atoms in a little more detail. Doubtless they are not like blocks of Lego! So what are they like?

In fact, every atom has a complex internal structure. Given the extremely small size of an atom, you may find it difficult to visualise any smaller bits inside it. However, you may already be familiar with some of the effects of one of these components – **electrons**. It is easy to do an experiment that shows the presence of electrons and, moreover, one of their important characteristics.

Activity 6.2   Detecting electrons

You should allow about 5 minutes for this activity.

The items you need for this small experiment are: a plastic comb (or plastic ruler or inflated balloon) and a small piece of tissue paper or newspaper.

Tear the tissue paper or newspaper into pieces about 1 cm square and leave them in a pile on a table. Rub the comb (plastic ruler or balloon) up and down several times on your clothes. (Some materials are better than others for doing this; wool and nylon are particularly good.) Now move the comb up to the paper and note what happens.

You should find that the paper is attracted to the comb. The explanation for this phenomenon is that the rubbing action transfers large numbers of the tiny electrons from the atoms of your clothes onto the plastic comb and vice versa. The plastic builds up *static electricity* which attracts the paper because the electrons have an electrical *charge*. You now need to look at the electrons in more detail.

Each electron carries a minute but standard amount of negative charge. Conventionally, chemists and physicists speak of an electron as having a charge of −1. The units do not matter in this case as the '−1' is a comparative amount such as a ratio: one electron has a charge of −1, two electrons a charge of −2 and ten electrons have a charge of −10.

Most objects – combs, people or atoms – do *not* usually have any net charge. They are described as electrically neutral. This is not a very hard concept to accept in the light of some intuitive ideas from mathematics or, indeed, bank balances! Something can be negative, positive or have a value of zero, which means no charge at all.

■ Atoms are neutral particles: that is, they carry no net charge. If an atom can be shown to contain negative particles (that is, electrons), what else must there be in an atom?

□ There must be some particles carrying a positive charge to balance the negative charge of the electrons. Moreover, the total negative charge of the electrons must just be balanced by the total positive charge in these positive particles, so that the whole atom has a net charge of zero.

These positive particles are known as **protons** and each one carries the same amount of charge as an electron but has the opposite sign, +1.

■ What is the relationship between the number of protons in an atom and the number of electrons in the same atom?

□ Since they have the same charge, but opposite signs, there must be the same number of protons as electrons.

Looking at a few atoms will put this important idea into perspective. The simplest element possible is hydrogen. It has just *one* proton and *one* electron. As +1 and −1 together give a charge of 0, it follows that the atom is neutral. Next there is helium, the light but non-flammable gas that is used to fill balloons at fairgrounds and for celebrations (Figure 6.11).

Each helium atom contains two protons and two electrons: together, +2 and −2 equal 0. Table 6.3 summarises this and gives three more examples of elements that you have already met. Note, in passing, two points: first, atoms with three, four and five protons are omitted from Table 6.3 for simplicity: they do exist! Indeed, the 100 different elements contain atoms with, progressively, 1 up to 100 protons.

Second, most atoms also contain electrically neutral particles called **neutrons**. These do not greatly affect the chemistry of elements and are not discussed further in this course. They are mentioned here in case you have already heard of them and wonder why they are omitted.

Table 6.3 The numbers of electrons and protons in five elements.

Element	No. of electrons	No. of protons
hydrogen	1	1
helium	2	2
carbon	6	6
nitrogen	7	7
oxygen	8	8

Figure 6.11 Helium-filled balloons.

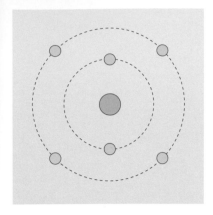

Figure 6.12 Chemists' simple representation of the carbon atom. The smaller dots represent electrons moving in concentric orbits around the central nucleus containing the protons.

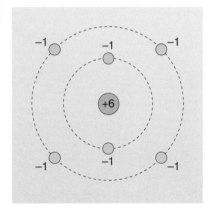

Figure 6.13 Labelled drawing of a carbon atom.

The number of protons determines the identity of each element. Thus, if an atom has six protons it *must* be an atom of the element carbon. If it has seven protons it *must* be nitrogen, and so on. As the number of protons increases so the mass of the atom increases. The number of protons in an atom also determines the number of electrons in that atom and it is the protons and electrons that give the atom its unique characteristics. Note that electrons have very little mass compared with protons.

Each element has a characteristic number of protons, e.g. hydrogen has one. In a neutral atom, the number of protons equals the number of electrons.

Chemists picture an atom as comprising a central **atomic nucleus**, which contains the protons, with electrons moving around it. In this picture (or model) the electrons are arranged in layers, like the layers in an onion. Figure 6.12 shows a simple representation of this for the element carbon.

■ Using Table 6.3 and the information in the last few paragraphs, label Figure 6.12 by writing the appropriate charge next to each dot.

☐ Figure 6.13 shows a labelled drawing of a carbon atom. The small blue dots represent electrons in layers around the central nucleus shown by a larger orange circle. There is a charge of +6 in the nucleus and 6 electrons each with a charge of −1.

The nature of atoms is described above. However, in Nature very few atoms ever exist entirely on their own: most atoms are joined to other atoms by some kind of *bonding*. In this course we consider two ways in which atoms can bond together. Both ways depend on 'interactions' between the outermost layer of electrons of each of the atoms that are bonding. One way is called **covalent bonding** (pronounced 'co-vay-lent') and the other is called **ionic bonding** (pronounced 'eye-on-ic'). They are discussed in Sections 6.4 and 6.6 respectively.

Question 6.12

The nucleus of each atom of the element gold contains 79 protons. How many electrons are there moving around each atomic nucleus in this element?

Question 6.13

Totally dry air, from which all carbon dioxide has been removed, contains the following gases – in decreasing order of concentration.

Nitrogen (7), oxygen (8), argon (18), neon (10), helium (2), krypton (36) and xenon (54). (*Note*: krypton is pronounced 'krip-ton', and xenon is pronounced 'zen-on'.)

All these gases are elements. The figures in brackets are the number of electrons in each kind of atom. How many protons are there in the nucleus of each kind of atom? How did you deduce these values?

6.4   Molecules and covalent bonding

Covalent bonding is one kind of linking that joins atoms together. The group of atoms held together by covalent bonds is a molecule. The example you are most familiar with is the compound water: water consists of covalent molecules, i.e. it is a **covalent compound**. Recall what is in molecules of water from Section 6.1.

■ Which atoms are in a water molecule? How are they bonded together?

☐ A water molecule comprises two hydrogen atoms and one oxygen atom and they are bonded covalently. (Look back at Figure 6.8.)

You have met three other compounds in the text so far: protein (Figure 6.10), methane (Question 6.10) and carbon dioxide (Question 6.11). These all involve covalent bonding and all exist as molecules. You have also met some gaseous elements that exist as covalent molecules. The oxygen gas in the air does not exist in the form of free individual oxygen atoms, but as pairs of oxygen atoms joined together by covalent bonds to give oxygen molecules. The same applies to the nitrogen in the air: here two nitrogen atoms join together to form a covalent molecule. (As noted earlier, very few elements exist as free, solitary atoms.)

Before going on, make sure that you are clear about three crucial points concerning molecules.

1   It is possible to have molecules that are elements (e.g. a molecule of oxygen) and molecules that are compounds (e.g. a molecule of water).

2   Molecules always consist of two or more atoms bonded together (e.g. two oxygen atoms bond together to make an oxygen molecule; two hydrogen atoms and one oxygen atom bond together to make a water molecule).

3   The kind of bonding in molecules is *always* covalent. If a compound or an element exists as *molecules*, the bonding *has to be* covalent.

Now consider the number of covalent bonds that different atoms like to form.

■ The element nitrogen exists as a covalent molecule. From what you have read above, what is in a molecule of nitrogen?

☐ Two nitrogen atoms joined together covalently.

■ Nitrogen molecules and methane molecules are both covalent but one is an element and the other is a compound. Why is one described as an element and one as a compound?

☐ Only one kind of atom is involved in the nitrogen molecule: nitrogen atoms. Two kinds of atom are involved in a methane molecule: carbon and hydrogen.

Look back at Figure 6.10. This is just *part* of a molecule of a protein. Recall that there are only four kinds of atom involved in a molecule of a protein: carbon, nitrogen, oxygen and hydrogen. The black lines in Figure 6.10 represent the covalent bonds. A protein molecule is always very large, and the dotted lines represent covalent bonds going to parts of the molecule not shown in the diagram. This may look very complex, but atoms obey fairly strict rules as to how they interconnect with other atoms. In particular, there is almost always a set *number* of covalent bonds that a given atom can form.

In the rest of this section, models of some of the more common atoms are used to show how more complex molecules, such as the protein in Figure 6.10, can be built up from simple atoms. This will show you how many different kinds of molecule can be built up from the same set of atoms; in short, from the chemists' Lego set!

Start by looking at the simplest atom. You have already seen that this is hydrogen and that it has one proton and one electron. Hydrogen likes to form just *one* bond with another atom. Visualising the bonding between atoms can be very difficult – unless, once again, a model is used. This time sketches of the different atoms somewhat similar to those used in the protein molecule in Figure 6.10 will be used, except that instead of straight lines hooks will be used. Thus, you might represent hydrogen as a sphere with one hook since it has one bond, as shown in Figure 6.14.

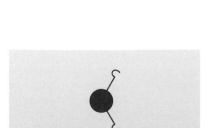

Figure 6.14 Representation of the hydrogen atom.

When linking atoms together to make molecules, the 'golden rule' is that no atom must ever have any spare hooks. A hydrogen atom all by itself has got a spare hook and that is *not* allowed.

■ What is the simplest molecule that hydrogen atoms alone can form? Use representations of the hydrogen atom, such as that in Figure 6.14, to sketch the molecule.

□ Hydrogen forms only one link with one other hydrogen atom, as shown in Figure 6.15a.

Chemists usually draw the links between the different atoms that form molecules in the form of straight lines. This is shown for hydrogen in Figure 6.15b. By comparing (a) and (b), you can see that 'two linked hooks' equals 'one covalent bond'.

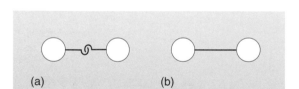

Figure 6.15 Two representations of the hydrogen molecule: (a) using hooks; (b) using bonds (with the two hooks redrawn as a line representing a single bond).

Now apply the model-building idea to a molecule of water. Oxygen has two hooks, as shown in Figure 6.16.

■ Sketch a representation of the water molecule, but this time leave out the 'joined hooks' stage and write down the straight lines of the covalent bonds.

□ Your answer should look similar to that shown in Figure 6.8a.

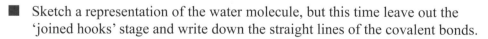

Now consider something slightly more complicated than a hydrogen molecule or water molecule. Methane, which is used in domestic heating and cooking, is a covalent compound that has been mentioned several times before. A molecule of methane contains only carbon and hydrogen. In fact, the molecule contains just one atom of carbon. Carbon atoms have four hooks as shown in Figure 6.17.

Figure 6.16 Representation of the oxygen atom.

■ Use the model atoms of hydrogen (Figure 6.14) and carbon (Figure 6.17) to obtain a representation of the methane molecule. How many hydrogen atoms can be attached to the one carbon atom?

☐ Your model should look similar to Figure 6.18a. Each of the four carbon hooks attaches to a hydrogen hook to produce a methane molecule in which four hydrogen atoms form bonds to one carbon atom. Figure 6.18b shows the same molecule using bonds; as before, two joined hooks equals one covalent bond. Figure 6.18c illustrates a ball-and-stick model of methane.

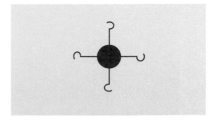

Figure 6.17 Representation of the carbon atom.

Note that methane isn't a flat molecule – it is described as tetrahedral in shape, as shown in the ball-and-stick model (Figure 6.18c). (The four hydrogen atoms form the four corners of a tetrahedron with the carbon atom at the centre.) However, this is difficult to draw, hence chemists often don't accurately depict the three-dimensional shapes of molecules in written representations.

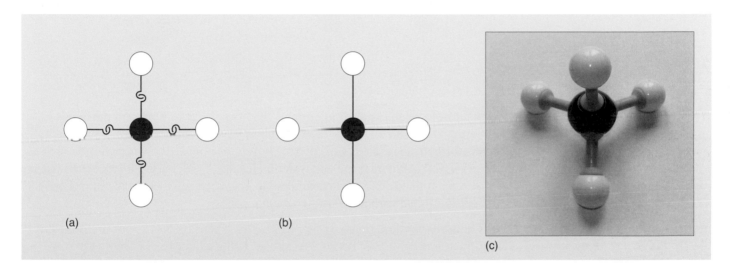

(a) (b) (c)

Figure 6.18 Models of the methane molecule: (a) using hooks; (b) using bonds; (c) using a ball-and-stick model.

Try another example: carbon dioxide. This is the molecule produced when carbon (in coal, wood or oil) is burned and when humans or animals breathe out. The name of a compound sometimes gives useful information. In this instance, the 'di' in front of the oxide of *di*oxide tells you that the molecule has *two* oxygen atoms. The carbon dioxide molecule demonstrates another feature of bonding between atoms.

■ How many bonds does carbon form? Look back at Figure 6.17 if necessary.

☐ Carbon forms four bonds.

■ How many bonds can oxygen form? Look back at Figure 6.16 if necessary.

☐ Oxygen forms two bonds.

So, how does one carbon atom bond to two oxygen atoms in this instance? Imagine that all the hooks sticking out of the spheres of the atoms of carbon and oxygen are flexible. Try to fix them together so there are no unsatisfied hooks.

The only way for all the carbon hooks to be used is (i) for the *two hooks* of one oxygen atom to link to *two of the four hooks* of the carbon atom and (ii) the second oxygen atom to link in the same way to the remaining two hooks of the carbon atom. The molecule is represented in Figure 6.19a.

Figure 6.19 A carbon dioxide molecule: (a) using hooks; (b) using bonds; (c) using a ball-and-stick model.

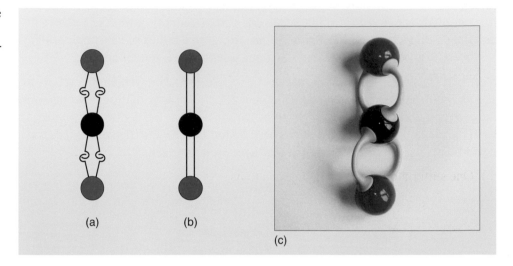

This type of sketch is quite clumsy and chemists prefer to represent the bonds as shown in Figure 6.19b. When atoms bond in the way shown in this figure, the bonds formed are referred to as **double bonds**, as opposed to **single bonds** such as those formed in the methane and water molecules. Look back at Figure 6.10 – part of a protein molecule. The vertical 'double lines' between the carbon atoms and the oxygen atoms are carbon-to-oxygen double bonds.

It is entirely possible to have other molecules where carbon atoms are joined to carbon atoms by double bonds – as shown in the example in Figure 6.20. (*Note*: Chemists have a special name for compounds that contain carbon-to-carbon double bonds. They are described as *unsaturated* compounds or sometimes as *unsaturates*. If there are several such double bonds in a molecule, they are often called *polyunsaturates*, where 'poly' simply means 'many'. You may have heard the term in expressions such as 'high in polyunsaturates' used to describe certain margarines and spreads.)

Figure 6.20 A carbon-to-carbon double bond in the ethene molecule:
(a) using bonds;
(b) using a ball-and-stick model.

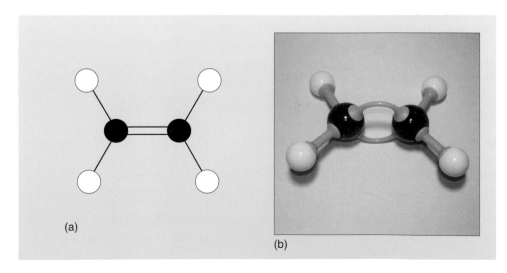

The number of covalent bonds that are normally formed by hydrogen, carbon, nitrogen and oxygen (the four atoms found in molecules of protein) are summarised in Table 6.4. To extend your 'chemistry Lego set' a little further, two other elements have been added to the table, namely sulfur and chlorine.

In concluding this section on covalent bonds, it is important to remember that it is not really hooks that hold atoms together! You learned from Figure 6.12 that the nucleus of every atom is surrounded by electrons. When two atoms link covalently some of these electrons are *shared* between them. This idea of 'electron sharing' in covalent bonds is an important one in chemistry.

Question 6.14

Using the information in Table 6.4, which of the following are likely to exist as covalent molecules?

(a) One sulfur atom and two hydrogen atoms

(b) One nitrogen atom and three hydrogen atoms

(c) One carbon atom and five chlorine atoms

Table 6.4 Usual number of covalent bonds formed by six elements.

Element	Usual number of bonds
hydrogen	1
carbon	4
nitrogen	3
oxygen	2
sulfur	2
chlorine	1

You will find it helpful to memorise this table.

6.5   Chemical language

The above sections include many terms which may have been unfamiliar to you: for example, atom, element, compound, molecule and bond. Chemistry has a language all of its own and grasping the terminology can be as much of a problem as understanding the chemistry itself. In this section, you will consider the language of chemistry before returning to the examination of bonding.

6.5.1   Chemical symbols

So far, atoms have been represented as labelled spheres or circles and the bonds that link atoms in molecules have been represented as lines. This is a rather cumbersome method of writing down molecules. Chemists have developed their own shorthand language for the names of the elements. It involves giving each element a **symbol** consisting of one or two letters. You can guess some of them, because they start with the *first letter* of the element's name. Thus oxygen is designated by the capital letter O and nitrogen by N.

■   The symbols of the following elements are all formed in this way: hydrogen, carbon and sulfur. Write down their symbols.

☐   The chemical symbols are H for hydrogen, C for carbon and S for sulfur.

However, there are about 100 elements and only 26 letters in the alphabet! So some elements such as calcium and aluminium are represented by the *first two* letters. Thus calcium is Ca and aluminium is Al. Note that the first letter is always a capital and the second is always written or printed as a small letter (lower case).

■ The symbols of the following elements are all of the type just described: helium, nickel, bromine and silicon. Write down their symbols.

☐ The chemical symbols are He for helium, Ni for nickel, Br for bromine and Si for silicon.

This may seem perfectly straightforward but, for historical reasons, some elements have unusual symbols. Sulfur had taken the symbol S and so an alternative was required for sodium.

Table 6.5 shows the symbols for a few of the more common elements, along with the origins of the element's name. As noted above, in any two-letter symbol, the second letter is *always* lower case.

Table 6.5 Name, origin and symbol* for 15 elements.

Element name	Origin of name	Symbol
hydrogen	from the Greek, *hydro* (water) and *genes* (forming)	H
helium	from the Greek, *Helios* (the Sun)	He
carbon	from the Latin, *carbo* (charcoal)	C
nitrogen	from the Greek, *nitron* and *genes* (soda forming)	N
oxygen	from the Greek, *oxys* and *genes* (acid forming)	O
sodium	from the English, *soda* (*natrium* in Latin)	Na
magnesium	from Magnesia, a district of Thessaly in Greece	Mg
aluminium	from the Latin, *alumen* (alum)	Al
silicon	from the Latin, *silex* (flint)	Si
sulfur	from the Latin name *sulphur* for the element	S
chlorine	from the Greek, *chloros* (yellowish green)	Cl
potassium	from the English, *potash* (symbol from *kalium* – Latin for alkali)	K
calcium	from the Latin, *calyx* (lime)	Ca
iron	Anglo-Saxon name for the metal; the Romans called it ferrum	Fe
bromine	from the Greek, *bromos* (stench)	Br

*It is recommended that you memorise the chemical symbols for the 15 elements in Table 6.5. This will help you read and write the chemical shorthand used in chemical formulas (Section 6.5.2), and in chemical equations used to describe chemical reactions (Section 6.5.3).

6.5.2 Chemical formulas

By using symbols, elements can be represented much more conveniently and much more briefly. This method of using symbols can be extended to compounds. You will now look further into this idea using a very familiar compound: water. Recall which atoms there are in a water molecule.

■ What symbols would you use to represent the water molecule?

☐ Since the water molecule has two hydrogen atoms and one oxygen atom, you might have written down HHO, HOH or OHH.

It is conventional to add up all the atoms of one type in a molecule, so it is written H_2O where the subscript 2 after the H indicates that there are two hydrogen atoms and the absence of a subscript after O indicates that there is only one oxygen atom. Such a representation is known as a **chemical formula**. Arguably, you should write H_2O_1 but for convenience and simplicity the subscript 1 is always omitted. Unfortunately, there is no obvious rule to indicate which element should be written down first in a chemical formula. Do you write H_2O or OH_2? You probably know the answer, of course; from saying 'aitch-two-oh': you would write H_2O. The reason is, essentially, a matter of convention: that's the way chemists do it. At first, you may find this system of writing formulas slightly awkward. Concentrate on remembering that the subscript refers to the symbol that *directly precedes it.* (There are two possible plurals for formula: we will use 'formulas' but you may also see 'formulae' in some textbooks.)

■ Write down the chemical formulas for carbon dioxide and methane. You may need to refer back to the text to remind yourself which atoms are present and in what proportions.

☐ The chemical formula for carbon dioxide is CO_2 (pronounced 'see-oh-two') and for methane is CH_4 (pronounced 'see-aitch-four').

The chemical formula of a covalent compound shows the number of each type of atom in one molecule of the compound. It is written using the symbols for the elements.

Having examined the naming of elements, their symbols and the formulas of compounds, what about the names of compounds? As with elements, the everyday names of some compounds have their origins in history. For example, words that *sound* like 'water' have been used for this liquid for thousands of years. The old English term was 'waeter', in old Saxon 'watar', in old German 'wazzar' and ancient Greek 'hudor'. For common compounds these old names linger on: water, ammonia, salt and alcohol are just some examples. However, there are millions of different compounds – if they all had common names you would never be able to remember them. A more simple, logical naming system is needed, which can be applied to any compound, so that everyone can understand which compound is being talked about.

The scientific name reflects the elements found in the compound. Where a compound contains just two elements, the name of the second element is usually modified slightly so that it ends in the letters '-ide' (pronounced as in 'side'). Thus, the compound HCl (pronounced 'aitch-see-ell') is hydrogen chloride not hydrogen chlorine. Similarly, CO_2 is carbon dioxide not carbon dioxygen. The 'di-' prefix indicates that there are two oxygen atoms and the '-ide' ending confirms that only two elements are involved in it.

Now try Questions 6.15 to 6.18, referring to Tables 6.4 and 6.5 where necessary.

Question 6.15

Using chemical symbols to represent the atoms and the information in Section 6.4, write structures for (a) a molecule of oxygen and (b) a molecule of nitrogen. Draw covalent bonds as straight lines and not joined hooks. For example, the structure for water would be written as H—O—H.

Question 6.16

Which elements make up the following compounds? What is the ratio of the constituent atoms within each molecule?

(a) Ammonia, NH_3 (pronounced 'en-aitch-three')

(b) Hydrogen sulfide, H_2S (pronounced 'aitch-two-ess').

Question 6.17

Write the chemical symbols for the elements that make up the following compounds.

(a) Hydrogen bromide

(b) Silicon dioxide

(c) Nitrogen trichloride ('tri-' is the prefix for three atoms).

Question 6.18

Given that bromine, silicon and nitrogen normally form one, four and three covalent bonds respectively, and drawing on knowledge you already have about hydrogen and oxygen, write down the chemical formulas of the compounds named in Question 6.17. (You *can* write down the formulas from the names alone by using 'di', 'tri' and 'ide'. If you do this, use your understanding of covalent bonding to check your answers.)

6.5.3 Chemical equations and chemical reactions

The previous section shows how different elements can either exist on their own or combine with other elements to make compounds. This section builds on these ideas by looking at chemical reactions in more detail. It also shows how chemical shorthand can be extended to describing chemical reactions.

First, consider some of the molecules described earlier: water, methane, carbon dioxide and ammonia.

■ What are the formulas for each of these four molecules?

☐ The formulas are H_2O, CH_4, CO_2 and NH_3, respectively.

Although you don't need to remember the chemical formulas of compounds introduced in this book, you'll probably find it useful to memorise a few such as those for the four molecules above, plus those for hydrogen (H_2), nitrogen (N_2) and oxygen (O_2) molecules. This will help you in reading and writing these chemical formulas without continually referring back to the text.

Now you will look at reactions involving the elements hydrogen, carbon and oxygen and the compounds methane, water and carbon dioxide.

Hydrogen will react with oxygen when it is ignited (it is quite explosive) to form water. To write such a reaction in terms of a **chemical equation**, the substances that undergo the reaction are put on the left and the substances that are produced in the reaction are put on the right. The **reactants** on the left are linked to the **products** on the right by an arrow.

The equation can be written as a word equation 'hydrogen and oxygen make water' or, using a little chemical shorthand, it can be written as:

hydrogen + oxygen ⟶ water

where the arrow mean 'goes to'.

Now, try using chemical shorthand to write the equation. Substituting symbols in the word equation gives:

hydrogen   +   oxygen   ⟶   water

H_2 + O_2 ⟶ H_2O

reactants   *product*

The equation shows the reactants on the left of the arrow being converted to the product on the right. However, there is something wrong with this equation. You can see what is wrong by looking at Figure 6.21 where the reactants and products are shown as a diagram.

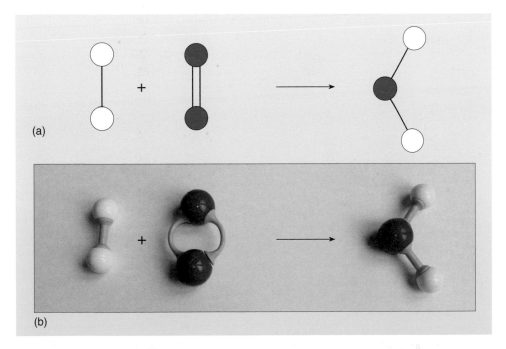

(a)

(b)

Figure 6.21 The unbalanced equation for the reaction between hydrogen and oxygen to give water: (a) diagrammatic representation; (b) ball-and-stick model. Note that the oxygen molecule comprises two oxygen atoms linked by a double bond. This is because each oxygen atom has two 'hooks' to link up.

Counting the numbers of atoms on each side of the equation shows that there are two oxygen atoms on the left compared with one on the right. The number of oxygen atoms on both sides of the equation must be equal – they can't magically appear and disappear during a reaction. It is not possible to change the composition of the water molecule on the right of the equation as the water molecule exists as a group of two hydrogen atoms and one oxygen atom all bonded together. Each oxygen molecule supplies two oxygen atoms so will always form two water molecules, provided there are two hydrogen molecules (each being a unit of two atoms) to react with it. Thus two *molecules* of hydrogen and one molecule of oxygen are needed to make two molecules of water. The reaction is accurately expressed by:

$$H_2 + H_2 + O_2 = H_2O + H_2O$$

There are now the same numbers of each type of atom on both sides of the equation: the chemical equation is *balanced*, so we can now replace the arrow with an equals sign.

A final tidy-up to avoid repeating the hydrogen molecules on the left of the equation and the water molecules on the right is to represent them by $2H_2$ rather than $H_2 + H_2$. So the balanced chemical equation becomes:

$$2H_2 + O_2 = 2H_2O$$

This is shown diagrammatically in Figure 6.22.

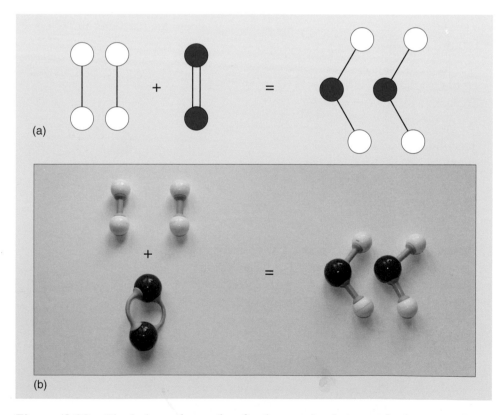

(a)

(b)

Figure 6.22   The balanced equation for the reaction between hydrogen and oxygen to give water: (a) diagrammatic representation; (b) ball-and-stick model.

Chemical equations show in a very concise way not only which atoms and molecules react together to form the products but also how many of each sort of atom and molecule are involved. It is important to remember that the number before a molecule means the number of that particular molecule. For example $3H_2O$ means three molecules of water, giving a total of six hydrogen and three oxygen atoms.

Chemical equations must balance; the number of atoms of each type of element on both sides of the equation must be equal.

You now know how to 'read' or interpret a chemical equation – and how it represents a chemical process. However, chemists are also very adept at writing chemical equations as a form of shorthand to describe various chemical processes or reactions. Writing chemical equations is like writing in any foreign language – it requires practice to become fluent. However, all budding scientists have to start somewhere and Box 6.4 shows you how to do this using a very familiar chemical reaction. If you wish to check whether you need to study Box 6.4, try Question 6.20 first.

Box 6.4 Writing a chemical equation to describe a chemical process

Natural gas, which is largely methane, is burned to provide heat for cooking and domestic heating and as an industrial power source. This process of burning involves the reaction of methane with oxygen in air to produce carbon dioxide and water.

A chemical equation can be constructed for the reaction of methane with oxygen to give carbon dioxide and water as the products.

1 The first step is to write the formulas of the reactants on the left and the products on the right:

$$CH_4 + O_2 \longrightarrow CO_2 + H_2O$$

2 At this point, all the products and reactants are featured, but the equation is not balanced; the numbers of hydrogen and oxygen atoms are not the same on both sides of the equation. Since oxygen atoms are in pairs in both carbon dioxide and oxygen, you know that you must have an even number of oxygens on the right-hand side of the equation too. To correct this 'odd oxygen' imbalance, add another water molecule to the right-hand side of the equation. Now count up the atoms on both sides of the equations.

$$CH_4 + O_2 \longrightarrow CO_2 + 2H_2O$$

There is now one carbon and four hydrogen atoms on each side of the equation. However, there are two oxygen atoms on the left-hand side and a total of $2 + 2 = 4$ oxygen atoms on the right.

3 To correct this, add another oxygen molecule on the left-hand side to give the balanced chemical equation:

$$CH_4 + 2O_2 = CO_2 + 2H_2O$$

The total number of atoms is the same on each side of the equation.

Balancing chemical equations is not always easy but it does come with practice. Try practising by doing Questions 6.19 and 6.20 before moving on to the next section which looks at ions and bonding.

Question 6.19

Balance the following equations. All the reactants and products are shown.

(a) Magnesium is burned in oxygen to give magnesium oxide:

$$Mg + O_2 \longrightarrow MgO$$

(b) Carbon and chlorine gas react to form carbon tetrachloride:

$$C + Cl_2 \longrightarrow CCl_4$$

(c) Potassium oxide is formed by burning potassium in oxygen:

$$K + O_2 \longrightarrow K_2O$$

(d) Hydrogen reacts with chlorine gas to form hydrogen chloride:

$$H_2 + Cl_2 \longrightarrow HCl$$

Now try writing a balanced chemical equation yourself by doing Question 6.20.

Question 6.20

Write a balanced chemical equation for the chemical reaction in which nitrogen, N_2, and hydrogen, H_2, react together to give ammonia NH_3. These are the only reactants and product involved.

6.6 Ions and ionic bonding

This section returns to bonding – the way in which atoms are joined to each other. You have already met one type of bonding involving covalent bonds, which is found in molecules. However, this is not the only bonding found in compounds. In this section you will look at ionic bonding and the **ionic compounds** that contain such bonding. What is the main *difference* between the covalent compounds you met in Section 6.4 and ionic compounds? Are there any *similarities* between these two enormous families of chemical compounds?

Glucose is a covalent compound and sodium chloride is an ionic compound. You meet glucose in solution in everyday life as it is the sugar in many sweet drinks (and is closely related to ordinary table sugar). You are certainly familiar with sodium chloride as it is the table salt used in kitchens. The formulas of both compounds tells you which atoms have combined together to make them. You can work this out for yourself in the following question.

■ The formula of glucose is $C_6H_{12}O_6$ and the formula of salt is NaCl. Which elements are combined to make glucose? Which elements are combined to make salt? Use Table 6.5 to help you if necessary.

□ The covalent compound glucose is formed from the elements carbon, hydrogen and oxygen. The ionic compound sodium chloride is formed from the elements sodium and chlorine.

If you bought some glucose tablets from a pharmacy or a sports shop and crushed them, you would have a fine, white, sweet powder – certainly not like the elements that form it: black carbon, gaseous hydrogen and gaseous oxygen.

Equally, sodium chloride is vastly different from the elements that combine to make it (Figure 6.23). Sodium chloride is a white solid that is used in food. Yet chlorine is an enormously reactive green gas, deadly poisonous in concentrated

Figure 6.23 (a) Sodium metal (immersed in oil to prevent reaction with oxygen and moisture in the air); (b) chlorine gas; (c) the reaction between sodium and chlorine; (d) sodium chloride (common table salt).

form, and an excellent disinfectant when dissolved in water, such as in swimming pools. You probably haven't seen sodium as this silvery metal catches fire in air and almost explodes in water. Once again, the compound – an ionic compound in this case – is completely different from its constituent elements.

If covalent and ionic compounds are similar in that they are unlike the elements that form them, in what key way do they differ? The answer is in the *nature of the bonding.* To understand ionic bonding, you need to recall what you learned in Section 6.3 about the internal structure of atoms.

■ Which kind of charge does an electron carry? In which way is the overall electrical neutrality of atoms achieved?

□ Each electron carries one negative charge that is represented as −1. An atom is neutral because the number of protons (each of which bears a positive or +1 charge) exactly equals the number of electrons.

Now apply this to the elements that are in common salt. Table 6.3 lists the number of electrons (and hence protons) in five elements. Table 6.6 shows the comparable information about sodium and chlorine.

Table 6.6 The number of electrons and protons in sodium and chlorine.

Element	No. of electrons	No. of protons
sodium	11	11
chlorine	17	17

How do these two elements bond together? Picture a sphere representing a sodium atom. The sphere isn't solid: it has a tiny central nucleus (with a charge of +11) and a cloud of electrons arranged in layers (with a total charge of −11). In many chemical reactions, an atom of sodium *very easily loses one electron* from the outer layer of this cloud of electrons. The loss of a single electron from a sodium atom makes it into a particle bearing a net *positive* charge of +1. This positive particle is termed an **ion** (pronounced 'eye-on'). By taking away one electron from a sodium atom, a sodium ion is formed:

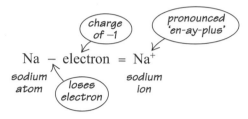

This equation can be easily explained. The sodium atom is electrically neutral; it comprises 11 protons (+11) and 11 electrons (−11). When it loses one electron with a charge of −1, by arithmetic, the particle that is left must have a charge of +1. Note that this is represented by the symbol for sodium with a small superscript 'plus' sign.

Now picture a chlorine atom. This is electrically neutral: it has 17 electrons and 17 protons. In its reactions a chlorine atom *likes to gain one electron.* Following the same line of reasoning as before, adding one electron to this atom gives one extra negative charge. Thus a chlorine ion (usually called a chloride ion) is formed. Once again, the ion is represented by the symbol for the element followed by the charge written as a superscript. Thus:

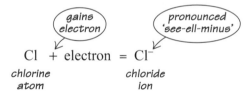

The next question covers the same ground but looks at the change from atom to ion in overall terms.

■ Look back at chlorine in Table 6.6. (a) What charge is in the nucleus after the electron is gained? (b) What total charge is there in the remaining set of electrons? (c) What, therefore, is the *net* charge on the ion as a whole?

□ (a) The protons are undisturbed; so the charge in the nucleus is still +17. (b) The electrons are one more than before; so their charge is −18. (c) The outcome of +17 and −18 is −1. So the *net* charge on the ion is −1.

The fact that a sodium atom likes to lose an electron and a chlorine atom likes to gain an electron means that they have a great potential for satisfying each other's 'needs'. This is what lies behind the violence of the reaction between shiny sodium metal and green poisonous chlorine gas (Figure 6.23c). If you dropped a lump of sodium into a container of chlorine gas (behind armoured glass as the reaction is very violent and involves flames) *electron transfer occurs.* Each sodium atom loses an electron (so forming Na^+) and each chlorine atom gains one (so forming Cl^-). On the bottom of the container of chlorine gas, there would be a trace of white powder: the compound sodium chloride, common table salt. The Na^+ ions and the Cl^- ions formed in the reaction attract each other in a similar way to a comb attracting paper. The positive ions are strongly attracted to the negative ions.

■ Suppose one billion sodium atoms lost one electron each to one billion chlorine atoms. (a) How many electrons move from Na atoms to Cl atoms? (b) How many sodium ions (Na^+) are formed? (c) How many chloride ions (Cl^-) are formed? (d) What is the net charge on the resulting sodium chloride? (e) How many molecules are formed?

☐ (a) One billion; (b) one billion; (c) one billion; (d) zero. The answer to (e) may surprise you: none!

The net charge on any ionic compound is always zero. The atoms, after all, start out neutral. All that happens is that some electrons move from one place to another. The total charge on the positive ions exactly equals the total charge on the negative ions.

The answer to (e) raises an important point. In ionic compounds such as salt, it is the attraction between the negatively charged chloride ions and the positively charged sodium ions which holds the substance together. This attraction *operates in all directions*, unlike the bonding in covalent compounds where the linking is directly between the atoms. Figure 6.24 shows this in a magnified piece of salt.

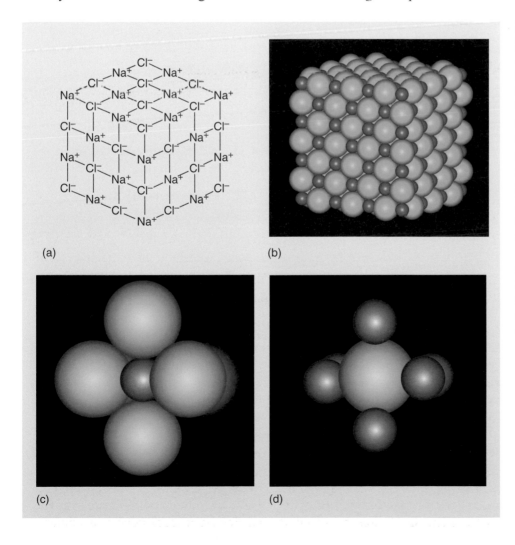

(a)

(b)

(c)

(d)

Figure 6.24 A magnified piece of salt. (a) Here the solid lines represent the electrical attraction between every Na^+ and each of its neighbouring Cl^- ions. In fact, this is a two-dimensional representation of a more complex three-dimensional structure. (b) The ions are shown in their space-filling representation. The larger spheres are chloride ions and the smaller ones sodium ions. (c) and (d) illustrate the 'ion packing' structure within sodium chloride – that each sodium ion is surrounded by 6 chloride ions, and that each chloride ion is surrounded by 6 sodium ions, respectively.

A distinct *molecule* of sodium chloride *cannot* exist because each sodium ion is attracted to more than one chloride ion and vice versa. Thus drawing directional bonds between atoms, as you did for the covalent molecules in Section 6.4, would be meaningless.

So far, you have considered the Na^+ ion and the Cl^- ion which have lost and gained one electron, respectively. Some atoms like to lose more than one electron or gain more than one electron. For example, atoms of the element calcium (another very reactive metal) always lose *two* electrons, so the calcium ion is always Ca^{++} normally written as Ca^{2+} (pronounced 'see-ay-two-plus'). In this case, the superscript '2+' tells you that there are two plus charges on this ion.

Another example of a 'two electron change' is shown by atoms of the element oxygen. Recall that an oxygen atom forms two covalent bonds in some reactions (you saw this in Section 6.5 in H_2O and CO_2). However, in some other reactions it prefers to gain two electrons and thus forms ions. When this happens, the ion formed is O^{2-} (pronounced 'oh-two-minus'). This is called the *oxide ion*.

This preference for forming oxide ions is shown by oxygen in the many reactions where metals burn in oxygen. For example, calcium metal burns in oxygen to form the ionic compound *calcium oxide*. The formula for calcium oxide is CaO. This means that there is exactly one calcium ion (Ca^{2+}) to every oxide ion (O^{2-}) in a piece of calcium oxide. Thus the overall neutrality of the compound is maintained: $(2+) + (2-) = 0$.

Note that the formula of an ionic compound gives the ratio between the two kinds of ions. By convention, charges are not written in the formula. Thus it is NaCl and CaO and not Na^+Cl^- and $Ca^{2+}O^{2-}$.

What happens in an ionic compound when an ion containing two charges is combined with ions bearing only one charge? The 'golden rule' is that electrical neutrality must be maintained.

■ Calcium chloride has the formula $CaCl_2$. Which ions are in this compound and what is their ratio?

☐ The subscript 2 in $CaCl_2$ means there are two Cl^- ions, each with a charge of $1-$, i.e. $2-$ in total. The single Ca in $CaCl_2$ means one Ca^{2+} ion, i.e. a total charge of $2+$. In the compound, the $2-$ charges and $2+$ charges add up to zero. Thus neutrality is maintained.

So far, this section has described simple compounds containing only two types of element: one forms the positive ion and one forms the negative ion. However, there are several ionic compounds that are more complex than this because one or both of the ions contain more than one element. An example is the nitrate ion, the principal culprit in water pollution by agricultural fertilisers. (You will find out a little more about the causes of pollution in Chapter 7, Section 7.2.1.)

The nitrate ion contains a cluster of atoms: one nitrogen and three oxygen atoms covalently bonded together inside the nitrate ion. However, the cluster of atoms as a whole bears just one negative charge just like the simple Cl^- ion. So the chemical formula for the nitrate ions is NO_3^-. Another ion that contains a cluster of atoms is the sulfate ion. Table 6.7 summarises the ions you have met in this section and in Section 4.4.1. You may find it useful to memorise the chemical formulas for these ions. You can see that the dissolved substances in bottled water in Figure 4.16 are ions.

Table 6.7 Summary of ions in Section 6.6.

Name	Formula
sodium ion	Na^+
potassium ion	K^+
calcium ion	Ca^{2+}
chloride ion	Cl^-
oxide ion	O^{2-}
nitrate ion	NO_3^-
sulfate ion	SO_4^{2-}
bicarbonate ion*	HCO_3^-

* Chemists prefer to call this ion hydrogen carbonate - but the 'old' name bicarbonate continues to be used in some areas such as food and household labelling.

■ The chemical formula for the sulfate ion is given in Table 6.7. How many sulfur atoms and oxygen atoms are covalently bonded within each ion?

☐ The sulfate ion contains one atom of sulfur and four of oxygen.

The negative nitrate ion pairs with a positive ion, of course. Sometimes this is a sodium ion (Na^+); alternatively, it could be potassium (K^+). Sodium nitrate ($NaNO_3$) and potassium nitrate (KNO_3) are, in fact, two of the commonest fertilisers containing the nitrate ion (Figure 6.1b). Sodium nitrate contains a vast number of sodium ions (Na^+) and nitrate ions (NO_3^-). As you can tell from the formula for sodium nitrate, these ions are present in equal numbers to give overall electrical neutrality.

The chemical formula of an ionic compound shows the ratio of ions (and atoms that form the ions) in that compound. It is written using the symbols for the elements.

The attraction of the positive and negative ions in sodium nitrate, in the solid form, holds the compound together in a similar way to that shown for NaCl in Figure 6.23. When sodium nitrate is added to water, the water molecules interpose themselves between the two types of ion reducing the attraction between them and allowing them to separate. The result is that the solid sodium nitrate dissolves in water (Figure 6.1c).

■ Which ions are present in potassium nitrate and in what ratio are they?

☐ Potassium nitrate contains the potassium ion (K^+) and the nitrate ion (NO_3^-). They are in the ratio 1 : 1.

A final point about the names of ionic compounds may be helpful. In some ionic compounds (e.g. sodium chloride and calcium oxide), the name of the negative ion ends in '-ide'. As you know from Section 6.4 on covalent compounds, this simply denotes 'two elements in the compound'. However, in ionic compounds where the positive ion is balanced by a negative ion containing oxygen and another element (such as in the ion NO_3^-), the ending usually changes to '-ate'. Thus the NO_3^- ion is called the *nitrate ion*; this tells you that the ion contains nitrogen and oxygen. Some general rules about the chemical names of different substances are summarised in Box 6.5.

Box 6.5 Endings in chemical names

You may have noticed that endings such as '-ide' '-ate' and '-ium' are used in chemical names: for example, sodium chloride and calcium sulfate. These endings give clues about the types of atom in a particular compound.

'-ide' This usually means that there are only two elements in a compound. The convention applies to both covalent and ionic compounds, e.g. carbon dioxide and sodium chloride, respectively. In ionic compounds, the name of the negative ion ends in '-ide', e.g. oxide and chloride.

'-ium' This usually signifies a part of a compound that comes from an element that is a metal, e.g. calcium and sodium. In ionic compounds, this part is the positive ion.

'-ate' This ending applies only to ionic compounds. It usually means that the negative ion itself consists of two elements, one of which is oxygen, e.g. the sulfate and nitrate ions.

Try the following four questions to practise your understanding of chemical formulas.

Question 6.21

What are the names of the following ionic compounds?

(a) CaO; (b) KCl; (c) Na_2SO_4; (d) MgO.

Question 6.22

Which ions are present in a solid sample of compounds (a) to (d) in Question 6.21? In each case, what is the ratio of positive ions to negative ions? (You may need to refer to Table 6.7.)

Check your answers to Questions 6.21 and 6.22 before trying Questions 6.23 and 6.24.

Question 6.23

Using your knowledge from this chapter so far (and your understanding of Questions 6.21 and 6.22), what are the chemical formulas of (a) calcium sulfate and (b) potassium sulfate?

Question 6.24

Magnesium sulfate is very soluble in water. Which ions from magnesium sulfate would be present in the solution and in what ratio would they occur?

In the next section you will see why ions are an important feature of the water around you.

6.7 Water and its impurities

The purity of drinking water was considered in Section 4.4.1. Water must be of a certain quality to be suitable for human consumption. No natural water found on Earth is pure; any sample of water contains more than just water molecules. Some materials, such as sodium nitrate, are very soluble and dissolve in water in large quantities, whereas other materials are much less soluble. This is just as well, otherwise rain would dissolve all the rocks and they would end up in the oceans!

Drinking water must not contain harmful materials, which means both harmful bacteria and dissolved material that could be dangerous. Water does not have to be absolutely pure to be drinkable and, indeed, not only would it be costly to make it so, but also water is an important source of many of the metal ions (such as Ca^{2+}) required in the human diet. Water must be processed to make it acceptable for consumption. However, water must have levels of impurities that are below a danger threshold. How such thresholds (recommended by the World Health Organization) are assessed can be contentious but, in order to make comparisons, some measure of the amount of a particular substance dissolved in water is needed. **Concentration** is the mass of a substance in a known volume of a liquid: for example, milligrams in a litre. The units of concentration are expressed as milligrams per litre (abbreviated to mg/l). Box 3.2 introduced the prefix 'milli' when it was used in conjunction with metres. Here it is used with grams.

■ What fraction of a gram is a milligram?

☐ A milligram is one-thousandth of a gram:

$$1\,mg = \frac{1}{1000}\,g = 1 \times 10^{-3}\,g$$

As noted above, tap water is never pure in the sense that it contains only water molecules and no other chemicals. Even bottled waters are not 100% water. Which substances are dissolved in water and in what concentrations?

If you drink bottled mineral water, look at the label and note down the contents. You will find that it contains a wide range of ions. Table 6.8 gives the concentrations of some ions in various bottled waters and two tap waters. Note that tap waters can vary substantially. You are already familiar with most of the ions listed.

■ What are the formulas for the following ions: calcium, sodium, potassium, chloride and nitrate?

☐ In Section 6.6 you saw that calcium is Ca^{2+}, sodium is Na^+, potassium is K^+, chloride is Cl^- and nitrate is NO_3^-.

To interpret Table 6.8, a few points need to be clarified. For example, what do the values in Table 6.8 mean? They are given as concentrations in mg/l.

Table 6.8 Concentrations of ions in bottled and tap waters.

Ion	Concentration/(mg/l)*					
	Volvic®	Vittel®	Buxton®	Evian®	Tap water	
					Area 1	Area 2
calcium	11.5	91	55	78	130	50.0
magnesium	8.0	19.9	19	24	9.4	6.6
sodium	11.6	7.3	24	5	51	128
potassium	6.2	–	1	1	9.4	1.6
chloride	13.5	–	37	4.5	82	27.1
nitrate	6.3	0.6	<0.1	3.5	26	17.6
sulfate	8.1	105	13	10	210	21.3
bicarbonate	71.0	258	248	357	?	?

< means 'less than'; – means too small to measure; ? means the values are not available.

*Note here that for clarity we have enclosed the units mg/l in brackets, i.e. the column heading is concentration divided by mg/l.

■ From Table 6.8 what is the concentration of chloride ions in Buxton water?

☐ The concentration is 37 mg/1, which means that in one litre of water there are 37 mg of dissolved chloride ions.

You may be wondering why ion concentrations in drinking water are deemed important enough to be measured by suppliers of both bottled drinking water and tap water. The following activity will help to clarify this.

Activity 6.3 Ions in drinking water

You should allow at least 30 minutes for this activity.

The aim of this activity is to access up-to-date information about ions in drinking water. You will access the web pages of the Drinking Water Inspectorate (DWI) of England and Wales and search for information to answer the following questions and make a note of the answers in your study folder.

(a) Which ions in Table 6.8 are responsible for the hardness of water?

(b) What is the World Health Organization's guideline value for nitrate concentration in drinking water?

(c) How does this concentration compare with the values for nitrate concentration in Table 6.8?

Further guidance on this activity is given on the course website.

When you accessed the DWI web pages on drinking water you may have noticed that it isn't just ion concentrations that are monitored. Water companies are also required to monitor their treatment works for the presence of *Cryptosporidium* (a micro-organism that can cause diarrhoea) and pesticides. You will take a closer look at water use and the effects of water pollution on the world's water supplies in Chapter 7.

6.8 Summary of Chapter 6

You have learned about the following concepts in this chapter.

Each type of atom contains a characteristic number of protons in a central nucleus and an equal number of electrons in layers surrounding the nucleus.

Elements are substances that consist of only one type of atom.

Compounds contain two or more elements combined together.

There are two kinds of bond between atoms: covalent and ionic.

Molecules are the smallest units in which elements and/or compounds can exist covalently bonded together.

Ions are formed by atoms or groups of atoms gaining or losing electrons.

Chemical formulas describe the number of atoms present in elements, ions and compounds.

Balanced chemical equations describe, using chemical formulas, the reactants and products in a chemical reaction.

Concentration is the mass of a substance dissolved in a given volume (usually 1 litre) of a liquid.

Learning outcomes for Chapter 6

When you have completed Chapter 6 you should be able to:

- Read data presented in tables.
- Use scientific notation to express both large and small quantities.
- Appreciate why chemists use different models to represent molecules.
- Identify the number and type(s) of atom present in a molecule from its chemical formula.
- Identify the reactants and products of a reaction in a chemical equation.
- Read and write using chemical notation.
- Write a balanced chemical equation to represent a chemical reaction.
- Access DWI website and retrieve information about ions in drinking water.

Activity 6.4   Water, molecules and ions

You should allow about 45 minutes for this interactive activity.

This interactive video sequence introduces issues associated with water purity and health in an overcrowded world. It also has animations of water molecules showing how they dissolve sodium chloride.

Activity 6.5   Further reflection on your study time plans

Now that you have planned your work for two chapters, and seen the results, you are in a good position to consider how your study time plans are working out. Compare your log of study time for Chapter 6 with your plan (including any revisions you made after studying Chapter 5). Had you set realistic plans and manageable targets? You might need to make some adjustments to your targets for each study session and your overall plan for Chapter 7. You may find it helpful to reread the comments for Activity 5.3.

Remember to bring your learning journal up to date before moving on to Chapter 7.

Chapter 7
Global water needs

This chapter looks at water needs in a global context. Chapter 2 considered domestic water use but this topic is now widened in scope to include the total water use of countries around the world. Section 7.1 considers the water used in industry to produce manufactured goods and that used in agriculture, particularly to irrigate crops. In theory, there should be plenty of water but pollution is a serious and ongoing problem that needs constant monitoring and action. This is exemplified by the case of the River Thames over the last 400 years, which you will study in Section 7.2. Section 7.3 considers how plants and animals are adapted to conditions where water is scarce. To study Section 7.4 you will need to have identified and listed the key points from Sections 7.1–7.3, as described below in Activity 7.1, and we return to the 'three Cs' of communication introduced in Section 5.2.

Activity 7.1   Listing key points

You should allow about 30 minutes for this activity.

Summarising is a very important activity because it not only gives you a written record of the key points that you have noted as you have been studying, but also it helps to reinforce your learning. You should practise summarising as you study Chapter 7 by identifying key points. You will be using your notes from this activity to produce a summary of the chapter in Activity 7.6 in Section 7.4. Further guidance on this activity is given on the course website.

7.1   You and your water footprint

About 1.1×10^5 km³ of water, in the various forms of precipitation, falls globally on the land surface each year but the majority of this evaporates back into the atmosphere. Only about 4×10^4 km³ of the total precipitation runs off into lakes and rivers or seeps into underground reservoirs and is potentially available for human use.

■ What percentage of the total global annual precipitation is potentially available for use?

☐ $\dfrac{4 \times 10^4 \text{ km}^3}{1.1 \times 10^5 \text{ km}^3} \times 100\% = 36.36\%$

which is about 36%.

However, the amount of this water that can be exploited in practice, for domestic use or for industry and irrigation, is estimated to be no more than about 1.4×10^4 km³.

■ What percentage of the total global annual precipitation can be exploited in practice?

□ $\dfrac{1.4 \times 10^4 \text{ km}^3}{1.1 \times 10^5 \text{ km}^3} \times 100\% = 12.727\%$

which is just under 13%.

■ You read in Chapter 6, Section 6.1 that the total volume of water on Earth is about 1.46×10^9 km^3. What percentage of this is usable?

□ $\dfrac{1.4 \times 10^4 \text{ km}^3}{1.46 \times 10^9 \text{ km}^3} \times 100\% = 9.589 \times 10^{-4}\%$

which is just under 0.001% or $1 \times 10^{-3}\%$ or 1 part in 100 000 of the Earth's total water.

This may not seem like very much but, shared out among the world's human population, it is still far more than is needed to ensure the basic survival and minimum domestic needs of everyone, as well as leaving plenty to sustain the other animals and plants which share the Earth.

The minimum water intake needed for survival varies for people in different countries, not least because of the sort of climate they live in. In Chapter 2 you were reminded that the average person in the UK has a daily water intake of about 2.5 litres.

■ Do you think this water intake would be enough to sustain someone living in Nigeria, during April, when the average temperature is about 30 °C? If not, why not?

□ No, it wouldn't. A much higher water intake would be needed to balance the amount likely to be lost through sweating at such high temperatures.

Depending on how hot it is, and how much physical work a person has to do, it is possible for their daily water requirement to rise to as much as 11 or 12 litres. Without adequate water intake, dehydration occurs very rapidly. With loss of water equal to 5% of body mass, you would feel incredibly thirsty, and with 10% loss, you would become very ill.

However, humans depend on water for rather more than drinking. The perception of *personal* need is likely to be far greater when water is freely available 'on tap' (Figure 7.1a and b) than when water must be carried from a well or river to the house, and the washing carried to the river (Figure 7.1c).

Not surprisingly, the daily consumption of water for domestic use is very much greater per person in the most developed areas of the world, such as Europe and North America, than in the least developed areas of Africa and Asia (Figure 7.2). In Question 2.7 you used the information in Table 2.1 to calculate that the domestic use of water in the UK is 150 litres per person per day. Contrast that figure with the estimate given by the charity WaterAid on their website (accessed April 2007) that the *average* domestic use in developing countries is about 10 litres per person per day. People in the most developed countries on average consume about 15 times more water than those in the least developed countries.

(a)

(b)

(c)

Figure 7.1 Contrasting uses of water in the most heavily developed and the least developed areas of the world: (a) car washes at service stations use large amounts of water; (b) loading a domestic dishwasher; (c) washing clothes in a river in Tanzania.

The difference between the most and least developed countries is less marked when the total water use is considered. The total use of water for all purposes, including industry and agriculture as well as domestic use, is known as a **water footprint**. The global water footprint, i.e. the total amount of water used globally, was estimated by UNESCO in 2004 as 7450 km^3 per year, which equates to about 3400 litres per person per day. Since countries vary in size and population density, comparison between them is most straightforward if the water footprints *per person* are compared. It is estimated that the average water footprint per person in the most heavily developed countries is around 4800 litres per day, compared with 2990 litres per day in the least developed countries.

There are larger differences between individual countries: for example, the USA has a water footprint of 6795 litres per person per day while China has one of 1918 litres per person per day. The water footprint total given here for individual countries includes water used wholly within that country (the internal water footprint) as well as water used in the country for goods that are then exported (the external water footprint). The water footprint is affected by several factors: the amount of industrialisation; high versus low meat consumption; the climate; and how efficiently water is used for agriculture. This means that countries which use a large amount of water for agriculture and are industrialised, such as Italy and Greece, have large water footprints. Even highly industrialised countries, such as the UK, the Netherlands, Denmark and Australia, may have a relatively small water footprint if the climate is favourable for crop production since this lessens the need for irrigation. Countries such as the USA and Canada, where there is a high proportion of meat in the diet and a high consumption of industrial products, have a large water footprint.

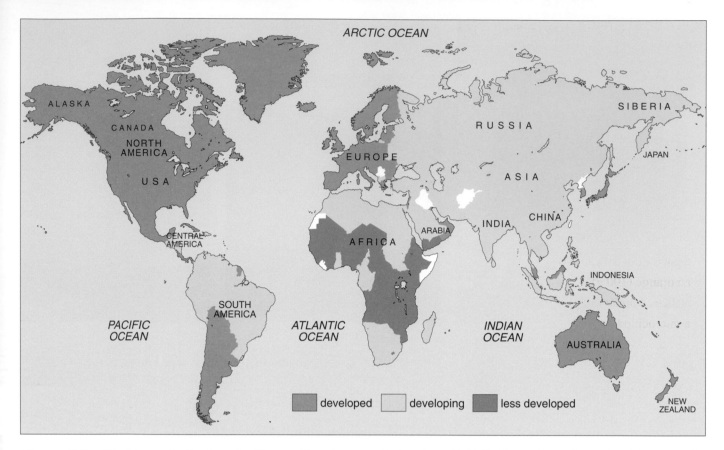

Figure 7.2 World map indicating the Human Development Index (as of 2006). Countries coloured red (e.g. North America, Europe, Australia, Japan, Chile and Argentina) exhibit very high human development and are generally recognised as heavily developed countries. Those in shades of yellow (including much of Asia, parts of the Middle East, South America and southern and Saharan Africa) are developing, and those in purple (parts of Africa) are the least developed (white areas – no data available).

Question 7.1

(a) Consider the figures given above for domestic water use. What is the domestic use of water per person per day in the least developed countries as a percentage of the domestic use of water per person per day in the UK? Give your answer to one decimal place.

(b) In Chapter 2 you learned that the *total* daily water requirement per person in the UK is 'more than 3000 litres'. In fact, it is about 3411 litres. What is the *domestic* use per person as a percentage of the *total* daily water requirement per person per day in the UK? Give your answer to one decimal place.

Worldwide, water for domestic use accounts for 4.6% of the *total* world water usage. So you can see from your answer to Question 7.1(b) that the UK figure is very similar to the global figure.

The needs of industry worldwide account for 9.6% which is more than twice as much as domestic use, but agricultural production uses 85.8% and is by far the most demanding. Table 7.1 gives the global average **virtual water content** – that is, the water associated with the production of various consumer goods.

Table 7.1 Examples of the global average virtual water content of consumer goods.

Product	Virtual water content/litres
average sized car, including tyres	148 000
1 kg coffee (roasted)	20 682
1 kg tea (loose)	9 205
a cotton T-shirt (medium sized)	4 100
a hamburger (250 g)	2 400
a glass of milk (200 ml)	200
a bag of potato crisps (200 g)	185
a cup of coffee (125 ml)	140
a glass of beer (250 ml)	75
an orange (100 g)	50
a slice of bread (30 g)	40
a microchip (2 g)	32
a sheet of A4 paper (80 g/m^2)	10

As you studied Table 7.1, you will have realised that when you eat an orange you don't consume 50 litres of water alongside it! Nor when you drink a glass of beer do you imbibe the 75 litres of water that went into its production! You drink only one-quarter of a litre. The water that is used in the production of goods and food is known as the 'virtual' or 'embodied' water content. In general, the more processing that is needed, the higher the virtual water content. For example, various materials are used to produce a car: metals have to be mined and smelted, rubber produced, fabrics made for upholstery, glass made for windows, and so on.

■ When you looked at Table 7.1, was it easy to compare the amount of virtual water needed to produce different items? For example, compare the amount of virtual water in: (a) a bag of potato crisps with that in a glass of milk; (b) a bag of potato crisps with that in an orange; (c) 1 kg of coffee with that in 1 kg of tea.

□ You probably found it simpler to make comparisons where you could compare like with like. In (a) you are comparing 185 litres of virtual water in a 200 g bag of potato crisps with 200 litres of virtual water in 200 ml of milk. Both products contain a similar amount of virtual water – slightly more in milk – but, for a more accurate comparison, you would have to do some calculations, for example, to find the exact mass of 200 ml of milk.

In (b) you are comparing 185 litres of virtual water in a 200 g bag of potato crisps with 50 litres of virtual water in a 100 g orange: a simpler calculation, perhaps in your head, shows that half of 185 litres, 92.5 litres, would be needed to produce 100 g of potato crisps, so you can make a direct comparison between that and the amount needed to produce an orange of the same mass.

In (c) you are comparing like with like: a *kilogram* of coffee with a *kilogram* of tea, and it should be immediately obvious that it takes more than twice as much virtual water to produce coffee.

The examples in Table 7.1 were produced with consumers in mind, so the data are presented in a way that will capture their interest. Scientists using data on virtual water content find it most useful to use figures that give a direct comparison.

Virtual water content is often exported and imported: for example, if you purchase a T-shirt in the UK it is fairly certain that the water that went to produce the cotton was not from the UK. The consumption of virtual water can considerably increase or decrease the apparent water footprint of a country. The number you used in Question 7.1(b) was the *total* water footprint for the UK, including the virtual water in imported agricultural and industrial goods, but excluding virtual water exported in goods produced in the UK. The breakdown by consumption category is shown in Table 7.2.

The volumes of water listed in Table 7.2 are very large: handling such large numbers is discussed in more detail in Chapter 9. All the quantities are given to the *same* power of ten in this table (rather than in scientific notation), to help comparison.

Table 7.2 The UK's annual water footprint by category.

Consumption category	Annual volume/ (10^9 m³/year)
domestic water withdrawal	2.21
agriculture for national consumption	12.79
industrial water for national consumption	6.67
Subtotal A: total internal water footprint for UK	**21.67**
agriculture for export	3.38
industrial water for export	1.46
Subtotal B: total UK water exported as virtual water	**4.84**
virtual water in imported agricultural goods	34.73
virtual water in imported industrial goods	16.67
Subtotal C: total virtual water footprint imported for UK	**51.40**
virtual water imported and then re-exported	12.83
Total: water footprint	**73.07**

Source: UNESCO, 2004.

■ The UK's total water footprint is the amount of water that is used annually by the UK, either virtually or actually. How is the total of 73.07×10^9 m³ per year arrived at?

☐ The total water footprint includes water used internally in the UK (subtotal A) and virtual water imported into the UK (subtotal C) but not water exported from the UK as virtual water (subtotal B). It also disregards virtual water imported and re-exported.

■ Supposing that it was not possible to import and export goods containing virtual water, would the UK be able to sustain water use at the present rate?

☐ Only 4.84×10^9 m^3 of water is exported in a year whereas 51.40×10^9 m^3 is imported. There is a deficit of 46.56×10^9 m^3. Unless this were available within the country, large-scale economies of water use would be needed.

In 2006, the United Nations calculated that over one-third of humanity is living in areas where water is scarce.

The world population is increasing but world water supplies are finite, so on a global scale the available water needs to be used to optimal advantage. By researching and using data on water availability, storage and use, scientists can recommend the best way to ensure that there is sufficient water worldwide.

Activity 7.1   Listing key points (continued)

Before you move on, remember to look back at your notes and highlighting in Section 7.1, and produce a list of the main points about water consumption, water footprints and virtual water content, as described in Box 3.1. You should aim to identify just five or six main points from the section, and your list need only be in note form at this stage.

7.2 'Sweet Thames run softly …'

Given humans' dependence on water for domestic use, you would think it would be important to keep lakes and rivers as clean as possible. Sadly, clean water has not always been a prime consideration for society. Too often, lakes and rivers have become a dumping ground for waste products, thereby polluting the very water that needs to be kept clean (Figure 7.3).

(a) (b)

Figure 7.3 Water pollution from factories in (a) the North West and (b) the Midlands of England.

■ Figure 7.3 shows examples of pollution from industrial waste. From what you know from your study of Chapters 4 and 6, what are the other two main sources of pollution likely to be?

☐ As well as industrial waste, there is domestic waste (sewage) and agricultural waste (such as the soluble waste from fertilisers).

You know already (from Chapter 4, Section 4.4.1) that water used for human consumption needs to be of a certain quality: in other words, it must be potable. Next you will look in more detail at the ways in which potable water may be rendered unfit for human consumption (or, indeed, for consumption by other animals) as the result of pollution.

7.2.1   The causes and effects of water pollution

Industrial pollution has often been caused in the past as the result of ignorance. Industries were frequently permitted to discharge their untreated waste products into lakes and rivers. Only later did the harmful consequences of these products become apparent. Figure 7.4 shows a warning notice advising people not to catch fish from a river in Florida, USA. For many years this river received untreated waste, containing dioxin, from a wood-pulp mill. Dioxin is a by-product of the chlorine bleaching process used to clean the pulp; it is an extremely toxic chemical that is thought to cause skin disease and increase cancer risk in humans, and has been shown to cause sterility in fish and alligators. Switching to an alternative technology that uses oxygen could avoid this. In other instances, the discharge of harmful substances into waterways is less obvious; for example, rainwater seeping through the waste-tips of old lead mines dissolves the lead, and carries it into rivers.

The pollutants from industry include metals such as lead and mercury, which are toxic above a certain concentration. Once they get into the water cycle, they begin to accumulate at various points along the way. They become incorporated into the muds of lakes and estuaries, and they build up in the tissues of plants and animals that live in the water or search in the mud for their food. As these organisms are eaten by others, the metals become steadily more concentrated in the tissues of the predators until they reach levels that may become life-threatening. If people eat fish and shellfish from these polluted waters, the lead and mercury will enter their bodies, too.

It isn't only industry that is responsible for polluting lakes and rivers with metals. Individual humans are equally culpable. In 1979, it was estimated that around 3000 mute swans in the UK could be dying of poisoning as the result of eating the lead weights that were carelessly discarded by anglers after fishing. Fortunately, this number has decreased significantly now that weights are made of different materials. You don't have to be an angler, however, to contaminate the water supply with lead. You may live in an older house that still contains lead water pipes. As water passes through the pipes, a little of the lead is dissolved and so enters the water cycle. One side-effect of both lead and mercury poisoning is brain damage. You may already know that the saying 'as mad as a hatter' is derived from the 19th century when mercury nitrate was used in the manufacture of men's top hats.

Figure 7.4 Warning notice by the side of a river in Florida, USA, where a wood-pulp mill was discharging high levels of dioxin and chlorine bleach into the water.

Pollution from domestic sewage can lead to more than one sort of problem. Most obviously, sewage is a source of water-borne diseases such as cholera and typhoid fever (Chapter 4, Section 4.4.1). A second problem with sewage is that the bacteria which break it down, during a process called respiration, use dissolved oxygen from the water to do so. (You will learn more about respiration in Chapter 8.) This same dissolved oxygen also supports the other aquatic life. The more sewage there is in the water, the more bacteria are required to break it down and the more dissolved oxygen they use, leaving less oxygen for fish and other aquatic animals. Once the oxygen in the water is used up, animals that need oxygen die. It isn't long before the water begins to smell distinctly unpleasant because of the gases released when the sewage begins to be broken down by bacteria that can live without oxygen. If you've ever stirred up the mud at the bottom of a stagnant pond, you will know what it smells like.

Agricultural activities cause problems through both crop spraying and the use of fertilisers. Crop spraying is carried out to prevent damage to crops from weeds and various pests (Figure 7.5a). However, spraying can disperse herbicides and pesticides over a wide area so that they end up in water that drains into rivers and lakes. In high enough doses, these pollutants may be toxic and, like lead and mercury, they can accumulate in the tissues of animals and so end up in human bodies, too.

(a)

(b)

Figure 7.5 (a) A tractor spraying pesticide onto fruit trees in the Po delta, northern Italy. Over 7000 kg of pesticide end up in the Po river every year. Underground water is also affected and hundreds of wells have become so contaminated with nitrate ions and other pollutants (which you read about in Section 6.6) that they have been sealed off. (b) Swans and cygnets on an algae covered urban canal in The Netherlands.

In Chapter 4, Section 4.4.1 and in Chapter 6, Section 6.6 one of the problems caused by pollution from fertilisers was mentioned. As well as nitrogen, fertilisers contain other nutrients, substances essential for the healthy growth of all plants and animals. One problem is that much of the fertiliser seeps into lakes and rivers by drainage off the land and it can lead to excessive plant growth (Figure 7.5b). As a lake surface becomes covered with water weed and algae, oxygen can no longer be dissolved in the water to replenish what is being used by fish and other aquatic animals. Once again, starved of oxygen, the animal life soon begins to die, and the water becomes stagnant and foul-smelling.

This discussion of the effects of water pollution takes up a lot of space with words. The notion that a single diagram can summarise a long piece of text was described in Chapter 4, Section 4.5. Figure 7.6 summarises how lead may get into lakes and rivers, and some of its effects. Figure 7.6 is a form of *flow diagram*. The arrows show the routes taken by lead from its various sources into the water cycle, and then into plant and animal life.

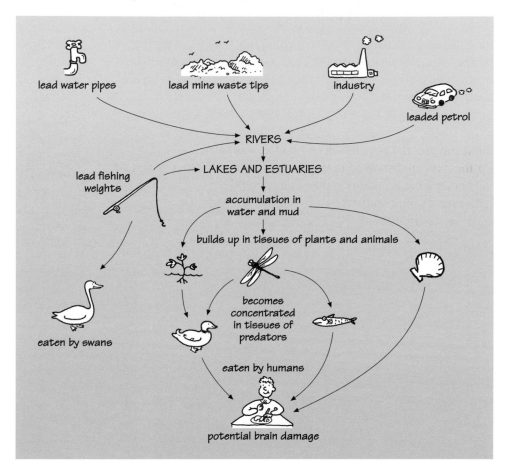

Figure 7.6 Diagrammatic summary of some sources of lead in lakes and rivers, and some of the organisms that accumulate the lead.

Activity 7.2 Summarising text with a diagram

You should spend about 15 minutes on this activity.

When you did Activity 4.3 you translated a diagram into text. In this activity you should do the reverse.

Using Figure 7.6 as an example, construct your own flow diagram to summarise the sources of domestic sewage in surface waters on the land, what happens to the polluted water when it enters the water cycle, and the effects it may have on the water, humans and other animal life. This process of producing a flow diagram can make it easier to follow a passage of text. (Note that pictures have been included in Figure 7.6 to make it more entertaining. You are *not* expected to do this.)

7.2.2 The pollution of the River Thames: a case study

As cities grew larger, pollution from domestic sewage entering waterways became a very serious problem, and in Britain this was not alleviated until late in the 20th century. Pollution of the River Thames in London is a good case in point. It will be used as a case study to explore the life of a large river that is typical of the conditions of large rivers around the world.

In 1596, when the poet Edmund Spenser penned the line 'Sweet Thames run softly, till I end my song' as the recurring refrain in 'Prothalamion', the Thames was probably a 'sweet' and clean-flowing river. Although it was common practice in Spenser's day for people to take their buckets of sewage down to the Thames to empty, and then refill with the river water for domestic use, the population of London was sufficiently small for the oxygen dissolved in the water to be replenished as fast as the bacteria breaking down the sewage could use up the oxygen. However, as the population of London expanded during the 19th century, when people were driven off the land by the Enclosure Acts, and as flush sanitation was installed in houses leading to the direct discharge of sewage into the river, a different story emerged. The unsanitary conditions of Thames water seriously affected the health of people living in London, with five cholera epidemics occurring between 1830 and 1871. The filthy state of the Thames was the focus of satire for cartoonists of this period (Figure 4.17 and Figure 7.7).

Figure 7.7 Cartoon from *Punch* in 1855, showing the physicist Michael Faraday greeting an offensive-smelling King Neptune in the Thames.

The oxygen levels in the water as the Thames passed through London became so depleted that in the drought summer of 1858 the river was rendered lifeless. The problem was exacerbated by the fact that the Thames is still tidal in central London. This means that some of the raw sewage transported down river from London was washed back up again on the incoming tide. The stench from the river became unbearable and on occasions Parliament had to be abandoned. This was not a bad thing because, after this so-called 'Year of the Great Stink', Parliament was forced to take steps to find a remedy.

Figure 7.8 is a graph showing the dissolved oxygen content of the Thames at various distances upstream and downstream from London Bridge in 1893, 1970 and 1992. Like several of the other illustrations in this book, this one requires close reading.

The vertical scale shows the dissolved oxygen content in the Thames, expressed as a percentage of the oxygen level at **saturation**. When the water is holding as much oxygen as it can, it is said to be saturated with respect to oxygen, and the saturation level is 100%.

The scale on the horizontal axis may appear strange to you, because the 0 km mark does not coincide with the intersection of the horizontal and vertical axes, as you might expect. London Bridge has been chosen as the zero reference point because it is not far from the centre of London. However, the changes in the oxygen content need to be recorded as relatively fresh Thames water flows into

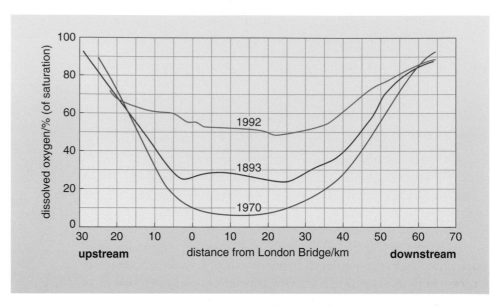

Figure 7.8 Graph showing the average dissolved oxygen content (as a percentage of saturation) of the River Thames at various distances upstream and downstream from London Bridge in 1893, 1970 and 1992. Measurements were taken during July–October, when pollution is greatest.

London, and as polluted water flows out of London. Consequently, the horizontal scale needs to extend some distance both upstream and downstream of London Bridge.

Each curve records measurements of dissolved oxygen in the Thames from July to October in a particular year. There are some similarities between all three curves. You can see that 20–30 km upstream of London Bridge the river is fairly rich in oxygen (70–90% saturation).

This is true for each of the three curves. As the water flows through London, the oxygen levels fall and it is about 20–25 km downstream from London Bridge before oxygen levels begin building up again. However, the curves for the three years do not coincide, showing that the oxygen levels in the Thames where it flows through London have varied considerably. There are historical reasons for these differences.

During 1858, when pollution from sewage was at its worst, the oxygen levels downstream of London Bridge reached zero, but by 1893 they had improved significantly as the result of government legislation.

Question 7.2

What was the dissolved oxygen level 20 km downstream of London Bridge in 1893?

Unfortunately, the very rapid growth of London in the first half of the 20th century meant that sewage treatment was unable to keep pace with the growing population, so oxygen levels plummeted once more, reaching zero again at London Bridge during the 1950s. However, after the 1960s, tighter controls on sewage discharge and improved treatment facilities brought about a steady improvement, which is reflected in the curve for 1970.

■ Does the curve for 1970 represent improvement or deterioration in oxygen levels since 1893?

☐ It represents deterioration because the curve for 1970 lies below that for 1893.

■ What were the oxygen levels between London Bridge and about 20 km downstream in 1970?

☐ They were between about 5% and 10% of the level at saturation.

Oxygen levels continued to improve during the late 20th century, and there was much rejoicing in the angling community when the first salmon for 141 years was caught in the Thames 20 km downstream of London Bridge in 1974. By 1985, migrating salmon and sea trout were regularly recorded (Figure 7.9). Even so, there were major fish mortalities in 1973, 1977 and 1986 due to low dissolved oxygen content in the water. In recent years not only have rainfall patterns changed, but urban development has increased and open ground has been built on or paved over. Rainwater is increasingly being channelled directly into sewers and then into the Thames rather than soaking into the ground and replenishing water in aquifers. This combination has increased the sewage problem and, even though the effluent is fully treated, there are still enough organic pollutants to have a significant effect on dissolved oxygen levels. The problem is most severe after heavy rainfall when storm water rushes through the sewers. When this happens, large quantities of effluent mixed with storm water and rubbish washed from the city's streets are dumped into the Thames, greatly reducing the dissolved oxygen in the water.

To combat this problem, in 1989 the Thames Bubbler, a vessel used to inject oxygen into the water, came into operation which achieved some improvement and by 1992 this same stretch of the Thames was recording dissolved oxygen levels of between 50% and 60% of saturation. In the first years of the 21st century up to 500 migrating fish were recorded annually. However, there is concern at the gradual decline in oxygen levels in the Thames Estuary since 1992 partially as a result of warmer water temperature speeding up the rate of bacterial breakdown. The story of the River Thames – a 'river returned from the dead' – is a successful one and, with continued careful monitoring, could continue this way. However, awareness of the problems of pollution has not been as high regarding some other rivers, as Figure 7.3 shows.

Figure 7.9 Two women fishing in front of Canary Wharf tower in London's Docklands in 1997.

Activity 7.1 Listing key points (continued)

Remember to look back at your notes and highlighting in Section 7.2, and once again produce a list of five or six main points.

7.3 When water is scarce: camels and cacti revisited

People who live in countries where water is in short supply are very careful about using it. However, many plants and animals have evolved various ways of surviving in conditions where there would not be enough water to sustain human life. Now that you have learned more about the science of water, this section returns to the desert organisms introduced in Section 3.3, to consider in more detail how they are adapted to conditions where water is scarce.

In Section 4.3 you learned that cooling by sweating is important because it prevents the body from overheating, which can damage its functioning. Humans readily sweat in order to maintain their normal body temperature of around 37 °C. This is important because, if the body temperature rises to as high as 39.5 °C and stays there, the body functions become impaired and death follows. Such an efficient sweating mechanism depends critically on the availability of drinking water to replace water lost by sweating. However, a camel's normal body temperature of 38 °C can rise to about 40 °C before it begins to sweat, and therefore the amount of water lost by sweating is reduced. In fact, its body temperature can rise even more than this – as high as 41.5 °C – without impairing its body functions. The inside of the lungs is a particularly vulnerable surface for water loss by evaporation. Large quantities of air are breathed into the lungs and out to the external world every minute of the day and night. The air passes from the nose through the nasal passages, which are tubes at the back of the nose that connect to a tube that leads to the lungs. In camels, the nasal passages are long, narrow and elaborately convoluted. This means that they have a large total surface area of more than 1.0×10^3 cm^2, which can be pictured as the area of a strip of ribbon 10 m long and 1 cm wide. The structure of the nasal passages helps to conserve water at night when the air temperature in desert regions is much lower than during the day. At night, when the air temperature is about 25 °C or less, the convoluted nasal passages are cooled each time the inhaled air passes through them. Once in the lungs, the cool night air is warmed to the camel's body temperature. However, as the warmed air is exhaled, it is cooled by the lower temperature of the nasal passages. In the camel, the air leaves the lungs at a body temperature of 38 °C but, after passing through the convoluted nasal passages, its temperature is reduced to 25 °C.

In animals such as humans, which have wide nasal passages, cooling of the nasal passages by the inhaled air is incomplete, and so the exhaled air leaving the nose is warmer than the surrounding air.

■ How does the process of cooling the exhaled air affect water retention in camels?

□ As you discovered in Chapter 4, Sections 4.1 and 4.5, cooler air cannot contain as much water vapour as warmer air. Consequently, some of the water vapour present in the air as it leaves the lungs will condense within the nasal passages instead of being lost to the atmosphere.

Although this water retention can only work when the surrounding air temperature is much lower than the body temperature, it makes an important contribution to overall water conservation in camels. In addition, the camel's nasal passages are lined with mucus that absorbs water from the exhaled air.

Like animals, plants generally have a vulnerable surface for water loss by evaporation. Pores, called **stomata**, are present on stems and are particularly common on the surface of leaves. Stomata can open and close, and are important for air exchange. When open, they expose the inner layer of the leaves, making them vulnerable to water loss. In cacti, water is conserved because they have far fewer stomata on stems than other kinds of plants, and the leaves are reduced to spines, which have no stomata at all. Cacti, like camels, also take advantage of the cool temperatures at night for conserving water. The stomata on the stems open only at night; during the heat of the day they remain closed.

You should now be in a position to pull together some of the threads of Chapter 7, along with information from earlier in this book (Chapter 3, Section 3), and to present them in writing in a concise and coherent way for someone else to read. In the next activity you will consider the problems of water loss for camels in a hot desert environment, and how these are overcome.

Activity 7.3   Writing a clear, coherent and concise account

You should allow about 30 minutes for this activity.

An assignment question will often require you to use material you have studied to write an account. Before you write the account, you need to plan it. Often there will be a word limit and you will usually be penalised if you do not keep to it. This activity will give you some useful practice in planning and writing a brief account (200 words) of the camel's ability to survive the shortage of water in a hot desert environment. Further guidance on this activity is given on the course website.

Did you find it difficult to keep your account within the required 200 word length? Perhaps you found it hard to know what to leave in and what to take out: this sort of judgement is easier with experience so, if you did have problems, you should find the activities in Section 7.4 particularly helpful.

Activity 7.1   Listing key points (continued)

Now you have completed Section 7.3, look back at your notes and highlighting of this section, and produce a list of the main points. Compare your list for Sections 7.1, 7.2 and 7.3 with the comments on this activity on the course website before you attempt Activity 7.6 at the end of Section 7.4.

7.4 The three Cs revisited

This section comprises activities aimed at helping you develop your science writing skills, introduced earlier in Section 5.2.

Activity 7.4 Writing concisely

You should allow about 20 minutes for this activity.

This activity requires you to read an extract from a student's overlong account of how camels survive the shortage of water, to consider how it could be made more concise. Nyasha's account may be downloaded from the course website. Further guidance on this activity is given on the course website.

Activity 7.5 Communicating science

You should allow about 30 minutes for this activity, including watching a video sequence.

Critical discussion of writing is a good way to develop writing skills. This activity requires you to read another student's account of how camels survive the shortage of water, to consider whether it measures up to the 'clarity, coherence and conciseness' criteria, and to criticise it constructively. You should then watch a video sequence of students discussing how Terry's account could be improved and compare their suggestions with your own. The account and further guidance on this activity may be downloaded from the course website.

Activity 7.6 Summarising material you have studied

You should allow about 20 minutes for this activity.

Summarising a piece of written material is a useful skill and one that you may be asked to do in an assessment: this activity gives you practice in summarising. You should use the notes you have made of the main points in Sections 7.1–7.3 from Activity 7.1 to produce a brief summary of Chapter 7. You should write the summary in clear, concise sentences (Box 5.1), rather than notes, and organise it into paragraphs (Box 5.2), one paragraph for each section. When you have completed your summary, compare it with the version in the comments on this activity on the course website.

7.5 Summary of Chapter 7

Water footprint is a measure of the total amount of water used for all purposes. The most heavily developed countries have a footprint on average some 1.6 times greater than that of developing countries.

The virtual water content of consumer goods is the water used to produce it.

Water pollution is caused by a number of activities including industrial effluent discharge into waterways (e.g. dioxins, mercury and lead), agriculture (e.g. soluble waste from fertilisers, herbicides and pesticides) and domestic waste disposal (sewage).

Pollution in the River Thames arising from low dissolved oxygen levels is caused by the bacteriological breakdown of discharged sewage by respiration.

Camels conserve water by not sweating until their body temperature reaches 40 °C, and by having long convoluted nasal tubes with high surface areas to absorb condensed water vapour from the exhaled moisture-laden air from their lungs.

Cacti conserve water by having fewer stomata than other kinds of plants, and leaves that are reduced to spines.

Diagrams can be used in scientific writing to summarise text for quick reference.

Summarising text in a diagram can make it easier to understand a passage of text.

Clarity in writing may be achieved by avoiding ambiguities, unnecessary repetition and redundant words.

Learning outcomes for Chapter 7

When you have completed Chapter 7 you should be able to:

- Understand the terms water footprint and virtual water content.
- Understand why sewage discharged into rivers can reduce the dissolved oxygen content of the water.
- Summarise text in a diagram.
- Summarise a piece of text within a given word limit.
- Summarise a chapter by means of key points.

You have been given numerous facts and figures about water use in this chapter, but now is the time to find some of your own.

Activity 7.7   Water facts

You should allow about 30 minutes for this activity.

You may have been surprised at the quantity of water needed for various domestic, industrial and agricultural needs. For this penultimate activity in Chapter 7, you should spend some time discussing water needs with other students in your tutor group – and perhaps trying to surprise *them*. First, you should find out some information about water and then post this information in a message on your tutor group forum.

Further guidance on this activity is given on the course website.

Activity 7.8   Updating your study time plans

You should allow about 10 minutes for this activity.

Before leaving Chapter 7 check your log of study time and compare it with your study plan. Now would be a good time to adjust your plans, if necessary.

Remember to bring your learning journal up to date before moving on to Chapter 8.

Chapter 8
Processes of life

This story about water has touched on some biology – the science that deals with living material (from the Greek *bios*, meaning 'life', and *–logy*, meaning 'study of'). All living things share fundamental properties that separate them from non-living materials. They have definite structures: for example, they are composed of small **cells**, the unit of life (Section 4.4.2); and they can carry out certain activities or processes, such as digestion and absorption of nutrients (Section 4.4.3).

■   What other activities or processes are characteristic of living materials?

☐   You may have thought of one or two of the following (there are others): most use oxygen; they 'grow' and reproduce themselves; they excrete waste products; and their behaviour is affected by their environment.

Non-living materials show none of these properties. From your everyday knowledge you are aware that there are very many different sorts of living material. Living individuals or organisms are divided into several groups according to how similar they are. For example, a tree has several features in common with grass, whereas both trees and grass are quite dissimilar to frogs. Cats share more features with elephants than they do with flowers. In science, trees, grasses, seaweeds and flowers are grouped together as plants; frogs, fish, cats, elephants, worms and humans are grouped together as animals.

So far, two groups of organisms have been mentioned: plants and animals. However, there are other major groups, one of which is fungi. This group includes toadstools, mushrooms, moulds (e.g. those which grow on bread), dry rot and yeast.

Two processes that are specific to living material, respiration and photosynthesis, are the main topic of this chapter. You will learn how water is involved in both these processes, beginning with an investigation of the process of respiration in yeast, and then move on to examine these processes in plants and animals. You will also carry out the second practical work of this course – an investigation to measure the quantity of gas produced by yeast. As you progress through the chapter you will extend some of the skills developed earlier in the course, particularly plotting graphs, balancing chemical equations, recording and analysing the results of an investigation, as well as summarising.

Activity 8.1   Planning your study
You should allow about 20 minutes for this activity.

To help you plan when you will do the practical work in this chapter, you should read the information in Activities 8.2 and 8.3 in this book and briefly survey the additional information for Activity 8.3 on the course website. You also need to allow some time for assembling the materials and equipment before doing the investigation. When planning your study of this chapter, check back to see how well you followed your study plans for Chapter 7 and, in the light of this experience, adjust your plans as appropriate.

8.1　Yeast

First, consider the structure of yeast. Yeast consists of separate, rounded cells, as shown in Figure 8.1a. Each individual yeast cell, or organism, looks identical to its neighbour and, since it is very small, you would need to use a microscope to study it. Yeast is a single-celled organism whereas flowers, fish, seaweeds and humans are made up of many millions of cells.

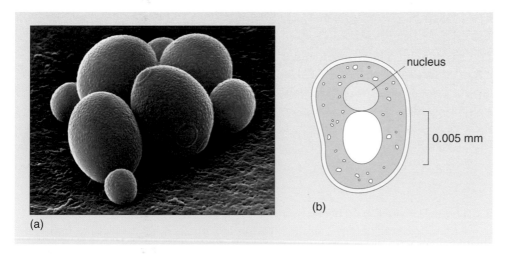

Figure 8.1　(a) A micrograph of yeast cells. (b) Schematic diagram of a 'slice' or section of yeast, a single-celled organism. Some of the cell contents can be seen. The scale bar shows the length on the figure that the bar represents. The cell dimensions are roughly twice the scale bar, i.e. 0.01 mm.

A yeast cell contains several different structures called **organelles**, each with a definite shape and function. The largest organelle is the **nucleus** (see Figure 8.1b), which plays an important role in controlling the activities or processes characteristic of living material. Look back at Figure 4.18 and you will see that each cell from inside a human cheek contains a nucleus (a pale yellow stained, round structure).

You are probably familiar with the fact that yeast is used commercially: for example, in bread making. Once yeast is added to the dough mixture (flour, sugar and water), large quantities of gas are produced, which make the dough rise. It is also used in the wine, spirit and beer industry where it is important in alcohol production. If you have ever made wine or beer, you will have noticed the gas bubbles that are produced. These gas bubbles result from the respiration process inside the yeast cells and they are released from the cells into the surrounding mixture.

8.2　An investigation of gas production by yeast

This section describes an investigation of the process of respiration in yeast. As you learned in Section 8.1, one of the characteristics of yeast is that it produces gas bubbles in beer and bread making. However, gas bubbles are produced only if certain conditions are met. When the conditions are ideal, large quantities of gas bubbles are produced; under less than ideal conditions, either only small quantities of gas bubbles are produced or none at all.

One condition that affects the quantity of gas produced is temperature. The aim of the investigation is to examine how temperature affects the rate of gas production. Two types of results will be collected: qualitative and quantitative (introduced in Chapter 3). Qualitative results are based on observations alone without taking any measurements, such as colour or smell. In contrast, quantitative results involve taking measurements or collecting data with numbers and units attached to them.

This investigation has been done for you at three different temperatures and recorded as a video sequence. However, some of the measurements have been left for you to record while you watch the video sequence as part of Activity 8.2, so that you are also involved in the investigation. In addition, you can carry out the investigation for yourself (see Activity 8.3). First, here is a summary of the investigation.

1   Some yeast cells and some sugar were measured into a standard kitchen measuring jug (Figure 8.2).

2   Then water, which had been heated to about body temperature (i.e. 37 °C), was added to the jug (Figure 8.2) to the 150 ml mark. Note that the scale on most measuring jugs is in millilitres (ml); 150 ml equals 150 cm^3. Ideally, the mixture should be left in a warm place to maintain a constant temperature inside the jug. The jug in the experiment was left standing in a bowl of water at the required temperature. (Alternative places include an airing cupboard, an oven at a very low temperature or even at room temperature.)

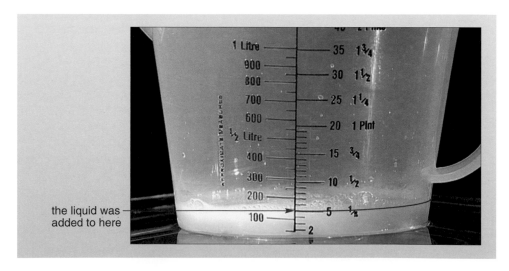

Figure 8.2   Volume of yeast mixture at the start of the investigation.

3   Having completed steps 1 and 2, the experiment was carried out again, but this time using water straight from a cold tap (about 10 °C) instead of warm water. The jug was left in a place that would maintain a constant temperature (i.e. standing in a bowl of cold tap water).

4   Finally, the experiment was carried out a third time, this time using boiling water (100 °C). The jug was left in a place that would maintain the temperature at 100 °C (i.e. standing in a pan of simmering water).

Activity 8.2 An investigation of the volume of gas produced by yeast at different temperatures

You should allow about 45 minutes for this activity.

The video sequence of the yeast investigation and its related activities are divided into three parts.

The first sequence demonstrates carrying out the investigation at the three temperatures: first 37 °C then 10 °C and finally 100 °C. The second sequence explores the qualitative results based on observations alone at three temperatures. The third sequence investigates the quantitative results relating to the rate of change of the volume of the yeast mixture at 37 °C alone.

Begin by watching the first sequence.

Qualitative results

1   Watch the second sequence in the yeast investigation, which shows the investigation into the amount of gas produced by yeast at 37 °C, 10 °C and then 100 °C. Note that the video sequence is considerably speeded up (time-lapse recording), so it will take about 3 minutes to watch rather than the 21 minutes it took to do each of the three investigations.

2   Observe the changes in the appearance of the yeast mixture inside each jug at each of the three temperatures.

3   Note down in Table 8.1 what you can see for each of the three temperatures:

   •   during the investigation (between 0 min and 21 min), and
   •   at the end of the investigation (i.e. after 21 min).

These are your qualitative results.

Table 8.1 Qualitative observations of gas production in yeast mixtures at different temperatures.

Time elapsed	Appearance of the yeast mixture		
	warm water (37 °C)	**cold water (10 °C)**	**boiling water (100 °C)**
at the start	Cloudy, Pale faun	Milky/flat ·	~~Broomy~~ / milly
between 0 and 21 min	Very frothy	Slight change Little froth	Little change .
after 21 min	‖ ‹	‹ ‹	‹ .

Quantitative results

1   Watch the third sequence in the yeast investigation, which repeats the recording of the investigation at 37 °C. Your task is to watch the investigation – which again has been speeded up – and to complete the table of results by taking measurements of the quantity of the mixture at fixed times. The video sequence reverts to normal speed for 30 seconds at 3-minute intervals from the start of the experiment for you to read the volume of yeast mixture inside the jug over a period of 21 minutes. When taking the readings, the volume of liquid plus froth (bubbles) should be measured where it touches the side of

Table 8.2 Quantitative measurements of gas production in yeast at 37 °C.

Elapsed time/min	Volume/ml
0	150
3	175
6	300
9	375
12	460
15	555
18	650
21	730

the jug, as shown in Figure 8.3. When the volume reading lies between markings, measure to the nearest half mark.

2 Note down the volumes in Table 8.2. You should begin by noting down the volume at the start of the investigation, i.e. at time 0.

Figure 8.3 Taking readings of the volume of yeast mixture: measure the level where the surface of the mixture touches the side of the jug.

At the end of this activity you should have completed both Table 8.1 and Table 8.2.

You are encouraged to carry out the investigation for yourself (Activity 8.3). Not only will you learn a lot from this but also it is fun and you will be able to observe the results directly, which are quite dramatic!

Activity 8.3 Carrying out the yeast investigation and collecting your own data

You should allow about 1.5 hours for part (a) of this activity (note this part of the activity is optional) and 15 minutes for part (b).

The best time to do part (a) of this activity is now whilst you have the video sequences fresh in your mind, and so that you can use the data you collect for part (b) of this activity.

(a) Details of the material and equipment you need and the procedures are given on the course website.

(b) Compare the results you collected from your investigation with the measurements made from the video, and discuss the differences (and possible reasons for these) online in your tutor group forum. Comment also on any changes you might make to improve the reproducibility of the results if you repeated the experiment. If you were unable to complete part (a) of this activity you should still participate in the online discussion of the investigation.

8.3   Interpreting the results of the investigation

When gas is produced, bubbles rise to form a layer of froth on top of the mixture of yeast, sugar and water. Measuring the volume of the mixture (including the froth which holds the gas) at various times throughout the investigation provides data which can be used to measure the rate of change in volume.

You should have noted that the rate of gas production was greatest when warm water (37 °C) was used and the largest quantity of bubbles collected on the surface at this temperature.

■ Did the same changes occur when (a) boiling water and (b) cold water were used?

☐ (a) When boiling water was used, no bubbles or froth were seen. (b) When cold water was used, a few bubbles and less froth were seen than at 37 °C. The rate of gas production was much slower at 10 °C than at 37 °C.

■ What do these observations suggest to you about the respiration of yeast at different temperatures?

☐ When warm water is used, the yeast is active in some way, producing a froth of gas bubbles. In cold water, yeast is less active, producing less gas, and in boiling water yeast appears to be inactive.

In answering this last question, you were attempting to *interpret* the observations. This is an important skill in science. It is not possible to give a more detailed interpretation from the qualitative results of the investigation alone. To fully understand the observations, you need to know more about the nature of living organisms and the process of respiration. However, before considering this process, you should first examine the quantitative results of the investigation.

Putting the readings of volumes in a table (as you did in Table 8.2) enables you to see more easily how the volume varies with elapsed time than if you had written them in no set order. You can do this by looking down the readings in the column. However, it is even easier to see the relationship between elapsed time and the volume of the mixture if the data are plotted on a graph. As you learned in Chapter 3, a graph makes it easier to interpret the results. Box 3.5 explained how to interpret graphs that had been plotted by someone else. This skill is now extended by exploring how to plot graphs in Box 8.1. To help you judge which parts of this box you need to study, try answering Question 8.1, which covers the same ground as Box 8.1.

Question 8.1

(a) Imagine you were asked to plot the variation of mass with volume for a series of blocks of aluminium, with volumes that varied from 0.005 m^3 to 0.050 m^3 and the corresponding masses that varied from 14 kg to 135 kg. Decide:

(i) which readings should be plotted on which axis

(ii) how the axes should be labelled

[handwritten: — horizontal 0.005 m^3 —0.010— — vertical 0, 10, 20 kg]

(iii) what scales you would use on each axis (assuming you were to use a sheet of graph paper similar in size to that given in Figure 8.4).

(b) Use the data in Table 8.3 opposite to:

(i) draw a graph on the graph paper in Figure 8.4 to illustrate the change in a baby's mass with age (take care with your choice of axes, scales and labels)

(ii) from your graph, decide which mass may have been incorrectly recorded in Table 8.3.

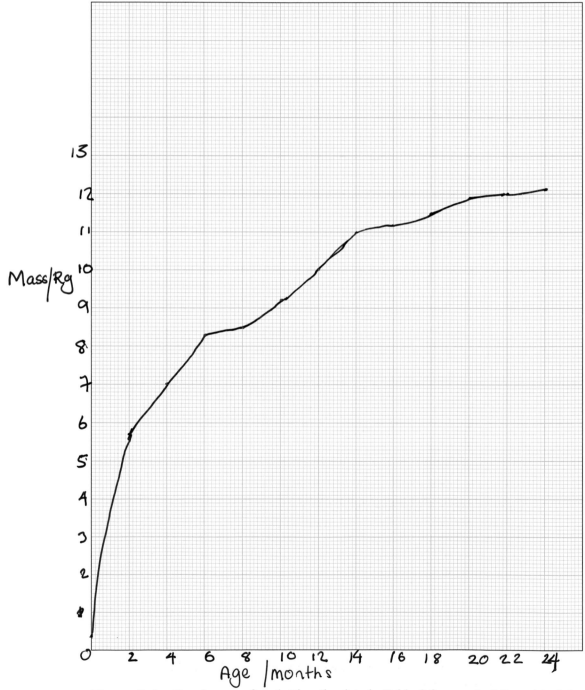

Figure 8.4   Graph paper for plotting the data in Table 8.3 as part of Question 8.1.

Table 8.3 A baby's mass measured every two months from birth to 24 months.

Age/months	Mass/kg	Age/months	Mass/kg
0	3.9	14	11.0
2	5.7	16	11.2
4	7.0	18	11.5
6	8.3	20	11.9
8	8.5	22	12.0
10	9.2	24	12.1
12	10.0			

Box 8.1   Plotting a graph

For this graph-plotting exercise, the experimental procedure for gas production in yeast (Section 8.2) was repeated but with water at 25 °C. The results are given in Table 8.4.

When plotting a graph of these results, or any similar data, you should work through the following stages.

Stage 1   Choose your axes

You may remember from Box 3.5 that two sets of readings (elapsed time and volume in this case) can be represented on the two axes of a graph. But which readings should go on which axis? In this experiment, the time intervals at which readings were to be taken had been decided in advance, before the investigation began, i.e. they were fixed. Such fixed information – termed the **independent variable** – is conventionally plotted on the horizontal axis, frequently referred to as the 'x-axis'. The volume readings depend on the time at which the reading was taken and, consequently, these are termed the **dependent variable**. Such quantities, which depend on other variables, are plotted on the vertical axis, frequently referred to as the 'y-axis'.

Stage 2   Choose your scale

Having decided that elapsed time should go on the horizontal axis and volume should go on the vertical axis, next you need to decide what scale to use on each axis. You should aim to use as much of the graph paper as possible (so that the graph is as large as possible, which makes it easier to read the values) while avoiding scales that are awkward to read and thus potentially confusing.

■ Look at the graph paper in Figure 8.4. How many of the larger (1 cm) squares does this show horizontally and vertically?

☐ There are thirteen 1 cm squares shown horizontally and seventeen 1 cm squares shown vertically.

Table 8.4 Volume of yeast mixture after various times with water at 25 °C.

Elapsed time/min	Volume/ml
0	150
3	150
6	155
9	170
12	200
15	215
18	245
21	275
24	305

■ Look at the data in Table 8.4 again. What ranges of values need to be represented horizontally and vertically?

☐ The horizontal axis needs to include times from 0 to 24 minutes. The vertical axis needs to include volumes from 0 to 305 ml (it would also be acceptable to plot a graph just showing volumes from 150 to 305 ml).

On the horizontal axis you could use each 1 cm to represent 2 minutes, as shown in Figure 8.5.

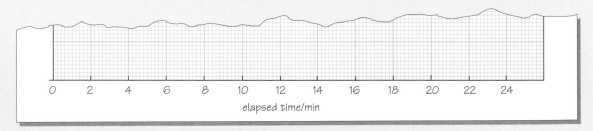

elapsed time/min

Figure 8.5   Choosing the scale for the horizontal (time) axis.

■ What scale would be appropriate for the vertical axis?

☐ One possibility is to use each 1 cm on the vertical axis to represent 20 ml, as shown in Figure 8.6, so each small 1 mm square represents 2 ml.

In this example, both scales start from zero (the origin of the graph) but this is not essential – the scale for the vertical axis could equally well start at, say, 140 ml, which would make better use of the graph paper.

You should aim to use as much of the graph paper as possible when plotting a graph. However, sometimes it is not possible to do this without using a different scale that is difficult to use. For example, the value for a volume of 215 ml at 15 minutes might fall between the labelled divisions in an awkward way, so it is best to aim for straightforward scales where the plot uses at least half the graph paper. In Figures 8.5 and 8.6, 1 cm represents 2 minutes on the horizontal scale and 1 cm represents 20 ml on the vertical scale, respectively. In general terms, multiples of 2, 5 and 10 are usually satisfactory; scales involving multiples of 3 are to be avoided!

One final point relates to the orientation of the graph paper. Sometimes simply rotating the graph paper from portrait to landscape can make it much easier to find suitable scales, as shown in Figure 8.7.

Stage 3   Label your graph

For a graph to convey meaning to other people, it must be completely labelled. A similar convention is used for the axes to the one for labelling headings of tables (Box 2.3); i.e. each axis should be labelled with the quantity it represents (elapsed time or volume in this case), followed by a forward slash (/), followed by the units (min or ml). So the vertical axis of

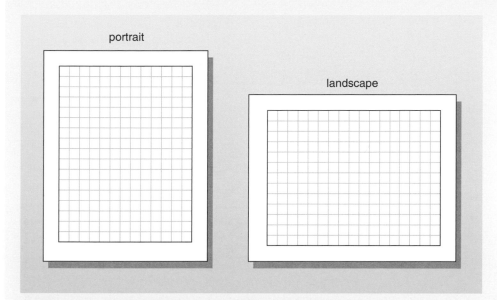

Figure 8.7   Changing the orientation of the graph paper from portrait to landscape can help in choosing appropriate scales for the axes.

the graph should be labelled 'volume/ml' and the horizontal axis should be labelled 'elapsed time/min'.

In addition to having labelled axes, the graph itself should have a title. This should include information about the content of the graph: for example, it needs to be clear that the graph illustrates the variation of the volume of the yeast mixture with elapsed time. The title should also include some information about the temperature.

■   What would be a suitable title?

☐   Here is one suggestion: 'Graph showing the variation of the volume of yeast mixture with elapsed time, at 25 °C'.

Stage 4   Plot the points

You are now ready to plot the points. Follow a procedure similar to the one you used to read the value from a graph in Chapter 3. So, to plot the point for which the elapsed time is 6 minutes, you should draw a real or imaginary line up from the horizontal axis for an elapsed time of 6 minutes (Figure 8.8). Similarly, since the volume of mixture was measured as 155 ml at this time, you should draw a real or imaginary line across from the vertical axis for a volume of 155 ml. Your point should be at exactly the place where the two lines meet.

Several different conventions are used to indicate points on a graph, ×, + and ⊙ being the best (Figure 8.9), but it does not matter which one you use. These marks make it clear exactly where the centre of the point is: for × and + it is where the two lines cross, and for ⊙ it is at the dot in the centre

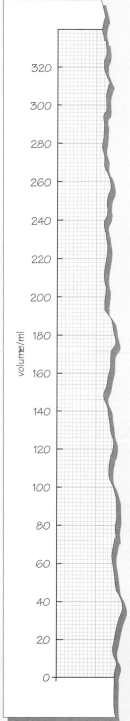

Figure 8.6
Choosing the scale for the vertical (volume) axis.

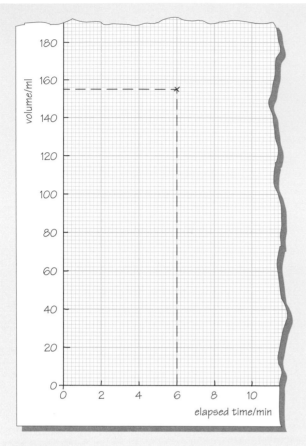

Figure 8.8 Plotting a point on a graph.

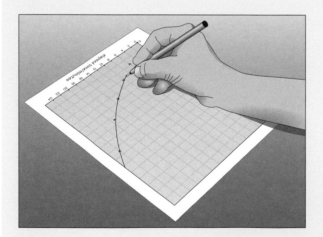

Figure 8.10 Drawing a smooth curved graph by placing your hand inside the curve.

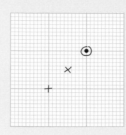

Figure 8.9 Different marks for indicating the points on a graph.

of the circle. The circle drawn around the dot simply makes the point clearer – it can be very difficult to see just a dot when you come to draw the curve. It also makes it difficult for other people to see where you have positioned the point.

It is very easy to make a mistake when plotting points and drawing a curve through the points, so you are advised to use a pencil rather than a pen for these tasks – and to have an eraser ready. There are computer programs which will plot points for you and draw the curve but, unless there is a reason why you cannot plot graphs by hand, you should make sure that you can do this. Many people find it easiest to draw a smooth curve if they place the graph so that their hand is inside the curve (Figure 8.10).

Stage 5   Draw a curve through the points

When you have plotted all of the points on the graph, all that remains to be done is to draw a curve that best represents the data. Before doing this, hold the graph paper at arm's length and look at the points. Most of the graphs that you draw will represent a general trend, for example the way in which a child's height increases with age, or the mass of a cucumber decreases as it is dried, or a yeast mixture increases in volume as time passes. These are all continuous processes: you would not expect the child's height to increase one month and then decrease the following month, or for the mass of the cucumber to increase and decrease randomly. However, with real experimental data, uncertainties in measurements sometimes lead to readings which vary in a rather erratic way (Figure 8.11). Provided you are sure that your graph represents a general trend (which is usually the case), you

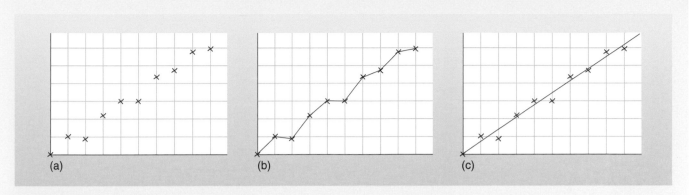

Figure 8.11   Graphs usually represent a general trend: (a) a series of points on a graph; (b) the points should not be joined by a series of short lines; (c) instead, a best-fit line should be drawn to represent all the data.

need to draw the smooth curve which best represents the data, *not* a series of short lines joining the individual points.

If the points appear to represent a uniform variation, the 'curve' which best represents them will be a straight line, as in Figure 8.11c. This is known as the **best-fit line**. If common sense tells you that the line should go through the origin, the line can be drawn in this way. (For example, if it represents the variation of mass with volume for a series of aluminium blocks, when there is no volume it is reasonable to assume that there is no mass either.) Apart from this, the line should be drawn so that there is approximately the same number of points above the line as below it, at approximately similar distances from the line. Note that, generally, it is not necessary for *any* of the points to lie right on the best-fit line.

If it seems that the data cannot be represented by a straight line, a smooth best-fit curve should be drawn. This is a more difficult skill, but the same general principles can be applied, leading to a curve which is the best representation of the data as a whole.

The completed graph for the data in Table 8.4 is shown in Figure 8.12 (overleaf), with a smooth curve drawn to represent the points. Note the point with an elapsed time of 12 minutes and a volume of 200 ml. This point does not seem to follow the general trend; it is probably the result of a measurement error during the experiment. It is best to ignore such points when drawing best-fit curves.

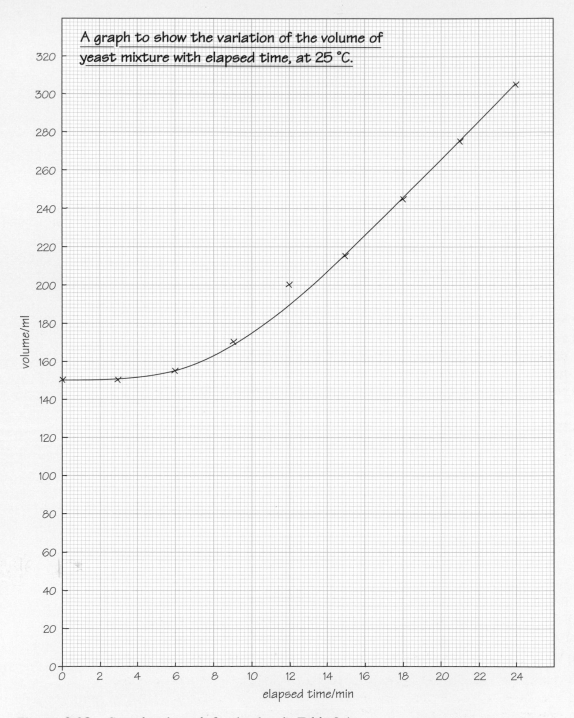

Figure 8.12 Completed graph for the data in Table 8.4.

8.3.1 Interpreting graphs

Having displayed the data in a graph, you now need to interpret the shape of the graph itself. Begin with the graph in Figure 8.12.

■ How does the slope of the graph in Figure 8.12 vary as time increases?

☐ The graph is initially flat, then it begins to slope up gently from left to right and, as time increases, the slope increases. From about 15 minutes onwards the graph slopes upwards at a constant rate.

■ What does the slope tell you about the variation of the volume of the yeast mixture with time at 25 °C ?

☐ When the graph is flat, the volume of the mixture is constant. Then it begins to increase, slowly at first but then more rapidly. From about 15 minutes onwards, the volume increases at a steady rate (you can tell this because the points fall on a straight line between 15 and 24 minutes).

The slope of a graph is more formally described as its **gradient**. The gradient of a graph is a measure of how rapidly the quantity plotted on the vertical axis changes in response to a change in the quantity plotted on the horizontal axis. If the graph is a straight line, the gradient is the same at all points on the line. In Figure 8.12 the gradient corresponds to the rate of change of volume of the yeast mixture – the steeper the gradient, the faster the rate of volume change, i.e. the faster the production of gas.

You will learn about a method of calculating the gradient of a straight-line graph in Chapter 9.

Having seen how to plot and interpret a graph, it is now a good time for you to plot a graph of your results of the yeast investigation at 37 °C (Section 8.2).

Activity 8.4   Plotting a graph to show the behaviour of yeast at 37 °C

You should allow about 40 minutes for this activity.

(a) Use the graph paper in Figure 8.13 (overleaf) to plot a graph for your data in Table 8.2.

(b) Write a sentence describing the shape of the graph as time increases.

(c) Discuss your results and the shape of your graph online with your tutor group. Your readings in Table 8.2 probably differ slightly from ours and those of other students and these differences may affect the shape of your graph.

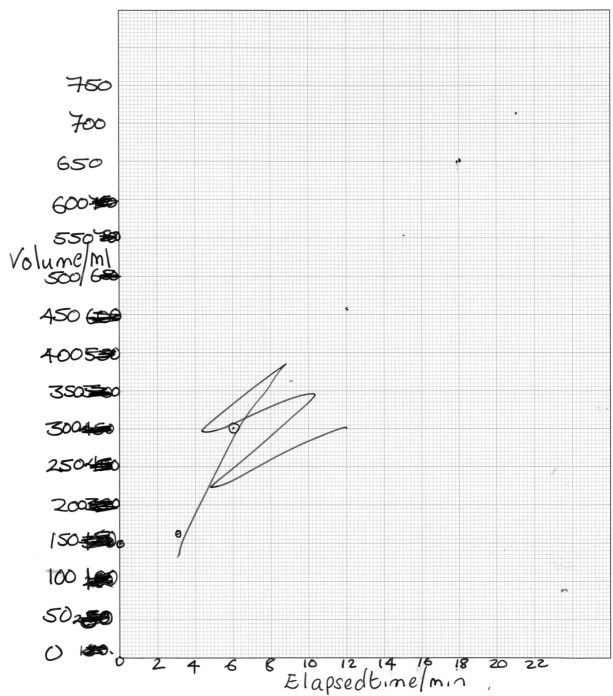

Figure 8.13   Graph paper for plotting the data in Table 8.2. For use with Activity 8.4.

So far, you have plotted the data from the investigation carried out at 37 °C. Now you should return to the investigations carried out at 10 °C and 100 °C. You could refresh your memory of your observations by reading your completed Table 8.1. Both the qualitative and the quantitative observations of the investigation at these two temperatures differed from each other and from that at 37 °C.

The course team took measurements of the volume of mixture over a period of 21 minutes at both 10 °C and 100 °C, and plotted the data on two graphs. These two graphs have been plotted on the same pair of axes, to make it easier to compare them (Figure 8.14). Note that different marks are used for the two graphs: × for the results of the investigation carried out at 10 °C and ⊙ for the results of the investigation at 100 °C to make it clear that each set of points represents a different experiment.

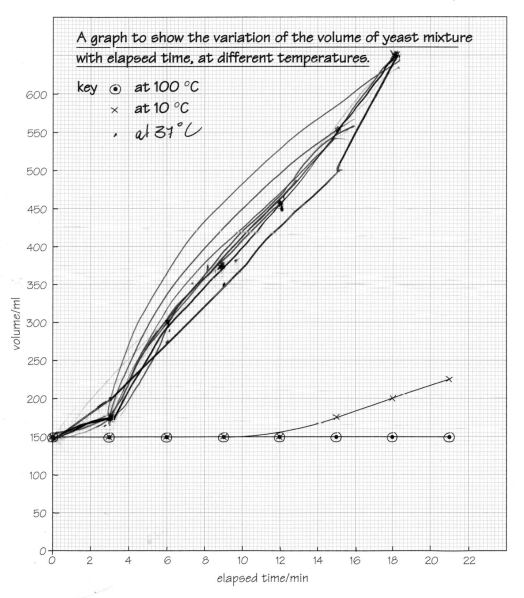

Figure 8.14   Results of the investigation into the quantity of bubbles and froth produced when the water was at 10 °C and 100 °C.

Activity 8.5   Interpreting the shapes of the graphs in Figure 8.14

You should allow about 20 minutes for this activity.

(a) In order to make it easier to compare the results of the investigation at all three temperatures, you should plot your data from Table 8.2 onto Figure 8.14 using + marks.

(b) Write two or three sentences comparing the variation in the shapes of the three graphs in Figure 8.14.

In Section 8.2 you saw the different appearances of the yeast mixture for three values of water temperature. Then, in Activities 8.4 and 8.5, you plotted graphs of the quantitative results and used these graphs to compare the different ways in which the volume of the yeast mixture changes for each temperature.

■ What can you conclude from the results of this investigation into the effect of water temperature on the production of bubbles by yeast?

☐ Clearly, the temperature of the water has a marked effect. There are no bubbles and no increase in volume with water at 100 °C, i.e. no changes are observed over the 21 minutes that the investigation ran. At 10 °C, some bubbles are produced, leading to a small increase in volume. However, at 37 °C, many bubbles are produced with a marked increase in volume.

Question 8.2

Figure 8.15 shows examples of graphs plotted for the data in Table 8.4 by three students – Chris, Ruth and Shamim. What comments or advice would you give to the person who plotted each graph on how they might improve them? (There is a good example of a graph of this data in Figure 8.12.)

Question 8.3

This question involves interpolation of the graph in Figure 8.12, i.e. estimating the intermediate values to those already measured and plotted. (Interpolation was defined in Box 3.5.)

(a) Estimate the volume of the yeast mixture after 23 minutes of elapsed time.

(b) Estimate the change in volume of the mixture between 0 and 20 minutes.

(c) One point on the graph looks as though it may have been incorrectly plotted. What is the expected value of the data for this point?

If you would like more practice at plotting graphs, there are further examples on the course website.

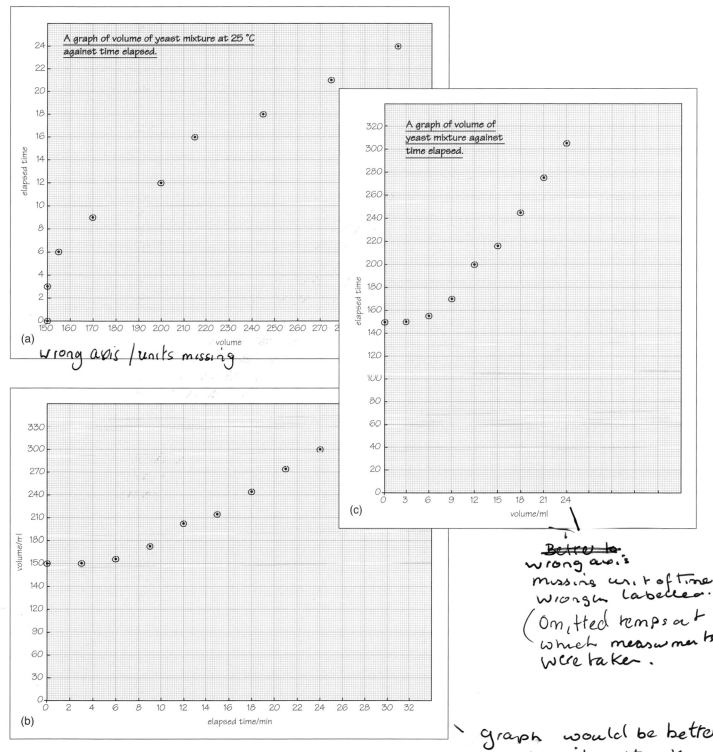

Figure 8.15   (a) Chris's graph; (b) Ruth's graph; and (c) Shamim's graph.

8.4 Explaining the results of the investigation

The conclusions drawn in Section 8.3 suggest that the yeast is more active in some way at around 37 °C than at either 10 °C or 100 °C. This may lead you to wonder why yeast cells produce bubbles of gas. What is this gas? Why is the quantity produced affected by temperature? This section explains the biology behind these observations. It is important to note that you could not derive these explanations from the observations of your investigation.

All living organisms need energy to survive and maintain themselves. The idea that food provides energy is often used in advertisements for chocolate and breakfast cereal. For example, you need energy to carry out activities and maintain your body from day to day. This is one of the important characteristics of living material that separates it from non-living material.

■ Which activities that you carry out every day involve the use of energy by your body?

☐ You might have thought of some of the following (but there are many others): movement, heartbeat, thinking and growth.

Figure 8.16 Yeast on the surface of plums.

Yeast also needs energy to survive and maintain itself. Recall that sugar was added to the yeast mixture in the investigation (Section 8.2); the yeast obtains energy from the sugar. Sugar is the only compound dissolved in the mixture and, since organisms are made largely of water, it is reasonable to assume that the yeast cells used the sugar for growth and transformed it into their own mass. Yeast cells live naturally in situations where sugar is readily available, such as in the nectar of flowers, and on the surface of fruit. You can see them on the surface of healthy grapes, plums or sloes, for instance, where they contribute to the grey film (Figure 8.16).

The process by which energy is released from food such as sugar is called **respiration**. You may be surprised to learn that, in biology, the term 'respiration' means the chemical breakdown of foods to release energy. In everyday life, the word is often used to describe the process of taking gases into and out of the body (i.e. breathing).

Depending on the environmental conditions, yeast cells use one of the two kinds of respiration. One depends on the reaction of food chemicals, such as sugar, with oxygen to release energy. This is called **aerobic respiration**. The other depends on the breakdown of food chemicals without involving oxygen at all. This is called **anaerobic respiration** or fermentation. In both types of respiration, carbon dioxide gas is produced. The bubbles and froth that appeared on top of the yeast mixture contained carbon dioxide, the product of yeast respiration.

Now look at the process of respiration inside the yeast cell in more detail, in order to understand the results of the investigation. Begin by concentrating on what was happening in the investigation at 37 °C. Sugar molecules are taken into the yeast cell where they are broken down to release energy. At the beginning of the investigation there would be some oxygen dissolved in the water, which the yeast cells could use for aerobic respiration. As long as oxygen is available, yeast cells respire aerobically to break down the sugar molecules to carbon dioxide and water.

A word equation can be used to summarise the chemical reaction of aerobic respiration:

> sugar and oxygen goes to carbon dioxide, water and energy

The above equation can be written as a chemical equation:

$$\underset{\substack{\text{one molecule}\\\text{of sugar}}}{C_6H_{12}O_6} + \underset{\text{oxygen}}{O_2} \longrightarrow \underset{\substack{\text{carbon}\\\text{dioxide}}}{CO_2} + \underset{\text{water}}{H_2O} + \text{energy}$$

There are three points to note about this equation. First, an arrow is often used in biological equations instead of the equals sign (even when balanced), and means 'goes to' or 'the reactants are changed to the products within living material'. Second, the idea that 'energy' is produced is noted down as part of the equation, as a reminder that this is the key to the process for living material. Third, water is a product of aerobic respiration, i.e. water is intimately involved in this process occurring within cells.

■ The equation above is not balanced. Try to balance it, as you learned in Section 6.5.3, so that there are equal numbers of each type of atom on each side.

☐ $C_6H_{12}O_6 + 6O_2 \longrightarrow 6CO_2 + 6H_2O + \text{energy}$ (8.1)

Equation 8.1 is the basic chemical equation for aerobic respiration which you will meet again if you study further biology.

In a relatively short period of time after the start of the investigation at 37 °C (in fact, only a few minutes), the oxygen in the water would be used up and the developing froth on top would prevent any further oxygen dissolving from the air into the mixture. At this point, the yeast cells would switch to anaerobic respiration. Again, in this process the sugar is broken down but this time its remains are released as carbon dioxide and ethanol.

A word equation can be used to summarise the chemical reaction of anaerobic respiration:

> sugar goes to carbon dioxide and ethanol and energy

This equation can be written as a chemical equation:

$$\underset{\substack{\text{one molecule}\\\text{of sugar}}}{C_6H_{12}O_6} \longrightarrow \underset{\substack{\text{carbon}\\\text{dioxide}}}{CO_2} + \underset{\text{ethanol}}{C_2H_6O} + \text{energy}$$

■ The above equation is not balanced. Try to balance it.

☐ $C_6H_{12}O_6 \longrightarrow 2CO_2 + 2C_2H_6O + \text{energy}$ (8.2)

Equation 8.2 is the basic equation for anaerobic respiration (fermentation) in yeast. If you had left the investigation for a longer period of time, you would have begun to notice the smell of ethanol, commonly known as alcohol (e.g. whisky contains 40% ethanol). Yeast is important in the wine, spirit and beer industry because of its remarkable ability to respire anaerobically and produce alcohol. However, it is important to note that the products of anaerobic respiration differ in the cells of other organisms.

Thus, at 37 °C yeast cells can carry on respiring even in the absence of oxygen, so carbon dioxide bubbles continue to be produced and consequently the volume of froth increases.

These chemical equations, Equations 8.1 and 8.2, like all the others you have met, involve the conversion of chemicals to new compounds without the loss of material. Energy is produced as a by-product of these reactions. In contrast to aerobic respiration, where the sugar molecule is completely broken down to water and carbon dioxide, in anaerobic respiration the breakdown is less complete. Consequently, less energy is derived from anaerobic respiration than aerobic respiration. Therefore, as long as oxygen is available, yeast cells respire aerobically ensuring the greatest production of energy. If you had passed air through the yeast mixture, or constantly shaken the jug, the yeast would have continued to respire aerobically.

You can now understand the origin of gas bubbles produced in the investigation, but why should different volumes of carbon dioxide be produced at different temperatures? Is temperature affecting the rate of respiration in some way? The answer to this question requires a deeper understanding of the process of respiration and the role of enzymes.

8.4.1 Enzymes

The conversion of many chemical compounds into new compounds is assisted by substances called **enzymes**. You may have noticed that manufacturers of 'biological' washing powders and liquids state that they contain enzymes, which help to remove dirt from clothes. Enzymes are found in all living materials and have the important property of speeding up chemical reactions, without themselves being used up. Thus they are used over and over again. Without enzymes, the chemical reactions on which living materials vitally depend would be very slow – too slow for survival. So, for example, the reactions in Equations 8.1 and 8.2 are speeded up by enzymes.

A crucially important point is that enzyme activity is affected by temperature. The effect of temperature on enzyme activity explains the difference in the quantity of gas produced in the yeast investigation. The enzymes in yeast, like many others, work best at about 37 °C, a temperature which results in the rapid breakdown of sugar and the high rate of production of carbon dioxide bubbles.

At lower temperatures, enzymes do not work so well. Consequently, sugar breaks down more slowly. Thus, in the investigation using cold water, fewer bubbles were produced. At very high temperatures, such as 100 °C, the structure of the enzymes is permanently damaged, so that they can no longer function; no energy is produced and the yeast cells die. This explains the results when boiling water was used: there was no breakdown of sugar and no carbon dioxide bubbles were produced.

8.5   A comparison of yeast with other living organisms

You have already learned about the cellular structure of yeast and how energy is released from sugar during respiration. This section compares some of the features of yeast with those of other organisms: which features are common to all organisms; and which features might be specific to yeast? It looks at how organisms obtain sugar for energy, their cellular structure and their method of respiration.

8.5.1   How organisms obtain sugar for energy

Organisms obtain energy in different ways. Section 8.4 noted that yeast obtains energy from sugars present in fruit and flowers. However, most other types of fungi feed mainly on dead plant and animal remains. Animals feed by eating other organisms. However, plants are quite different in that they obtain energy from sunlight and produce their own sugar by a process known as **photosynthesis**. This process occurs in green organelles called **chloroplasts** which are present inside plant cells (Figure 8.17).

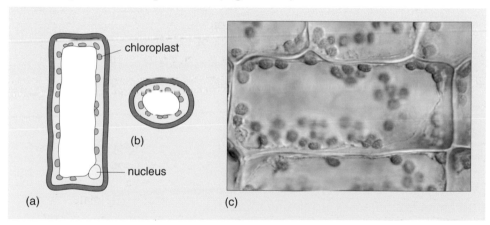

Figure 8.17   A single chloroplast-containing leaf cell: (a) and (b) schematic drawings of a cell cut lengthways and cut across, respectively; (c) a micrograph, where parts of the surrounding cells can be seen. Magnification in (c): approximately 700 times life size.

Sugars are made by combining carbon dioxide with hydrogen from water, which can be written as a chemical equation:

$$CO_2 + H_2O \longrightarrow C_6H_{12}O_6 + O_2$$

■ Try to balance the above equation.

☐ $6CO_2 + 6H_2O \longrightarrow C_6H_{12}O_6 + 6O_2$

The process becomes more understandable if you analyse the word 'photosynthesis': 'photo' means light and 'synthesis' means the process of building complex substances from simpler substances.

Green plants obtain the energy needed to make sugars (and other substances) by the chloroplasts trapping the energy of sunlight. You should not be surprised to learn that this is also assisted by enzymes, although they are different from the ones involved in respiration.

Equation 8.3 is the basic chemical equation for the process of photosynthesis.

$$6CO_2 + 6H_2O \xrightarrow{\text{sunlight}} C_6H_{12}O_6 + 6O_2$$

(8.3)

Note that this process can only occur in sunlight, hence this term is included in the equation. Once plants have produced sugar, they use it in the same way as animal cells do to release energy.

■ What is the name of the process that releases energy from sugar in living organisms?

☐ Respiration.

Hence, green plants carry out both the process of photosynthesis and the process of respiration.

Returning to the theme of water: you have learned that water is essential for living material. Equation 8.3 shows that water enters *directly* into one of the many chemical reactions that occur within cells. In fact, it enters into many such reactions within cells. Equation 8.1 shows that water is sometimes a *product* of chemical reactions. Water also plays an important *indirect* role within cells in that it provides the medium in which other molecules chemically interact.

8.5.2   Cellular structure of organisms

Having looked at how groups of organisms obtain sugar, now consider the structure of yeast and how it differs from that of other organisms. You may recall from Section 8.1 that yeast is a single-celled organism (see Figure 8.1) and that each individual cell looks identical to the others.

However, the majority of organisms which are familiar to you are **multicellular**, i.e. they consist of many cells. In multicellular organisms, cells are of different types. They may have quite strikingly different structures, as regards shape, size and content. For example, a human skin cell (Figure 8.18a) is quite different in appearance from a nerve cell (Figure 8.18b), a cell lining the human gut (Figure 8.18c), or a human muscle cell (Figure 8.18d).

One consequence of being a larger multicellular organism is that different cells take on different functions. The shape or appearance of the human cells shown in Figure 8.18 is related to the different functions, or work, that they carry out. A muscle cell changes shape; a cell lining the gut is protective, but it also plays a very important role in taking in food that has been digested or broken down inside the gut; a nerve cell is very long because it transmits messages along its length to adjoining nerve cells.

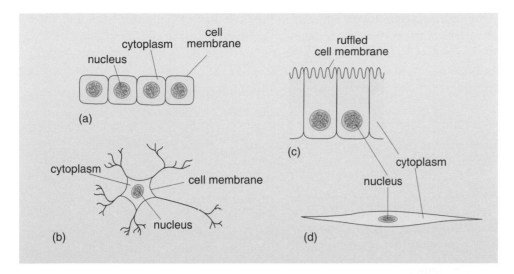

Figure 8.18   The diversity of human cells: (a) skin cells; (b) a nerve cell; (c) cells that line the gut; (d) a muscle fibre cell. (*Note*: these are not drawn to the same scale.)

8.5.3   Methods of respiration in organisms

Another important comparison that can be made between yeast and other organisms relates to the breakdown of sugar to provide energy – the process of respiration. You might ask whether this process is common to all living organisms. In fact, respiration is universal and occurs within each individual cell of a multicellular organism as well as within cells of single-celled organisms.

The process of respiration is the same in animal, plant and yeast cells. They all use oxygen to assist in the breakdown of sugar. Recall the equation for aerobic respiration:

$$C_6H_{12}O_6 + 6O_2 \longrightarrow 6CO_2 + 6H_2O + energy \tag{8.1}$$

■ Compare the process of aerobic respiration in Equation 8.1 with the process of photosynthesis in Equation 8.3.

☐ The process of aerobic respiration is the *opposite* of photosynthesis. Photosynthesis involves green plants trapping the energy of sunlight to produce sugars and oxygen from carbon dioxide and water. Respiration releases energy by converting the sugar back to carbon dioxide and water, using up oxygen in the process.

The scientific observation you have just made is an extremely important one.

The process of photosynthesis replaces the oxygen in the atmosphere that is used up by the process of respiration.

What is happening during the process of respiration is that energy locked up in sugar (derived from sunlight) is now released when organisms need it. Like yeast, plants and animals use the released energy to maintain themselves, to grow and to reproduce.

Although only a limited number of living organisms were considered in this chapter, life exists in many forms. It is estimated that the current number of living species on Earth is about 3×10^7. However, all living material has certain features in common (such as cellular structure) and functional properties (such as respiration) which separate it from non-living material.

Question 8.4

Based on the information given in Section 8.5, write down a list of the similarities of living organisms and another of the differences between living organisms.

8.6   Summary of Chapter 8

All living organisms are composed of cells.

Respiration is a universal process, which occurs within single-celled organisms such as yeast, and in the individual cells of multicellular organisms.

Enzymes speed up chemical reactions without themselves being changed in anyway. Their activity is affected by temperature.

Photosynthesis is a process by which plants obtain energy from sunlight to produce their own sugar; it also replaces the oxygen used in respiration.

Plotting the results of the yeast investigation on a graph facilitates the comparision and interpretation of the effect of temperature on the activity of yeast.

Learning outcomes for Chapter 8

When you have completed Chapter 8 you should be able to:

- Describe some of the similarities and differences in cellular structure between plants, animals and yeast.
- Describe how energy is released from sugar in living organisms and distinguish between the processes of aerobic respiration and anaerobic respiration.
- Outline the role of enzymes in bringing about the conversion of chemical compounds that occur in cells.
- Compare the process of aerobic respiration with the process of photosynthesis.
- Understand the notation used in the chemical equations used to describe both respiration and photosynthesis.
- Carry out qualitative observations and quantitative measurements.
- Plot graphs using a suitable scale, label axes and add a title.
- Interpret simple graphs and use them to establish the relationship between two variables, and to predict intermediate values by interpolation.

Chapter 9
From raindrops to oceans

This chapter provides an opportunity for you to practise many of the skills, especially the mathematical skills, which you have learned throughout the course, and to develop some of these skills a little further. In particular, you will learn how to find the gradient of a graph, how to add, subtract, multiply and divide fractions, and how to express equations in terms of symbols rather than words. You will also be encouraged to write out your answers to mathematical questions carefully, a skill that will be useful not only as you prepare for the final assessment of the course but also throughout your study of science.

All of this will be done in the context of a consideration of the size of objects, from the astronomically big to the infinitesimally small. This means departing briefly from the theme of 'water', and then returning to it to consider various volumes of water on Earth – from raindrops to oceans. This chapter also considers the speed at which objects move. Much of the water on Earth is not stationary: for example, oceans have currents; rivers and glaciers flow; and blood, which is approximately 83% water, is pumped around your body.

Towards the end of the chapter you will have an opportunity to review your progress in all of the mathematical skills that have been developed in the course.

9.1   Big and small

Scientists frequently deal with enormous quantities – and with tiny ones. Chapter 6 introduced scientific notation as a way of expressing these numbers. You may recall that the total volume of water stored on Earth, 1460 000 000 km^3, can be written as 1.46×10^9 km^3 and that the width of a water droplet, approximately 0.002 m, can be written as 2×10^{-3} m. However, the use of scientific notation is not limited to water falling to and being stored on the Earth.

Consider some distances. By the most direct route, it is just over 9600 km (9600 000 m) from London in England to Cape Town in South Africa. This is a long way by everyday standards, but small in comparison to the distances involved in space travel. The Moon is approximately 380 000 000 m away and Mars at its closest is about 56 000 000 000 m from the Earth.

■ Convert the distances in metres from London to Cape Town, and from the Earth to the Moon and Mars respectively, into scientific notation.

□ It is 9.6×10^6 m from London to Cape Town, 3.8×10^8 m from the Earth to the Moon and 5.6×10^{10} m from the Earth to Mars. If you had any difficulty with these conversions you should look back at Box 6.1 'Going up: using scientific notation for large numbers'.

The outer ranges of the Solar System are even more distant (Pluto is 4.3×10^{12} m away) and beyond the Solar System the distances are truly vast. The Solar System lies in the Milky Way Galaxy, and the centre of this galaxy is 2×10^{17} m from the Earth, the Andromeda Galaxy is 2.4×10^{22} m away and the galaxy Abell 1835 is estimated to be 1.2×10^{26} m from the Earth.

Scientific notation can also be used to represent small lengths and distances. A human hair is approximately 8×10^{-5} m thick, a yeast cell is about 1×10^{-5} m long, the rhinovirus (responsible for the common cold) is about 2.5×10^{-8} m in size and, as discussed in Box 6.2 'Going down: using scientific notation for small numbers', the width of a water molecule is around 2×10^{-10} m. Going even smaller, an atom of oxygen is about 6×10^{-11} m across and quarks, believed to be the fundamental particles of which atoms are comprised, are less than 1×10^{-18} m in size.

■ Express the thickness of a human hair and the width of an oxygen atom in ordinary decimal numbers (i.e. not in scientific notation).

☐ A human hair is approximately 0.000 08 m thick and the width of an oxygen atom is about 0.000 000 000 06 m. If you had any difficulty with these conversions you should look back at Box 6.2.

When considering very small and very large lengths and distances, frequently there is no interest in the *exact* size – and sometimes the size isn't known very precisely in any case. It may be adequate simply to give the number to the nearest power of ten; so the rhinovirus is about 10^{-8} m in size and it is about 10^{22} m to the Andromeda Galaxy. This is known as the **order of magnitude** of a number. Note that the distance from London to Cape Town (9.6×10^6 m) is nearer to 10^7 m than to 10^6 m, so would be given as 10^7 m to the nearest order of magnitude.

■ Express 3.8×10^8 m and 8×10^{-5} m to the nearest order of magnitude.

☐ 3.8×10^8 m is 10^8 m to the nearest order of magnitude; 8×10^{-5} m is closer to 10^{-4} m than to 10^{-5} m, so it is 10^{-4} m to the nearest order of magnitude.

The text above included the values of many lengths and distances in scientific notation or to the nearest order of magnitude, some of which are illustrated in Figure 9.1. It can be easy to forget the significance of these numbers: 10^{26} m is an extremely long way and 10^{-18} m is unimaginably small. Also, although distances such as 10^{22} m and 10^{23} m are both vast, remember that 10^{23} m is ten times further than 10^{22} m.

Time and mass can also be represented in scientific notation.

■ What are the SI units of time and mass?

☐ The SI unit of time is the second (s) and the SI unit of mass is the kilogram (kg). (See Box 3.2 'Units of measurement'.)

An African elephant such as the one shown in Figure 4.21 has a mass of about 7×10^3 kg and the mass of the Earth itself is about 6×10^{24} kg. This contrasts with the mass of an electron, one of the components of an atom (Section 6.3), which is just over 9×10^{-31} kg.

The Earth's age is estimated to be about 4.6×10^9 years, which is about 1.5×10^{17} s. There is much debate about the age and history of the Universe but the conventional view is currently that the Universe came into being with a 'big bang' about 1.4×10^{10} years ago – about 4.4×10^{17} s. However, it is thought that many of the important processes in the evolution of the Universe happened at incredibly short times after the big bang – times such as 10^{-32} s, 10^{-36} s and even down to 10^{-44} s.

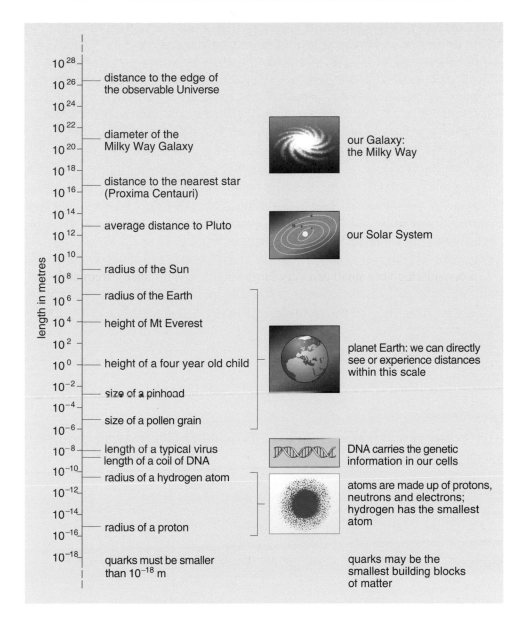

Figure 9.1   Examples of lengths and distances. (Radius is defined in Box 9.5.)

Box 3.2 introduced kilometres, centimetres and millimetres and the prefixes 'kilo', 'centi' and 'milli', which mean 1000, $\frac{1}{100}$ th and $\frac{1}{1000}$ th, respectively. So, 1 kg = 1000 g, 1 cm = $\frac{1}{100}$ m and 1 ms = $\frac{1}{1000}$ s .

■ What is the total volume of water stored on the Earth (1.46×10^9 km^3) in m^3?

☐ Using the method developed in Box 4.3, 1 km = 1000 m, so

1 km^3 = 1000 m × 1000 m × 1000 m = 1000 000 000 m^3, or 1×10^9 m^3.

So, the total volume of water stored on the Earth

$$= (1.46 \times 10^9) \times (1 \times 10^9) \text{ m}^3$$
$$= 1.46 \times 10^{18} \text{ m}^3.$$

When dealing with measurements as tiny as 10^{-18} m and as large as 10^{12} m, other prefixes are used in addition to 'kilo', 'centi' and 'milli'. Table 9.1 lists the complete range of prefixes used with SI units. So, for example, 2 Ms (2 megaseconds) is 2×10^6 s, which is about 23 days; 45 nm (45 nanometres; the typical width of a transistor in an integrated circuit) is 45×10^{-9} m. However, remember that scientific notation requires the number accompanying the power of 10 to be less than 10 and equal to or greater than 1. So, 45×10^{-9} m should be written as 4.5×10^{-8} m in scientific notation.

Some of the prefixes in Table 9.1 are associated with modern scientific disciplines, for example nanotechnology. Nanotechnology is concerned with sizes of about 100 nanometres or less. At this scale, we are dealing with small numbers of molecules or atoms, and materials have some interesting properties and useful applications. For example, carbon nanotubes, which have a thickness of a few nanometres, exhibit extraordinary strength and are good conductors of electricity.

Question 9.1

Express the following lengths to the nearest order of magnitude.

(a) 1.2×10^{26} m
(b) 2×10^{-10} m
(c) 8.7×10^9 m

Question 9.2

Express each of the following values in metres, giving your answers in scientific notation.

(a) 72 Tm
(b) 1.2 pm
(c) 36 μm

Table 9.1 Prefixes used with SI units.

Prefix	Symbol	Multiplying factor
tera	T	$10^{12} = 1000\,000\,000\,000$
giga	G	$10^9 = 1000\,000\,000$
mega	M	$10^6 = 1000\,000$
kilo	k	$10^3 = 1000$
—	—	$10^0 = 1$
deci	d	$10^{-1} = 0.1$
centi	c	$10^{-2} = 0.01$
milli	m	$10^{-3} = 0.001$
micro	μ*	$10^{-6} = 0.000\,001$
nano	n	$10^{-9} = 0.000\,000\,001$
pico	p	$10^{-12} = 0.000\,000\,000\,001$
femto	f	$10^{-15} = 0.000\,000\,000\,000\,001$
atto	a	$10^{-18} = 0.000\,000\,000\,000\,000\,001$

* The Greek letter μ is pronounced 'mew'.

9.2   How fast?

The average speed with which an object moves is the total distance travelled divided by the time taken. This can be written as a word equation:

$$\text{average speed} = \frac{\text{distance travelled}}{\text{time taken}}$$

So when the athlete Yuliya Nesterenko won the women's 100-metre final at the 2004 Athens Olympics in 10.93 s, her average speed was:

$$\text{average speed} = \frac{100 \text{ m}}{10.93 \text{ s}}$$

100 divided by 10.93 gives 9.15 to two decimal places.

■   What are the units of the answer?

☐   The answer should have units of metres divided by seconds, written as $\frac{\text{m}}{\text{s}}$ or m/s, and said as metres per second.

An answer of 9.15 m/s is correct but scientists conventionally use a slightly neater notation involving negative powers of the type introduced in Box 6.2. This notation is explained in Box 9.1. You are advised to read this box even if you have met negative powers notation previously.

Box 9.1   More about powers and units

Box 6.2 introduced some important general results, namely that:

$$10^0 = 1 \text{ and } 10^{-1} = \frac{1}{10^1}, 10^{-2} = \frac{1}{10^2}, 10^{-3} = \frac{1}{10^3}, \text{ etc.}$$

Note that 10^1, 10^0 and 10^{-1} are rarely used in scientific writing; it is usual to write simply 10, 1 or 0.1 instead. However, the use of zero, positive and negative powers in this way provides a useful notation which can be used with all numbers and with units and symbols too.

Note that any number to the power zero is one. For example

$$\frac{5}{5} = 5^1 \times 5^{-1} = 5^0 = 1$$

So, $5^0 = 1$ and $2^0 = 1$, $\frac{1}{3^2}$ can be written as 3^{-2} and $\frac{1}{7^3}$ can be written as 7^{-3}.

Also, $\frac{1}{\text{m}^3}$ can be expressed as m^{-3} and $\frac{1}{\text{s}}$ (which could be written as $\frac{1}{\text{s}^1}$) can also be expressed as s^{-1}.

■   How would you rewrite $\frac{\text{m}}{\text{s}}$ using a negative power?

☐   Since $\frac{1}{\text{s}} = \text{s}^{-1}$, $\frac{\text{m}}{\text{s}}$ can be written as m s^{-1}.

The conventional scientific way of expressing the SI unit of speed is m s^{-1}.

However, note that whether the SI unit of speed is written as m/s or as m s^{-1}, it is usually said as 'metres per second'. Note also that there is a space between m and s^{-1}, and you should do this whenever you write a unit that is a combination of two or more other units. This is different from how prefixes for multiples of units are written; they are always written *without* a space between the prefix and the basic unit. Thus 'ms' means 'millisecond' but 'm s' means 'metre second'. This separation of the different components of a unit, but not for multiples of units, avoids confusion.

A variety of units of measurement can be expressed in a similar way using negative powers. The SI unit of density was given in Chapter 4 as kg/m³. Since $\frac{1}{m^3} = m^{-3}$, $\frac{kg}{m^3}$ can be written as $kg\ m^{-3}$, although again this is usually said as 'kilograms per metre cubed'.

The conventional scientific way of writing the SI unit of density is $kg\ m^{-3}$.

Recall from Chapter 6 that the concentration of a solution is the mass of a substance in a given volume of a liquid. The units of concentration used in Chapter 6 (mg/l) are more correctly written as $mg\ l^{-1}$ (said as 'milligrams per litre'). However, frequently the interest is in very small concentrations, so units of $\mu g\ l^{-1}$ (micrograms per litre) are sometimes used. Recall from Table 9.1 that 1 μg is 1×10^{-6} g.

Question 9.3

Write down each of the following expressions using both positive and negative power notation.

For example, $\dfrac{1}{5 \times 5} = \dfrac{1}{5^2} = 5^{-2}$

(a) $\dfrac{1}{2 \times 2 \times 2 \times 2}$

(b) $\dfrac{1}{m \times m}$

Question 9.4

What is the value of the following expressions?

(a) 7^0

(b) 2^{-3}

In calculating the speeds of various objects, you may also need to input numbers in scientific notation into your calculator and to interpret the results. If you are not sure how to do this you should look back to the section of Box 6.1 on 'Using a calculator for scientific notation' before proceeding.

- It takes the space shuttle 120 s to reach an altitude of 4.50×10^4 m. What is its average speed?

$$\text{average speed} = \frac{\text{distance travelled}}{\text{time taken}} = \frac{4.50 \times 10^4 \text{ m}}{120 \text{ s}} = 375 \text{ m s}^{-1}$$

or 3.75×10^2 m s^{-1} in scientific notation.

- It takes light about 500 s to travel the 1.5×10^{11} m from the Sun to Earth. What is its speed?

$$\text{average speed} = \frac{\text{distance travelled}}{\text{time taken}} = \frac{1.5 \times 10^{11} \text{ m}}{500 \text{ s}} = 3.0 \times 10^8 \text{ m s}^{-1}$$

It probably doesn't surprise you that the space shuttle travels at a much faster speed than an athlete, even a world class one, and that the speed of light is considerably faster than either of these. Light travels a staggering distance of 9.5×10^{15} m in one year – this is a so-called 'light-year'.

Many objects move in the world around you, but their speeds are not always measured in SI units. If you measure the distance moved by a train or a car in kilometres and the time taken in hours, the speed will be in kilometres per hour, km h^{-1}. (Speeds are still sometimes quoted in miles per hour or mph but these units will not be considered further in this course.) So, if you drive 102 km in 2 h, your average speed is given by:

$$\text{average speed} = \frac{\text{distance travelled}}{\text{time taken}} = \frac{102\text{ km}}{2\text{ h}} = 51\text{ km h}^{-1}$$

Suppose you had driven 39 kilometres in $\frac{3}{4}$ hour. One way of finding your average speed on this occasion is to divide 39 by $\frac{3}{4}$, i.e. to divide by a fraction. Check that you can add, subtract, multiply and divide with fractions by attempting Question 9.5 and, if necessary, you should then study Box 9.2.

Question 9.5

Work out the following calculations, leaving your answers as the simplest possible fraction in each case.

(a) $\dfrac{2}{5} + \dfrac{1}{7}$

(b) $\dfrac{2}{5} - \dfrac{1}{7}$

(c) $\dfrac{2}{5} \times \dfrac{1}{7}$

(d) $\dfrac{2}{5} \div \dfrac{1}{7}$

Box 9.2 Doing calculations with fractions

Adding and subtracting fractions

Suppose you want to add the following two fractions:

$$\frac{3}{4} + \frac{2}{5}$$

You cannot just add the 3 and the 2. The 3 represents 3 quarters and the 2 represents 2 fifths, so adding the 3 to the 2 would be like trying to add 3 apples and 2 penguins – you just can't do it!

In order to add or subtract two fractions, they must both have the same denominator (bottom line).

Fractions with the same denominator are said to have a 'common denominator'. One way to find a common denominator when adding or subtracting two fractions is to multiply the top and bottom of the first fraction by the denominator of the second fraction, and the top and bottom of the second fraction by the denominator of the first fraction. A return to the example will make this clearer:

multiplying top and bottom by 4 (the denominator of the first fraction)

$$\frac{3}{4} + \frac{2}{5} = \frac{3 \times 5}{4 \times 5} + \frac{2 \times 4}{5 \times 4} = \frac{15}{20} + \frac{8}{20} = \frac{23}{20}$$

multiplying top and bottom by 5 (the denominator of the second fraction)

Note that $\dfrac{3}{4}$ and $\dfrac{15}{20}$ are equivalent fractions (see Box 2.5 'Fractions, percentages and ratios'); as are $\dfrac{2}{5}$ and $\dfrac{8}{20}$, and that $\dfrac{15}{20}$ and $\dfrac{8}{20}$ can be added without difficulty because they have a common denominator of 20.

Question 9.6

Work out the following calculations, leaving each answer as the simplest possible fraction.

(a) $\dfrac{2}{3} + \dfrac{1}{6}$ (b) $\dfrac{3}{4} - \dfrac{1}{6}$

Multiplying fractions

The expression 'three times two' just means there are three lots of two (i.e. $2 + 2 + 2$). So, multiplying by a whole number is just a form of repeated addition. For example:

$$3 \times 2 = 2 + 2 + 2$$

This is equally true when multiplying a fraction by a whole number:

$$3 \times \frac{4}{5} = \frac{4}{5} + \frac{4}{5} + \frac{4}{5} = \frac{12}{5}$$

The 3 could be written in the form of its equivalent fraction $\frac{3}{1}$ and it is then clear that the same answer is obtained by multiplying the two numerators together and the two denominators together:

$$\frac{3}{1} \times \frac{4}{5} = \frac{3 \times 4}{1 \times 5} = \frac{12}{5}$$

In fact, this procedure holds good for any two fractions.

To multiply two or more fractions, multiply numerators (top lines) together and also multiply the denominators (bottom lines) together.

So

$$\frac{2}{5} \times \frac{3}{7} = \frac{2 \times 3}{5 \times 7} = \frac{6}{35}$$

Sometimes cancelling is possible:

$$\frac{1}{4} \times \frac{2}{5} = \frac{1 \times \overset{1}{\cancel{2}}}{\underset{2}{\cancel{4}} \times 5} = \frac{1 \times 1}{2 \times 5} = \frac{1}{10}$$

Dividing fractions

The meaning of an expression such as $4 \div \frac{1}{2}$ is not immediately obvious, but a comparison with a more familiar expression, say $6 \div 2$, may help. The expression $6 \div 2$ asks you to work out how many twos there are in 6 (the answer is 3). In exactly the same way, $4 \div \frac{1}{2}$ asks how many halves there are in 4. Figure 9.2 illustrates this in terms of circles.

Each circle contains two half-circles, and four circles therefore contain eight half-circles. So:

$$4 \div \frac{1}{2} = 4 \times \frac{2}{1} = 8$$

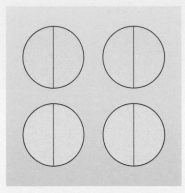

Figure 9.2 Four circles each containing two half-circles.

This can be extended into a general rule:

To divide by a fraction, turn it upside down and multiply.

So

$$5 \div \frac{8}{3} = 5 \times \frac{3}{8} = \frac{5 \times 3}{8} = \frac{15}{8}$$

and

$$\frac{2}{3} \div \frac{4}{5} = \frac{2}{3} \times \frac{5}{4} = \frac{\overset{1}{\cancel{2}} \times 5}{3 \times \underset{2}{\cancel{4}}} = \frac{1 \times 5}{3 \times 2} = \frac{5}{6}$$

Finally, remembering that 3 can be written as $\frac{3}{1}$

$$\frac{1}{2} \div 3 = \frac{1}{2} \div \frac{3}{1} = \frac{1}{2} \times \frac{1}{3} = \frac{1 \times 1}{2 \times 3} = \frac{1}{6}$$

Question 9.7

Work out the following calculations, leaving each answer as the simplest possible fraction.

(a) $\dfrac{2}{7} \times \dfrac{1}{4}$

(b) $\dfrac{2}{3} \div \dfrac{3}{4}$

(c) $\dfrac{3}{4} \div 5$

Returning to the example of the car that is driven 39 kilometres in $\frac{3}{4}$ hour, the average speed is:

$$\text{average speed} = \frac{\text{distance travelled}}{\text{time taken}}$$

$$= \frac{39 \text{ km}}{\frac{3}{4} \text{ h}}$$

$$= 39 \text{ km} \div \frac{3\text{h}}{4}$$

$$= \frac{39 \text{ km}}{1} \times \frac{4}{3\text{h}}$$

$$= \frac{\overset{13}{\cancel{39}} \times 4}{1 \times \underset{1}{\cancel{3}}} \frac{\text{km}}{\text{h}}$$

$$= 13 \times 4 \text{ km h}^{-1}$$

$$= 52 \text{ km h}^{-1}$$

So, the car's average speed is 52 km h^{-1}.

In addition to being quoted in km h^{-1}, speeds are sometimes given in other units. Returning to the theme of water, this time in the form of frozen rivers of ice – glaciers. It is not normally possible to detect the motion of a glacier by eye, and there is considerable variation in the speed at which they move but a typical glacier, such as the one shown in Figure 9.3, moves at about 12 cm each day. So its average speed can be written as 12 cm day^{-1}. Similarly, stalactites typically grow just 0.1 mm in a year, so their average growth rate is 0.1 mm year^{-1}. (Stalactites are formed when water drops from the roof of an underground cave, depositing the compound calcium carbonate in an icicle-shaped formation as it does so – see Figure 9.4.)

To compare the speed of a glacier with the growth rate of a stalactite, or with the speed of any other object, the speeds need to be given in the same units, preferably the SI unit of speed, m s^{-1}. To convert the average speed of the glacier (12 cm day^{-1}) to m s^{-1}, it is easiest to treat the distance and time components separately.

On average, a glacier moves 12 cm in one day:

$$12 \text{ cm} = 12 \times 10^{-2} \text{ m} = 0.12 \text{ m}$$

Since there are 24 hours in one day, 60 minutes in one hour and 60 seconds in one minute, 1 day = $24 \times 60 \times 60$ s = 8.64×10^4 s.

Figure 9.3   The Saskatchewan Glacier, Banff National Park, Canada.

Figure 9.4 Stalactites growing (very slowly!) in the Treak Cliff Cavern, Derbyshire, UK.

So, the glacier moves a distance of 0.12 m in a time of 8.64×10^4 s. Its average speed is therefore:

$$\frac{0.12 \text{ m}}{8.64 \times 10^4 \text{ s}} = 1.388\,888\,889 \times 10^{-6} \text{ m s}^{-1}$$

It is not sensible to give all those decimal places – the speed of the glacier won't be known that accurately! Remembering the rules for rounding (see Box 3.4), it is more reasonable to quote the average speed of the glacier as 1.4×10^{-6} m s^{-1}.

■ What is the typical growth rate of a stalactite (0.1 mm year^{-1}) in m s^{-1}?

□ The stalactite grows an average of 0.1 mm in one year, so:

$$0.1 \text{ mm} = 0.1 \times 10^{-3} \text{ m} = 1 \times 10^{-4} \text{ m}$$
$$1 \text{ year} = 365 \times 24 \times 60 \times 60 \text{ s} = 3.1536 \times 10^7 \text{ s}$$

So the stalactite grows an average of 1×10^{-4} m in 3.1536×10^7 s, i.e. its average growth rate is:

$$\frac{1 \times 10^{-4} \text{ m}}{3.1536 \times 10^7 \text{ s}} = 3.170\,979\,198 \times 10^{-12} \text{ m s}^{-1}$$

or, more sensibly, about 3×10^{-12} m s^{-1}.

Note that the stalactite grows at a very much slower rate than the glacier moves, and both speeds are tiny in comparison with the more 'everyday' speed of a 100-metre sprinter (recall this was about 9 m s^{-1}).

How do these speeds compare with examples of liquid water in motion? Blood in a human aorta (the main blood vessel leading from the heart) has an average speed of 0.35 m s^{-1} and the Mississippi River at New Orleans flows at about 1.3 m s^{-1}. However, it isn't usually possible to give a single value for the speed of water in a river – the value varies, depending on various factors.

■ What factors might cause the speed at which water flows in a river to vary?

□ You may have thought of the following factors.

- The river will flow more rapidly after heavy rain or when snow or a glacier is melting in the catchment area.
- The speed will vary at different positions across the river. Generally, the rate of flow will be greatest close to the surface of the river and in the middle of it. When the water comes into contact with the river bottom or banks, it is slowed down by friction.
- The river will flow more rapidly on the outside of bends.
- The river will flow more rapidly when it is flowing down a steep slope than when the slope is gentle. The term 'gradient' (introduced in Chapter 8) can also be applied to the slope down which a river flows.

Figure 9.5 illustrates the way in which the gradient of a typical river changes as it flows from its source to the sea. The river in question is the River Sprint which rises at Brown How, high in the English Lake District, then flows in a generally southerly direction, joining the River Kent before passing through the town of Kendal en route to the Irish Sea at Morecambe Bay. The graph in Figure 9.5 shows elevation (i.e. height above sea level) against distance from the river's source.

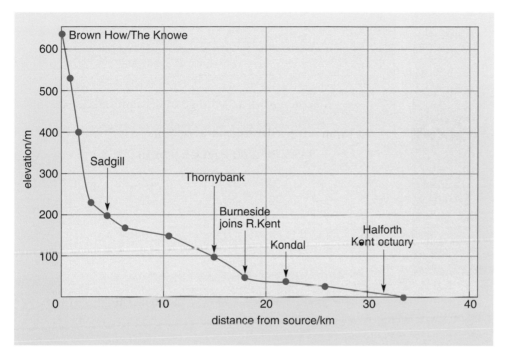

Figure 9.5   Graph showing the variation in elevation of the River Sprint (and River Kent) as it flows from its source in the English Lake District to the sea.

■   What is the general trend in the river's gradient as it flows from its source to the sea?

☐   Although the gradient does not decrease smoothly from source to mouth, there is a clear overall fall, the river becoming less steep towards the river mouth. If you had difficulty interpreting Figure 9.5, you may find it helpful to look back at Box 3.5.

All rivers have the same general variation of gradient shown in Figure 9.5, which leads to a characteristic change in form along the length of the river. Near its source, the River Sprint is a small stream, flowing rapidly down a hillside (Figure 9.6a). By the time it reaches the sea, the river (now joined with the River Kent) takes a slow, meandering path across the flat sands of the estuary (Figure 9.6b).

The word 'gradient' also has a strict scientific meaning, related to the slope of a plotted graph. The gradient of a graph is a measure of how rapidly the quantity plotted on the vertical axis changes in response to a change in the quantity plotted

(b)

(a)

Figure 9.6 (a) The River Sprint near its source; (b) the River Kent close to the sea.

on the horizontal axis. This idea was introduced in Chapter 8 in the context of the variation in the gas produced by yeast (see Section 8.3.1 and Figure 8.12).

If a graph is plotted of the distance travelled by an object against the time taken, the gradient of the graph gives the object's speed. The graph in Figure 9.7 shows the distance that a pole hammered into a glacier has moved from a fixed point. The distance has been measured every 10 days. Note that the points that have been plotted do not lie *exactly* on the straight line that has been drawn. This is because the glacier (and therefore the pole) does not move by exactly the same amount every day. However, the best-fit line (as defined in Box 8.1) is clearly a straight line. This means that, on average, the glacier moves by the same amount in each 10-day period. In other words, its average speed is constant.

The gradient of the best-fit line shown in Figure 9.7 can be used to find the glacier's average speed. The method for finding the gradient of any straight-line graph is described in Box 9.3.

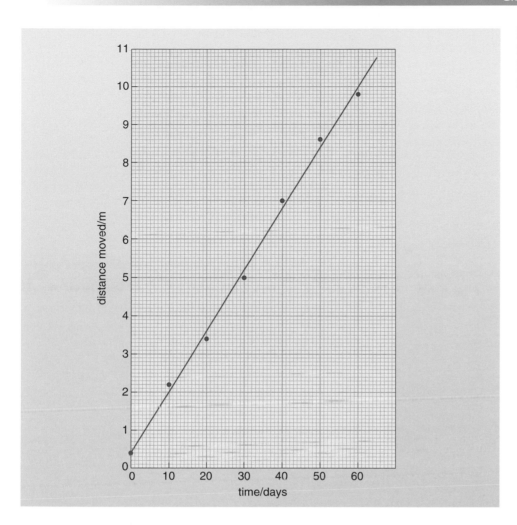

Figure 9.7 Graph showing the distance that a pole hammered into a glacier has moved from a fixed point.

Box 9.3   Finding the gradient of a straight-line graph

Scientists frequently want to know how one quantity varies with respect to another. They may be interested in the actual value of one quantity for a particular value of the other quantity but, more often it is the *rate* at which one quantity varies with respect to another that is more important. The slope or *gradient* of a graph gives a method for finding the rate of change.

This course will only consider how to find the gradient of simple, straight-line graphs, such as the ones shown in Figure 9.7. A straight-line graph is one in which the quantity plotted on the vertical axis varies at a steady rate with respect to the quantity plotted on the horizontal axis. In other words, the gradient of the line is constant.

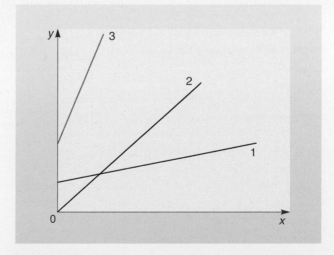

Figure 9.8 Graph of three lines with different gradients.

■ Which of the lines in Figure 9.8 has the largest gradient and which has the smallest gradient?

☐ Line 3 has the largest gradient – this is the steepest slope. Line 1 has the smallest gradient – it has the smallest change in the vertical direction for any particular change in the horizontal direction.

The gradient of a straight line is defined as:

$$\text{gradient} = \frac{\text{change in vertical value}}{\text{change in horizontal value}}$$

This is illustrated in Figure 9.9 and can be stated as:

$$\text{gradient} = \frac{\text{rise}}{\text{run}}$$

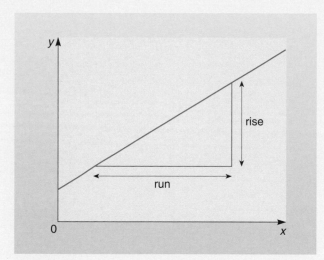

Figure 9.9   Finding the gradient by dividing rise by run.

To work out the gradient of a straight line on a graph, you simply need to take any two points on the line (to increase the precision of the calculation the points should be quite well separated) and find the change in vertical value (the rise) corresponding to a particular change in horizontal value (the run). As an example, consider the gradient of the graph shown in Figure 9.10.

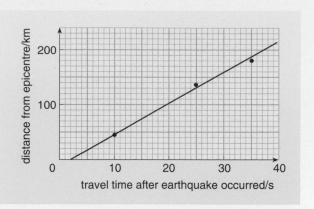

Figure 9.10   Graph showing how long it takes for seismic waves from an earthquake to reach three detectors at different distances from the epicentre. (Note that the focus is the point within the Earth at which the earthquake takes place, and the epicentre is the point on the Earth's surface vertically above the focus.)

Figure 9.11 shows that, as the horizontal value increases from 4 s to 32 s, the vertical value increases from 10 km to 170 km. Thus the run is (32 − 4) s = 28 s and the rise is (170 − 10) km = 160 km and the gradient is given by:

$$\text{gradient} = \frac{\text{rise}}{\text{run}} = \frac{160 \text{ km}}{28 \text{ s}} = 5.7 \text{ km s}^{-1}$$

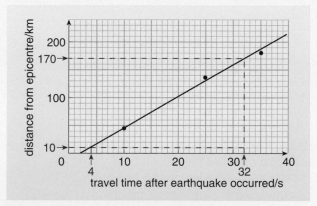

Figure 9.11   Finding the gradient of the graph in Figure 9.10.

The gradient of a graph can have units, just like any other calculated quantity. In this example, kilometres have been divided by seconds so the unit of the gradient is km s^{-1}. Note that this is a unit of speed, as expected.

Figure 9.12 is the same graph as in Figure 9.7, with some additional lines drawn to help you calculate the gradient. Note that when finding the gradient, values should be read from the line rather than from the plotted points (some of which do not lie on the line). Figure 9.12 shows that, as the horizontal value increases from 10 days to 60 days, the vertical value increases from 2 m to 10 m. Thus the run is (60 − 10) days = 50 days and the rise is (10 − 2) m = 8 m and the gradient is given by:

$$\text{gradient} = \frac{\text{rise}}{\text{run}} = \frac{8 \text{ m}}{50 \text{ days}}$$

■ Divide 8 by 50 to obtain a value for the gradient and divide m by days to obtain the correct units.

□ $\frac{8}{50} = 0.16$ and $\frac{\text{m}}{\text{days}} = \text{m day}^{-1}$, so the line has a gradient of 0.16 m day^{-1}.

Therefore, the glacier moves with an average speed of 0.16 m day^{-1}, which is 16 cm per day.

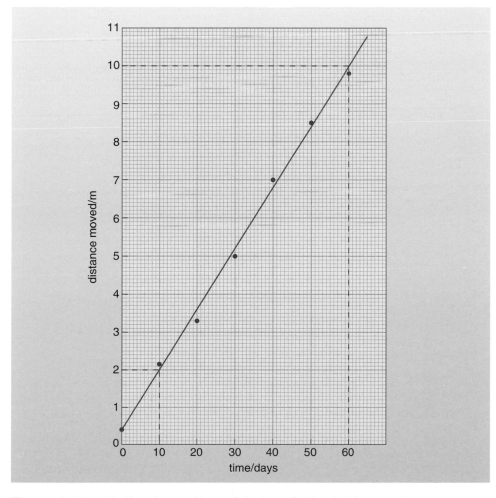

Figure 9.12 Finding the gradient of the best-fit line in Figure 9.7.

What is the gradient of the graph in Figure 9.13, which shows the variation of distance moved with time taken for a package on a conveyor belt?

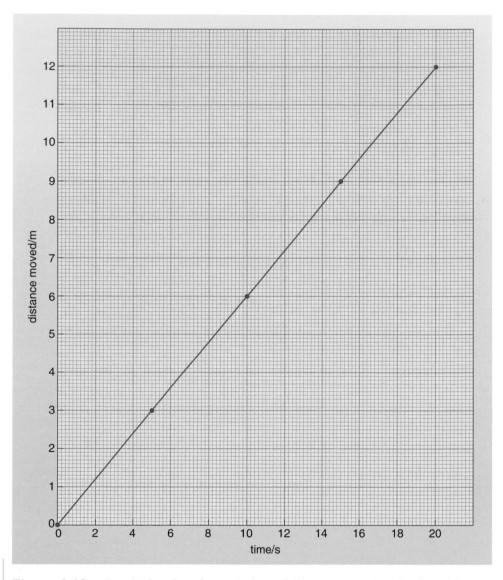

Figure 9.13 Graph showing the variation of distance moved with time taken for a package on a conveyor belt.

9.3 Calculating with symbols

So far in this course you have seen the word equations for density and average speed:

$$\text{density} = \frac{\text{mass}}{\text{volume}} \quad \text{(Section 4.2.1)}$$

and

$$\text{average speed} = \frac{\text{distance travelled}}{\text{time taken}} \quad \text{(Section 9.2)}$$

In addition, you know (from Box 4.3) that, for squares and rectangles, the area is found by multiplying the length by the width and that, for rectangular block-like structures, the volume is found by multiplying its length by its width by its height.

■ Write word equations (i.e. expressions involving an equals sign like those given above for density and average speed) for the area of a rectangle and the volume of a rectangular block.

☐ Area = length times width,
i.e. area = length × width (or equivalently, area = width × length).

Volume = length times width times height,

i.e. volume = length × width × height

Writing out all of these words is rather tiresome. However, equations can be expressed far more compactly if each word is replaced with a single letter, so the equation for the volume of a rectangular block might become:

$$V = l \times w \times h$$

where V represents volume, l represents length, w represents width and h represents height.

■ Rewrite the equation for density, using letters instead of words.

☐ The choice of letters was left up to you, so there is no single right answer. If you chose the symbol d to represent density, m to represent mass and v to represent volume, your equation will be $d = \dfrac{m}{v}$. (Note in this book we write the letter representing a quantity such as mass using an italic letter (m in this case) – this is particularly important where a symbol is also used as an abbreviation for a unit, for example, m for metre.)

It is reasonable to use the first letter of each quantity (e.g. m for mass). It makes the choice of letter more memorable and this is a perfectly acceptable answer. However, d for density might be confused with d for distance and v for volume might be confused with v for velocity. So, scientists try to reserve one letter for each commonly used quantity. Unfortunately, there aren't enough letters in the alphabet, so it is conventional to use the Greek letter ρ (pronounced 'rho') to represent density and a capital V to represent volume, so the equation for density becomes:

$$\rho = \frac{m}{V} \tag{9.1}$$

Similarly, speed is conventionally represented by v (for 'velocity'), so using d for distance travelled and t for time taken, the equation for speed becomes:

$$v = \frac{d}{t} \tag{9.2}$$

Note that the word 'velocity' has a precise scientific meaning, which you will learn more about if you go on to study S104 *Exploring science*. The velocity of an object is closely linked to its speed, and in everyday use the two words are used interchangeably.

There is one more convention that you need to know about:

> When using symbols instead of words or numbers, it is conventional to omit the multiplication sign, '×'.

So, the equation for the volume of a rectangular block becomes:

$$V = lwh \tag{9.3}$$

where V represents volume, l represents length, w represents width and h represents height.

Equations 9.1, 9.2 and 9.3 will enable you to calculate density, average speed and the volume of a rectangular block. The word **equation** is used for any expression containing an equals sign. The important point to remember is that what is written on the left-hand side of the '=' sign must *always* be equal to what is written on the right-hand side. Thus, as explained in Box 9.4, you should never use '=' as a shorthand for anything other than 'equals'.

Equations are very useful to scientists because the same equation is true in all sorts of circumstances, so you can calculate, for example, the density of one of the ice cubes shown in Figure 4.5a or of a huge block of stone using exactly the same equation. Question 9.9 is an opportunity to practise substituting values into equations for yourself. In doing this you should note the advice given in Box 9.4 for good practice when answering mathematical questions. You will find this advice useful throughout your study of science.

Question 9.9

(a) What is the volume of one of the 'cubes' of olive oil shown in Figure 4.5b? The illustrated cube can be considered to be a rectangular block with a length of 3 cm, a width of 2 cm and a height of 15 mm.

(b) The largest recorded iceberg in the Northern Hemisphere was approximately rectangular in shape with a length of 13 km, a width of 6 km and an average height of 125 m. What is the volume of the iceberg?

Box 9.4 Writing answers to mathematical questions

Writing maths

1 Always write down your working as well as your final answer (an example of how to do this is shown in the answer to Question 9.9(a) showing how the answer 9 cm³ was calculated). If you need to send your answer to your tutor, it will help them to see what you did right and (if you made a mistake) where you went wrong. Furthermore, most of the marks for mathematical questions in assignments are likely to be for the intermediate steps of working (i.e. the method you have used) rather the final answer. Even if no one else looks at your working, writing it down will make it clearer to *you* if you need to refer back to the question later. Also, if your answer is written down in a methodical way you are less likely to make a mistake and more likely to get the correct answer.

2 It is perfectly acceptable to write *words* of explanation in your answer – it doesn't all have to be symbols and numbers!

3 Remember that the symbol '=' means 'equals' and should *never* be used to mean 'thus' or 'therefore'. The symbol '∴' can be used to mean 'therefore', or just write the word 'therefore' or 'so' in your answer. It can make a calculation clearer if you align the = symbols vertically, to indicate that the quantity on the left-hand side is equal to or approximately equal to each quantity on the right-hand side. Figure 9.14 shows some examples of good and bad practice in the use of equals signs.

Taking care with units

1 Throughout this course the importance of giving appropriate units with all physical quantities is emphasised. So, when you work out the value of something, each line of your calculation should include units as well as numbers.

2 The units of your answer should be consistent with the units attached to the values you are using in the calculation. So, if you are multiplying three lengths, measured in metres, the units of the answer will be m³; if you are

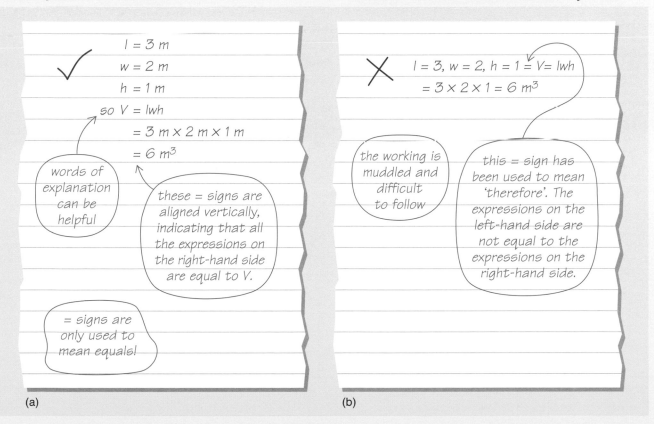

(a) (b)

Figure 9.14 Using equals signs in calculations: (a) example of good practice; (b) example of bad practice.

dividing a distance in m by a time in s, the units of the answer will be m s^{-1}.

3 Make sure that the values you have been given are in units that are consistent with each other. For example, it doesn't make sense to multiply one length given in mm by another length given in cm. It is easier to convert all values to the same unit (frequently the SI base unit) *before* doing a calculation.

Ensuring your answer makes sense

1 Is your answer about the size you expected? In Question 9.9, your answer to part (a) should be very much less than your answer to part (b). Is it? If you were finding the volume of a cube with sides each 1.57 m long, you would expect the answer to be between 1 m^3 (1 m × 1 m × 1 m)

and 8 m^3 (2 m × 2 m × 2 m). If your answer was 3870 m^3, you would know that you had made a mistake.

2 Are the units sensible? If you follow the advice in point 2 of 'Taking care with units', the units of your answer will be consistent with any equation that you used. So, if you used the equation $V = lwh$, your answer is probably in m^3 (or km^3, cm^3 or mm^3). However, if you were trying to find a speed (correct SI unit m s^{-1}) and your answer is in units of m^3, you would know that something had gone wrong – perhaps you used the wrong equation.

These checks won't guarantee that your answer is correct, but they will frequently highlight when mistakes have been made.

In Chapter 2 Question 2.8, you were asked to write down arithmetic expressions for various situations and then to work out the answers. Now try your hand at writing mathematical expressions using symbols.

Question 9.10

Using the letter b to represent the average volume of water used per day per person in the UK for baths and showers, f to represent the equivalent water usage for flushing toilets and c for washing clothes:

(a) Write an expression for the average volume of water used per day per person in the UK for *all* of these activities.

(b) Using your answer to part (a), write an equation for the total volume of water, T, used each day for these activities by a typical family of p people. You may find it helpful to look back to your answer to Question 2.8(b).

9.3.1   Earth and water

Now look at one final equation which gives the volume, V, of a sphere of radius r:

$$V = \frac{4}{3}\pi r^3 \tag{9.4}$$

where π is a constant (π is the Greek letter *pi*, pronounced 'pie'). The constant π has a value of 3.141 592 654 (to 9 decimal places) but you don't need to remember this as it is stored in your calculator – look for the π button now!

You can use Equation 9.4 to find the volume of *any* sphere anywhere in the Universe. In the final section of this chapter, you will use it to estimate the volumes of raindrops, hailstones and Earth itself. However, before you do this, you need to look more closely at the equation. First, if you are not sure of the meaning of the words 'circle', 'sphere', 'radius', 'diameter' and 'circumference', look at Box 9.5 now.

Box 9.5   Circles and spheres

The size of a sphere is specified by its **radius**, which is a quantity closely related to the radius of a circle.

Circles

Figure 9.15a shows a **circle**. The distance from the curve to the centre is called the radius of the circle, and it has the same value for all points around the curve, as you can readily check. The distance across the circle is twice the radius and is called the **diameter** of the circle.

■ What are the radius and the diameter of the circle in Figure 9.15a, in millimetres?

☐ Measured with a ruler, the radius is 13 mm and the diameter is 26 mm.

The distance around the outside edge of an object is its **circumference**. It has been known since ancient times that the ratio of a circle's circumference to its diameter is a constant value, π. Thus, for any circle:

$$\pi = \frac{\text{circumference of the circle}}{\text{diameter of the circle}}$$

Spheres

A **sphere** is the three-dimensional version of a circle in that all points on the surface of a sphere are the same distance from the centre of the sphere (Figure 9.15b). This distance is also called the radius, in this case the radius of the sphere. The diameter of a sphere is twice its radius.

■ What are the radius and the diameter of the sphere in Figure 9.15b, in millimetres?

☐ The radius is 12.5 mm and the diameter is 25 mm.

If a sphere is cut in half, the resulting flat surface is a disc with the same radius as the sphere (Figure 9.15c). This is also the shape that you think you see when looking at a sphere, such as the Moon, failing to notice that the surface curves away from you.

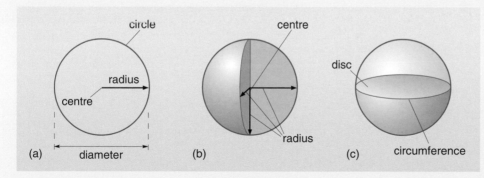

Figure 9.15   (a) A circle is the curve that is always the same distance from a point at its centre. This distance is known as the radius, and the diameter of the circle is twice its radius. (b) A sphere is the three-dimensional version of a circle in that all points on the surface of a sphere are the same distance from the centre of the sphere. This distance is also called the radius, in this case the radius of the sphere. (c) If a sphere is cut in half, the resulting flat surface is a disc with the same radius as the sphere.

Equation 9.4 is more complicated than any of the equations introduced earlier in the course, so it needs a closer look. First, the multiplication signs have been omitted, i.e. the equation could be written as:

$$V = \frac{4}{3} \times \pi \times r^3$$

Also, note that the radius term, r, is cubed: the powers notation, already introduced for numbers and units, can be used for symbols too.

$$r^3 = r \times r \times r$$

However, note that only the r is cubed, not the $\frac{4}{3}$ or the π, so when you substitute values into Equation 9.4, you need to take care to calculate:

$$V = \frac{4}{3} \times \pi \times r \times r \times r$$

Raindrops are approximately spherical and you know (from Chapter 6) that they have a diameter of about 2 mm, i.e. a radius of about 1 mm. Using Equation 9.4, find the volume, in m^3, of a typical raindrop:

$$r = 1 \text{ mm} = 1 \times 10^{-3} \text{ m}$$

so

$$
\begin{aligned}
V &= \frac{4}{3}\pi r^3 \\
&= \frac{4}{3} \times \pi \times (1 \times 10^{-3} \text{ m})^3 \\
&= 4.188\,790\,205 \times 10^{-9} \text{ m}^3
\end{aligned}
$$

 This is about 4×10^{-9} m^3. Check that you can obtain this value for yourself, taking special care to cube both 1×10^{-3} and its units (m).

■ The Earth can be thought of as a sphere with a radius of 6.4×10^6 m. Use Equation 9.4 to find a value for the volume of the Earth.

☐ Using Equation 9.4:

$$
\begin{aligned}
V &= \frac{4}{3}\pi r^3 \\
&= \frac{4}{3} \times \pi \times (6.4 \times 10^6 \text{ m})^3 \\
&= 1.098\,066\,219 \times 10^{21} \text{ m}^3
\end{aligned}
$$

So, the Earth has a volume of about 1.1×10^{21} m^3. In Chapter 6, you learned that there is about 1.46×10^9 km^3 of water on the Earth (including oceans, lakes, rivers and what is stored underground). Since 1 km = 1×10^3 m, 1 km^3 = $(1 \times 10^3)^3$ m^3 = 1×10^9 m^3. So, there is $(1.46 \times 10^9) \times (1 \times 10^9$ $m^3)$ of water on Earth, which is 1.46×10^{18} m^3.

■ What is the volume of water on Earth expressed as a percentage of the Earth's total volume?

☐ Using the guidance in Box 2.5, the volume of water on Earth can first be given as a fraction of the Earth's total volume:

$$\frac{1.46 \times 10^{18} \ \text{m}^3}{1.1 \times 10^{21} \ \text{m}^3}$$

The units (m^3) cancel and, as a decimal number, the answer is about 1.3×10^{-3}. To convert this into a percentage, multiply by 100, which gives:

$1.3 \times 10^{-3} \times 100\% = 0.13\%$

Thus about 0.1% of the Earth's total volume is water.

Question 9.11

Using Equation 9.4, what is the volume of a hailstone with a diameter of 1 cm? Write out your calculation in the style recommended in Box 9.4 showing each step of the calculation, and give your answer to one decimal place.

Activity 9.1   Auditing your mathematical skills

You should allow about 15 minutes for this activity.

This chapter has revised many of the mathematical skills you learned earlier in the course, and you have probably gained some new mathematical skills while studying this chapter. You may be pleased to know that you have now met all the mathematical concepts that are introduced in S154! You have probably already been reflecting in your learning journal on how well (or otherwise!) you are coping with the maths in this course, and you will be encouraged to complete this reflection at the end of Chapter 10. For now, look at Table 9.2 which lists all the mathematical skills developed in this course and see how much you have learned (these are just the maths skills – you have learned much else too). You might have found some of the maths difficult, so the purpose of this activity is to help you to identify any areas that are still causing you problems.

Rate your own ability in each skill by ticking the appropriate cell in each row of the table. In judging your ability, you could think about whether you were able to do the relevant questions in this book. It doesn't matter if you couldn't do them, or if you found them hard – did you manage to do them in the end? Also, how well did you get on with relevant questions in the interactive assessments? What comments did you get from your tutor on the assignment?

There is an electronic copy of Table 9.2 for downloading on the course website and, if possible, you are advised to complete that version.

The comments on this activity include some suggestions for what to do if you are lacking confidence in any of the mathematical skills taught in this course.

Table 9.2 Mathematical skills developed in this course.

Skill	Where taught	Very confident	Confident	Fairly confident	Still struggling	Having major problems
reading values from a table	Box 2.3					
using correct order of arithmetic (BEDMAS)	Box 2.4					
using powers notation	Box 2.4					
using fractions	Box 2.5					
using percentages	Box 2.5					
using ratios	Box 2.5					
using SI units of measurement	Boxes 3.2 and 4.3					
using decimal numbers	Box 3.3					
using decimal places and rounding	Box 3.4					
reading information from a graph	Box 3.5					
constructing a table of data	Activity 3.4					
using negative numbers	Box 4.2					
calculating area and volume	Box 4.3					
calculating density	Section 4.2.1					
reading bar charts	Activity 5.1					
using scientific notation	Boxes 6.1 and 6.2					
plotting graphs	Box 8.1					
interpreting graphs	Section 8.3.1					
calculating order of magnitude	Section 9.1					
using prefixes with SI units	Section 9.1					
using negative powers notation	Box 9.1					
doing calculations with fractions	Box 9.2					
finding the gradient of a straight-line graph	Box 9.3					
using symbols in equations	Section 9.3					
writing answers to mathematical questions	Box 9.4					

9.4   Summary of Chapter 9

Powers notation is used for units of measurement, for example, the SI unit of speed is m s^{-1} and the SI unit of density is kg m^{-3}.

When adding or subtracting two fractions, they must both have the same denominator (bottom line).

To multiply two or more fractions, multiply the numerators (top lines) together and multiply the denominators (bottom lines) together.

To divide by a fraction, turn it upside down and multiply.

The gradient of a straight-line graph can be found by dividing the increase in its vertical value (the 'rise') by the corresponding increase in horizontal value (the 'run').

An equation is an expression that contains an equals sign. Equations can be written with words or symbols. When using symbols instead of words or numbers, it is conventional to omit the multiplication sign, '×'.

π is the ratio of a circle's circumference to its diameter; it has a value of 3.14 when rounded to two decimal places.

The radius of a circle or sphere is half its diameter.

Learning outcomes of Chapter 9

When you have completed Chapter 9 you should be able to:

- Express a numerical quantity to the nearest order of magnitude, i.e. the nearest power of ten.
- Use a range of prefixes with SI units.
- Calculate the average speed with which an object moves, i.e. the total distance travelled divided by the time taken.
- Apply powers notation to units and symbols as well as to numbers.
- Calculate using fractions.
- Calculate the gradient of a straight line.
- Write answers to mathematical questions, showing your working as well as your final answer, with appropriate units.
- Check that your answers to calculations are reasonable.
- Substitute numerical values into mathematical expressions containing symbols.
- Write mathematical expressions using symbols for quantities.

Chapter 10
Water on Earth: the activities and responsibilities of scientists

As you approach the end of S154 *Science starts here*, this is a good time to reflect on what you have learned as you studied the course. At the end of this brief chapter, you will have the opportunity to reflect on the new skills you have learned, whether they are mathematical skills, communication skills, computer skills or simply the skills involved with becoming a more effective Open University (OU) student.

However, during this course, you have also learned a lot about water and its importance to life. Undoubtedly, water shortages cause inconvenience in the more developed areas of the world – at the beginning of the 21st century hosepipe bans, parched land and forest fires are becoming familiar (Figure 10.1). However, drought conditions in less developed areas cause tragedy on an unimaginable scale, as crops fail and thousands of people starve to death.

Figure 10.1 Drought conditions in southern Spain in 2005: (a) low reservoir levels at Embalse de Iznájar, Andalucía; (b) a forest fire.

(a)   (b)

However, Chapter 7 showed that the Earth isn't short of water but rather the water is in the 'wrong' place. The images in Figure 10.1 contrast markedly with Figure 10.2.

At the time of writing (2007), the Greenland ice sheet was estimated to be melting at a rate of 2.5×10^9 m^3 *per year* which, without considering any other ice sheets or glaciers, leads to a rise in sea level of 0.5 mm per year.

Figure 10.2 Extensive flooding destroyed homes and made streets impassable when Hurricane Katrina hit New Orleans in 2005.

If you think of the Greenland ice sheet as a rectangular block 2×10^6 m long, 1×10^6 m wide and 2.3×10^3 m thick, you can use Equation 9.3 to find its total volume:

$$V = lwh$$
$$= (2 \times 10^6 \text{ m}) \times (1 \times 10^6 \text{ m}) \times (2.3 \times 10^3 \text{ m})$$
$$= (2 \times 10^6) \times (1 \times 10^6) \times (2.3 \times 10^3) \text{ m}^3$$
$$= 4.6 \times 10^{15} \text{ m}^3$$

It takes some imagination to think of this ice sheet as a rectangular block but the volume calculated is about right. That is a lot of ice and, as the meltwaters flow down off the land into the sea, a potential increase in sea level of perhaps 7 m. This would have a significant effect on low-lying areas in places such as Bangladesh, the Netherlands and the east of England (Figure 10.3), which are already increasingly threatened by flooding. Although the catastrophic flooding in New Orleans in 2005 was caused primarily by the impact of Hurricane Katrina, rising sea levels and the fact that New Orleans is low-lying were contributing factors. Indeed, many scientists think that the increased incidence of hurricanes is, like rising sea levels, a consequence of the climate change caused by human activity on the Earth.

One reason for studying science is to help you to discover what is happening to this planet – and perhaps what needs to be done about it. There are many other good reasons for learning more about science. We hope that this course has helped you to begin the learning process and we conclude with a brief look at the main activities of science and scientists, and the responsibilities of scientists.

Figure 10.3 Rising sea levels mean that many low-lying areas, such as this one in Lincolnshire, UK, are likely to be flooded in the future.

10.1   The activities of scientists

If you look up the word 'science' in a dictionary, generally the most common definition is: the organised body of information about the material world that has been obtained by experiment and observation. There are other, older meanings. At one time, science meant all knowledge. Indeed, this is where the word comes from: the Latin for 'knowledge' is *scientia*.

People acquire knowledge as scientists by engaging in four fundamentally important activities. You have been introduced to these activities while working through this book.

1   Scientists observe the natural world around them and describe what they see.

2   They try to construct hypotheses to explain or make sense of what they see; the archaeologists who discovered the skeleton in the Egyptian desert (Figure 2.1) may have constructed more than one hypothesis to explain how it came to be buried there.

3   They carry out experiments, where possible, to test their hypotheses. The experiment you did in Activity 3.2 not only tested the hypothesis that potatoes, like cabbages and cucumbers, contain water, but also helped to establish roughly what percentage of a potato's mass is water. Once a hypothesis has been tested, by experiments where possible, and is found to be consistent with a wide range of observations, it becomes a scientific theory.

4   Scientists must be able to communicate their findings to other people, both to raise public awareness of new science and so that other scientists can build on their work to extend knowledge still further. The importance of scientists being able to explain their science to other people must not be underestimated. This is why great emphasis has been placed, throughout this course, on developing your communication skills.

In his novel *Dune* (first published in 1965) Frank Herbert explored the possibility of humans living on other planets and surviving by wearing a 'stillsuit' which collects and recycles water from the body. In the mid 1960s this was definitely in the realms of science fiction (the first human had gone into orbit round the Earth, but no one had yet landed on the Moon) but such is the pace of technological development that the notion of maintaining viable space stations on the surface of a planet such as Mars is now a serious scientific possibility, and not just a novelist's fantasy. Currently (2007), NASA (the National Aeronautics and Space Administration) has plans to establish a surface habitat on the Moon. The possibility of living in space or on other planets in a closed ecological system has now been researched by computer modelling and by experiment. This is the 'stillsuit' idea expanded to enclose a whole community rather than a single person, and extending to the atmosphere and the plants and animals in it as well. Planet Earth is essentially a closed system: almost nothing comes in, except energy in the form of heat and light from the Sun, and nothing leaves, except heat and reflected light. However, the Earth's system is made up of four major components: the atmosphere, water (the hydrosphere), living material (the biosphere) and the solid Earth (the geosphere). The balance between these four systems is very delicate, so large-scale experimentation on the planet itself would be highly complex and could be disastrous if it went wrong!

In the late 20th century smaller, closed ecological systems were extensively researched. These are small communities of plants and animals (including humans), closed off from the outside world, in which oxygen, water and nutrients are recycled. One system modelled by computer in 1992 involved reclaiming water from both plant and animal waste. In this model, the inedible matter from plants in the system's crop-growing unit was processed to remove the water. The residue, together with paper and plastic waste and faeces, was incinerated. Water lost through breathing, sweating and urinating, together with domestic waste water from showers, etc., was collected in an evaporator. Here it came into contact with hot gases produced during the incineration of the solid waste. The heat evaporated the water, leaving insoluble and unwanted residues. The water vapour was condensed and the resulting, purified water could then be reused for human consumption.

Perhaps one of the best known experiments was Biosphere 2, which was constructed in Arizona in the USA between 1987 and 1989 (Figure 10.4). During two sealed missions (the first for two years from 1991 to 1993 and the second for six months in 1994) teams of scientists lived in the closed biosphere while carrying out scientific experiments which studied and manipulated their environment. The first mission was eventually abandoned as oxygen levels became dangerously low and supplies had to be pumped in from outside. This was possibly because of insufficient oxygen production by photosynthesising plants combined with greater than expected oxygen use by microbes in the soil. Although the site was used for several years afterwards by college students, it has now been sold and is currently being run as a visitor centre.

The closest approach to a closed ecological system in the UK is perhaps the biomes of the Eden Project in Cornwall (Figure 10.5 overleaf). Although each dome mimics the conditions on a particular part of the Earth's surface, they are not true *closed* systems because people, water, air and even small animals and insects move into and out of the structures.

Figure 10.4   Biosphere 2, a closed ecological system which was constructed in Arizona, USA in the late 1980s.

Figure 10.5 The Eden Project in Cornwall, UK. A series of large plastic greenhouses – 'biomes' – were built to enclose areas with different climates. The Humid Tropics biome shown here is 200 m long and up to 50 m high – large enough to contain the Tower of London. The second biome Warm Temperate is not shown. At the time of writing, a third biome is planned – 'The Edge' will focus on the challenges of water and energy use, and security and climate change.

10.2   The responsibilities of scientists

The activities of scientists have led, and will continue to lead, to ever-increasing knowledge of the world. This knowledge has the potential to create untold benefits for humanity, but it also has the potential to inflict unimaginable harm. For example, a closed ecological system experiment on a global scale could be catastrophic for humans if it went wrong. Therefore, it is an important responsibility of scientists to try to maximise the benefits of scientific knowledge while they minimise any potential harm.

We hope that you will keep in mind the idea that scientists have responsibilities to society as you work through future courses. Scientists mostly want their discoveries to be used to benefit humanity. Occasionally, choices are made that result in knowledge being used in ways that might be considered detrimental.

■   Think of one or two examples of ways in which science has been used specifically to benefit humanity, and one or two ways in which its use has been detrimental.

☐   You might have thought of the science associated with medical research or some aspects of agriculture as being beneficial, and developments in atomic, biological and chemical warfare as detrimental.

There are many instances where scientific knowledge has been used in what scientists believed were our best interests, but that later turned out to have some damaging consequences for the environment. One such example is the use of fuels, such as coal and oil, to generate electricity. Most people would regard electricity as beneficial to society. However, burning these fuels releases the gas carbon dioxide into the atmosphere, which may be influencing world climates adversely.

■ From what you have read in this book, try to recall some other examples of areas where scientific developments have had unintentionally damaging consequences.

☐ You may have thought of fertilisers, which are intended to help grow healthier crops to feed more people but end up depleting rivers and lakes of oxygen and killing the animals that live there. Another example is the industries that manufacture goods intended to raise people's standard of living: these industries may discharge waste products, not known to be toxic at the time, into rivers.

Unintentional damage is an ongoing hazard of scientific and technological development. In the mid to late 1990s, scientific research began to uncover an increase in sterility and sexual abnormality in male fish living in rivers and lakes polluted by certain types of industrial chemicals. Parallel studies of human males across Europe, including the UK, also suggested an increase in potential sterility, and an increase in babies born with sexual abnormalities, since the 1970s. The chemicals suspected of causing these harmful effects have a structure which is very similar to that of oestrogen (pronounced 'east-roe-jen'), the predominantly female hormone used in many women's contraceptive pills. As these chemicals are very widespread – from the manufacture of plastics, carpets and wood-pulp to ingredients in paints, industrial detergents and pesticides – eliminating them from the environment is not easy.

Fortunately, the great increase in environmental awareness since the 1980s has encouraged many scientists to use their knowledge to find ways of correcting past damage and of managing the environment more effectively. However, it isn't only scientists who have a part to play in this. From the discussion of water usage in Chapter 2 (Section 2.3) and Chapter 7 (Section 7.1), and of water pollution in Chapter 7 (Section 7.2), you will be aware that everyone has a responsibility to use knowledge to manage the environment and its resources more effectively.

Part of the responsibility of being a scientist is trying to predict the long-term effects of the possible uses of scientific discoveries. This raises the question of whether knowledge should ever be suppressed if its resulting effects might prove harmful to society. You might like to think about this question now that you have almost completed S154 and when you study future courses.

10.3   Summary of Chapter 10

Science is the organised body of information about the material world that has been obtained by observation and experimentation. The four main activities of scientists are observing, constructing hypotheses, testing by experiment and communicating knowledge.

An example of scientific activity is the way in which the possibility of humans spending long periods in space has encouraged research into the development of closed ecological systems.

Scientific discoveries can be used to benefit or harm humanity, although harmful outcomes are sometimes unintentional.

It is everyone's responsibility to manage the environment and its resources effectively.

Learning outcomes for S154

In all the earlier chapters we have listed the specific learning outcomes for each chapter. However, in this the final chapter of the course book, we list the overarching learning outcomes for the whole course. These are listed below under four skills categories. On completion of S154 you should be able to:

Knowledge and understanding (Kn)

Kn1   Understand some of the basic terminology, nomenclature and conventions appropriate to science.

Kn2   Read and write in chemical notation.

Cognitive skills (C)

C1   Make sense of the information presented in a variety of ways appropriate to scientific topics (texts, tables, graphs, diagrams and figures, numerical and mathematical descriptions, computer-based interactive activities).

Key skills (Ky)

Ky1   Demonstrate basic numeracy, mathematical and computational skills.

Ky2   Apply basic arithmetic to solve problems.

Ky3   Process, analyse, interpret and present data using appropriate qualitative and quantitative techniques.

Ky4   Communicate scientific information clearly and concisely in writing and graphically.

Ky5   Reflect on the experience of learning in order to develop more effective learning strategies.

Ky6   Employ time-management and organisational skills.

Ky7   Use information technology to learn and communicate with others.

Practical and/or professional skills (P)

P1   Make and record observations and measurements.

Now that you have almost completed S154, you probably want to know how successful your learning has been! You can do this now in the following activity.

Activity 10.1   Reviewing your study of S154

You should allow at least 45 minutes for this activity.

As you studied this course, several skills were introduced to help you study and learn more effectively. Your assessment scores and the feedback from your tutor will give you an indication of this. However, the end of the course is also a good time to reflect on which techniques have worked well for you, to review how well you have achieved the course learning outcomes, and to do a little more work on any areas that you are unsure about. This should help you to decide what your strengths are and what you could study next and be useful preparation for your future studies.

S154 *Science starts here* is designed to prepare you for further study of science at Level 1 with the OU. As well as introducing scientific knowledge linked to the theme of 'water for life,' and helping you to understand the concepts involved, this course has shown you how to interpret this knowledge when it is presented in a variety of ways. You have also had an opportunity to learn some key skills connected with mathematics, communication, learning and organisation. Before you continue with further Level 1 science courses, you would be wise to check that your work in all these areas has been successful.

There are three stages to checking whether you have achieved what you set out to do when you began to study this course:

(a) reflect on planning and finding time for study

(b) review the techniques that you have developed for improving your learning skills

(c) consider how well you have met the course learning outcomes and consider, with the help of the comments, ways in which you can improve your performance in any outcomes that you have not achieved to your satisfaction.

(a) Planning and finding time for study

OU courses are valued according to a nationally agreed system of credit points in which one credit point equals 10 hours of study. Most OU undergraduate courses are worth either 30 points (300 hours) or 60 points (600 hours). So, studying a 30-point course over nine months will take about eight hours of study a week; for a 60-point course, you need to set aside about 16 hours a week. Students don't usually do more than 60 points of courses a year and most take at least six years to complete their degrees. So, if you now plan to move on to a 30- or 60-point course, you will need to find about 8 hours or 16 hours of study time respectively each week for the duration of the course. You might want to revise these numbers depending on how the time it took you to study S154 matched our estimates.

Forward planning and setting targets are important. You have started to develop these skills during your study of S154: activities helped you to plan your study time; you kept a log of the time you took to study the material; and you reflected on whether your plans were realistic and amended them accordingly.

In Activity 5.1 you set yourself study targets. In Activity 5.3 you reflected on whether you had met these targets and, if you thought it necessary, you revised your plans for studying later chapters. You were encouraged to discuss time-planning problems with other students in your tutor group to identify strategies to help you to meet your targets. In the comments on the time-planning activities, you were advised to note down your thoughts about successful time planning in your learning journal.

With reference to your learning journal, consider the following three questions and note down your responses in your journal if you haven't already done so.

1   Reflect on the targets you set yourself in Activity 5.1. How successful were you at meeting these targets?

2   Where you met or even improved on your targets, what was the reason for this? What did you do that helped you to be successful?

3   Where you missed your targets, what was the reason for this? Think about the advice you can give yourself about planning and managing your study of future courses and note this down. You may find it helpful to share this advice with other students in your tutor group and to see whether their advice would help you. It can also be comforting and reassuring when you find that other people have similar time-planning problems!

(b) Reviewing learning techniques

This course introduced several techniques to help you to study actively; the main ones are listed below.

- Highlighting and annotating text
- Scanning text to get an idea of what lies ahead
- Rephrasing a difficult concept or paragraph in your own words
- Identifying key points
- Summarising a section in words or a diagram
- Turning a diagram into words

Spend a few minutes thinking about these techniques and for each one try to note down:

- whether you used the technique a lot, sometimes, a little or not at all while studying S154
- whether you found the technique helped you to learn
- a specific example of when you used the technique and how you decided to use it, e.g. what to highlight, how you identified key points
- how you could improve your use of the technique in future study.

Now look at the comments on this part of the activity.

(c) Reviewing learning outcomes

The learning outcomes which you should have achieved through your study of S154 are given in the Summary section for this chapter (Section 10.3).

Take some time now to reflect on where your strengths and weaknesses lie and what progress you have made in each of these areas.

In your learning journal make a note of your conclusions and then read the comments on this part of Activity 10.1. After you have read the comments, access the Level 1 Science interactive quiz via the link on the course website. This quiz will enable you to confirm your own assessment of your strengths and highlight any areas that would repay further work, which will help you to plan any future study.

It only remains for us, the course team, to congratulate you on finishing S154 and to wish you luck with your result for this course, and success in your future OU studies!

Answers to questions

Question 2.1

(a) The number given in the second column of Table 2.1 on the same line as 'flushing toilet' is 37, and the units 'litres' are attached to this. So the average person uses 37 litres of water per day for this purpose.

(b) The entry in the third row from the bottom of the first column of the table is 'drinking and cooking', so the number 6, together with the table title and the column heading, should tell you that the use of water for cooking and drinking in the home in the UK is equivalent to 6 litres per day for each person in the country.

Question 2.2

(a) $3 \times 10 \div 2 = 15$

(b) The multiplication should be done before the addition, so
$$8 + 2 \times 5 = 8 + 10 = 18$$

(c) The 2^2 should be calculated first, so
$$3 \times 2^2 = 3 \times 4 = 12$$

(d) The calculation inside the brackets should be done first, so
$$(5 + 3) \div 2 = 8 \div 2 = 4$$

(e) Using the rules of BEDMAS (Box 2.4)
$$(2 + 3)^2 \times 2 = 5^2 \times 2 = 25 \times 2 = 50$$

(f) 10 litres + 5 litres − 2 litres = 13 litres

(Note that your answer is not correct unless it includes the units; litres in this case.)

Question 2.3

(a) $38 + 92 - 61 = 69$

(Note that you do not have to press '=' after the addition of 38 and 92 but, if you do, the final answer should be the same; check this for yourself.)

(b) $24 \times 32 \times 8 = 6144$

(c) $24 \times 32 \div 8 = 96$

Question 2.4

(a) The multiplication should be done before the addition, so
$$3 \times 4 + 2 = 12 + 2 = 14$$

(b) The multiplication should be done before the addition, so
$$2 + 4 \times 3 = 2 + 12 = 14$$

(Note that the answer to parts (a) and (b) is the same. This is because addition and multiplication are individually *commutative*, i.e. 3×4 is the same as 4×3, and $12 + 2$ is the same as $2 + 12$. Remember, though, that the multiplication must be done before the addition.)

(c) The division and multiplication should be done before the subtraction, so
$$4 \times 2 - 21 \div 7 = 8 - 3 = 5$$

(Note subtraction and division are *not* individually *commutative*, i.e. $21 \div 7$ is not the same as $7 \div 21$, and $8 - 3$ is not the same as $3 - 8$.)

Question 2.5

(a) $3^3 = 3 \times 3 \times 3 = 27$

(b) The 5^2 should be evaluated first, and $5^2 = 5 \times 5 = 25$. Then $3 \times 5^2 = 3 \times 25 = 75$

(c) The 3^2 and 4^2 should be evaluated first:
$$3^2 = 3 \times 3 = 9 \text{ and } 4^2 = 4 \times 4 = 16$$
Then $3^2 + 4^2 = 9 + 16 = 25$

Question 2.6

(a) Working from left to right gives
$$150 \div 10 \times 3 = 15 \times 3 = 45$$

(b) The bracket should be evaluated first, so
$$(2 \times 3)^2 = 6^2 = 36$$

(c) The term including an exponent, 3^2, should be evaluated first, so
$$2 \times 3^2 = 2 \times 9 = 18$$

(d) The innermost brackets should be evaluated first, so
$$[(10 - 5) \times (3 + 1)] + 4 = [5 \times 4] + 4 = 20 + 4 = 24$$

(e) $\dfrac{18 + 6}{3} = \dfrac{24}{3} = 8$

(f) $\dfrac{18}{3} + 6 = 6 + 6 = 12$

Question 2.7

(a) The total domestic use of water per person per day in the UK is found by adding all the values given in Table 2.1, i.e. 50 litres + 37 litres + 21 litres + 12 litres + 9 litres + 6 litres + 1 litre + 14 litres, which equals 150 litres.

(Note that in order to be correct, your answer must be '150 litres' not just '150'.)

(b) The total daily amount of water used per person outdoors is 9 litres + 1 litre = 10 litres. Thus the difference between the total domestic water use and the amount used outdoors is 150 litres − 10 litres = 140 litres.

(Note that you could have obtained the same answer by adding all the figures from Table 2.1 apart from those for garden watering and car washing. There are frequently several ways in which the same correct answer can be obtained, but the worked solutions in this book will generally show just one method.)

(c) The weekly usage will be seven times greater than the daily usage (assuming the same amount of water is used every day), so a week of baths and showers will require 50 litres × 7 = 350 litres. The annual usage will be 365 times greater than the daily usage, so this is 50 litres × 365 = 18 250 litres.

(*Note*: if your answer is 18 200 litres, i.e. 350 litres × 52 weeks, this is not accurate since 365 days = 52 weeks + 1 day. You need to add another 50 litres to your answer.)

Question 2.8

(Note that there are many different ways in which the expressions required in this question could be stated. Also, your final answers are not correct unless they include units; litres in this case.)

(a) The three people use 145 litres of water each, or 145 × 3 litres in total. The amounts that they use for baths and showers must be subtracted from this, so the calculation is: 145 × 3 − 15 − 25 − 40 = 355. So 355 litres are used for all other purposes.

(Note that you could have inserted brackets for clarity: (145 × 3) − 15 − 25 − 40 = 355, but in this case the brackets are not essential because the multiplication should be done before the subtractions.)

(b) Table 2.1 shows that each day a 'typical' person uses 50 litres of water for baths and showers, 37 litres for toilet flushing, and 21 litres for washing clothes. Written mathematically this is 50 + 37 + 21. Since a family of four 'typical' people would use four times this amount, the complete equation is (50 + 37 + 21) × 4 = 108 × 4 = 432, so a family of four will typically use 432 litres per day for these purposes.

(Note that the brackets mean that the *total* use of water for these three purposes per person is multiplied by 4, and they are essential for indicating that the addition must be carried out before the multiplication.)

Question 2.9

(a) From Table 2.2, the saving from not using any water outside is 20 litres per day. Before the savings, the total daily use is 400 litres (found by adding all the values in Table 2.2). Therefore, the saving is:

as a fraction: $\dfrac{20 \text{ litres}}{400 \text{ litres}} = \dfrac{20}{400} = \dfrac{2}{40} = \dfrac{1}{20}$

(note that the unit cancels out)

as a percentage: $\dfrac{1}{20} \times 100\% = 5\%$

(note that this could have been calculated directly: $\dfrac{20}{400} \times 100\% = 5\%$)

(b) The reduced daily amount of water used for baths and showers will be:

$$\frac{2}{3} \times 96 \text{ litres} = 64 \text{ litres}$$

The saving is therefore 96 litres − 64 litres = 32 litres. An alternative way to get to this answer is to recognise that if the water use is reduced to $\frac{2}{3}$ of its normal value, the saving must be $\frac{1}{3}$ of the normal value. So the daily saving is:

$$\frac{1}{3} \times 96 \text{ litres} = 32 \text{ litres}$$

This saving is:

as a fraction: $\dfrac{32 \text{ litres}}{400 \text{ litres}} = \dfrac{32}{400} = \dfrac{16}{200} = \dfrac{8}{100} = \dfrac{4}{50} = \dfrac{2}{25}$

as a percentage: $\dfrac{2}{25} \times 100\% = 8\%$

(c) By putting a 1-litre 'save-a-flush®' bag in the cistern, the amount of water used per flush is reduced from the normal 10 litres to 9 litres, a saving of 1 litre. This saving is:

as a fraction: $\dfrac{1 \text{ litre}}{10 \text{ litres}} = \dfrac{1}{10}$

as a percentage: $\dfrac{1}{10} \times 100\% = 10\%$

(d) The daily saving will be $\frac{1}{10}$ of the initial daily use for flushing the toilet, so this is

$$\dfrac{1}{10} \times 120 \text{ litres} = 12 \text{ litres}$$

This saving can again be expressed as a fraction or percentage of the initial total daily use:

as a fraction: $\dfrac{12 \text{ litres}}{400 \text{ litres}} = \dfrac{\overset{6}{\cancel{12}}}{\underset{200}{\cancel{400}}} = \dfrac{\overset{3}{\cancel{6}}}{\underset{100}{\cancel{200}}} = \dfrac{3}{100}$

as a percentage: $\dfrac{3}{100} \times 100\% = 3\%$

Question 2.10

Your completed Table 2.3 shows that the savings are much easier to compare when expressed as percentages. The savings on water for toilet flushing is lowest – 3% of the total use – followed by outside use (5%), and the largest saving, of 8%, is for baths and showers. The savings are not so easy to compare when expressed as fractions. For example, you probably can't tell from a quick glance which of $\frac{1}{20}$, $\frac{2}{25}$ and $\frac{3}{100}$ is the largest and which is the smallest.

Question 2.11

(a) Before implementing their water-saving measures, the Browns' water use for baths and showers was 96 litres per day and their water use for flushing the lavatory was 120 litres per day. As a ratio this is

96 : 120 or, by repeatedly dividing both numbers by two and then by three, it can be simplified to 48 : 60 then 24 : 30 then 12 : 15 and finally 4 : 5. This is the simplest form in which this ratio can be expressed.

(b) With the water-saving measures in place, 64 litres per day are used for baths and showers (from the answer to Question 2.9(b)).

If 12 litres per day are saved in toilet flushing (from the answer to Question 2.9(d)), the daily water use for this purpose is

120 litres – 12 litres = 108 litres

Thus the ratio of water use for baths and showers to that for toilet flushing is 64 : 108 which simplifies, by twice dividing both numbers by two, to 32 : 54 then 16 : 27. This is the simplest form in which this ratio can be expressed.

Question 2.12

The Browns save 20 litres on outside use, 32 litres on baths and showers and 12 litres on toilet flushing each day, which is a total saving of 64 litres. As a percentage of their normal daily use of 400 litres per day this is:

$$\dfrac{64 \text{ litres}}{400 \text{ litres}} \times 100\% = 16\%$$

Their neighbours' savings are:

$$\dfrac{70 \text{ litres}}{500 \text{ litres}} \times 100\% = 14\%$$

So the Browns make the greater saving as a percentage, even though they save 6 litres less each day than the Patels. Note again that it is easier to compare the savings expressed as percentages than if they were quoted as fractions.

Question 2.13

(a) Dividing the numerator and denominator of $\frac{6}{8}$ by 2 gives

$$\dfrac{\overset{3}{\cancel{6}}}{\underset{4}{\cancel{8}}} = \dfrac{3}{4}$$

(b) Cancelling the three zeros in the numerator and denominator of $\frac{3000}{4000}$ (i.e. dividing by 10 three times) gives

$$\frac{3\cancel{000}}{4\cancel{000}} = \frac{3}{4}$$

(c) Dividing the numerator and denominator of $\frac{6}{12}$ by 2 and then by 3 gives

$$\frac{\overset{3}{\cancel{6}}}{\underset{6}{\cancel{12}}} = \frac{\overset{1}{\cancel{3}}}{\underset{2}{\cancel{6}}} = \frac{1}{2}$$

(d) Dividing the numerator and denominator of $\frac{75}{100}$ by 5 two times gives

$$\frac{\overset{15}{\cancel{75}}}{\underset{20}{\cancel{100}}} = \frac{\overset{3}{\cancel{15}}}{\underset{4}{\cancel{20}}} = \frac{3}{4}$$

(e) $\frac{3}{8}$ is already in its simplest form.

$\frac{6}{8}$, $\frac{3000}{4000}$ and $\frac{75}{100}$ can all be simplified to $\frac{3}{4}$, so (a), (b) and (d) are equivalent fractions:

$$\frac{6}{8} = \frac{3000}{4000} = \frac{75}{100} = \frac{3}{4}$$

Question 2.14

From Table 2.1 you can see that an average of 50 litres of water are used per person per day for baths and showers, etc., and from the answer to Question 2.7(a) you know that the total domestic water use is 150 litres per person per day. Thus the fraction of domestic water use that is for baths and showers, etc. is

$$\frac{50 \text{ litres}}{150 \text{ litres}} = \frac{\cancel{50}}{\cancel{150}} = \frac{\overset{1}{\cancel{5}}}{\underset{3}{\cancel{15}}} = \frac{1}{3}$$

So $\frac{1}{3}$ of domestic water use is for baths and showers, etc.

Question 2.15

(a) $\frac{7}{10} \times 100\% = 70\%$

(b) $\frac{13}{25} \times 100\% = 52\%$

(c) $\frac{3}{2} \times 100\% = 150\%$

(Note that this answer is greater than 100% since the fraction $\frac{3}{2}$ is greater than 1.)

Question 2.16

(a) $60\% = \dfrac{60}{100} = \dfrac{\overset{3}{\cancel{6}}}{\underset{5}{\cancel{10}}} = \dfrac{3}{5}$

(b) $64\% = \dfrac{64}{100} = \dfrac{\overset{32}{\cancel{64}}}{\underset{50}{\cancel{100}}} = \dfrac{\overset{16}{\cancel{32}}}{\underset{25}{\cancel{50}}} = \dfrac{16}{25}$

(c) $67\% = \dfrac{67}{100}$

(Note that there are no whole numbers which can be divided into both 67 and 100, so this fraction is in its simplest form.)

Question 2.17

(a) $\dfrac{2}{5} \times 20 = 8$

(b) $\dfrac{7}{8} \times 24 = 21$

(c) 15% of 60 is $\dfrac{15}{100} \times 60 = 9$

(d) 60% of 5 is $\dfrac{60}{100} \times 5 = 3$

Question 2.18

(a) The ratio of women to men in the group is 8 : 15.

(b) The total number of students is $15 + 8 = 23$, so $\frac{8}{23}$ of the group are women.

Question 3.1

(a) 5 km = 5000 m = 500 000 cm = 5 000 000 mm

(b) 3 kg = 3000 g = 3 000 000 mg

(c) 25 s = 25 000 ms

Question 3.2

(a) 4000 g = 4 kg, since 1000 g = 1 kg. So the calculation becomes 7 kg + 4 kg = 11 kg. Alternatively, you could calculate the answer in grams. In this case, 7 kg = 7000 g, and 7000 g + 4000 g = 11 000 g. (*Note*: the two answers are clearly equivalent: 11 kg = 11 000 g. Either one is correct.)

(b) 55 cm − 40 mm = 55 cm − 4 cm = 51 cm. Alternatively, 550 mm − 40 mm = 510 mm.

(c) 20 s − 1000 ms = 20 s − 1 s = 19 s. Alternatively, 20 000 ms − 1000 ms = 19 000 ms.

Question 3.3

(a) $\frac{3}{8} = 0.375$

(b) $\frac{7}{10} = 0.7$

(c) $\frac{3}{100} = 0.03$

(*Note*: in each case, you can convert the fraction to the equivalent decimal number simply by dividing the numerator by the denominator. The answer to part (b) highlights the fact that the first number after the decimal point gives the 'number of tenths'. Similarly, the answer to part (c) shows that the second number after the decimal point indicates the 'number of hundredths'.)

Question 3.4

(a) $0.7 = \frac{7}{10}$

(b) $0.2 = \frac{2}{10} = \frac{1}{5}$

(c) $0.222 = \frac{222}{1000} = \frac{111}{500}$

(*Note*: remember that, to convert a decimal number between 0 and 1 to a fraction, you write the digits that follow the decimal point on the top of the fraction, and on the bottom of the fraction you write a 1 followed by the same number of zeros as there are digits after the decimal point. So for 0.222, you write 222 on the top of the fraction, and 1000 on the bottom – three zeros on the bottom because there are three digits on the top of the fraction.)

Question 3.5

(a) $79\% = \frac{79}{100} = 0.79$

(b) $35\% = \frac{35}{100} = 0.35$

(c) $3\% = \frac{3}{100} = 0.03$

Question 3.6

(a) 24.31 − 13.94 = 10.37

(b) 3.05 × 2.2 = 6.71

(c) 499.56 ÷ 27.6 = 18.1

Question 3.7

(a) 0.2648 is 0.3 to one decimal place; 0.26 to two decimal places; 0.265 to three decimal places.

(b) 0.825 51 is 0.8 to one decimal place; 0.83 to two decimal places; 0.826 to three decimal places.

(c) 21.1184 is 21.1 to one decimal place; 21.12 to two decimal places; 21.118 to three decimal places.

Question 3.8

Following a vertical line upwards from 11 years on the horizontal axis to the curve and then following a horizontal line left from this point on the curve to the vertical axis gives a value of approximately 122 cm.

Question 3.9

(a) The subject of this graph is the volume of water flowing each second over a 24-hour period, past a point in a stream after heavy rain.

(b) Water flow, measured in litres per second, is plotted on the vertical axis.

(c) Time is plotted on the horizontal axis, and this is measured in hours.

(*Note*: the 24-hour clock has been used, so the period covered is 1 day.)

(d) At 12.00 hours, the water flow was about 95 litres per second.

(*Note*: this is found by following a line vertically upwards from 12.00 hours to the curve, then following a horizontal line left from this point on the curve to the vertical axis and reading from the scale. In this case, the line intersects the scale one division below 100. Since 10 divisions correspond to 50 litres per second, 1 division corresponds to 5 litres per second, and so the flow is (100 – 5) litres per second, or 95 litres per second.)

(e) The maximum flow was about 155 litres per second, which occurred at approximately 08.00 hours.

(*Note*: the maximum flow corresponds to the peak of the curve; by drawing horizontal and vertical lines from the peak to the axes, you can read off the flow and the time respectively.)

(f) The flow was steady until 04.00 hours, and then it increased very rapidly for about two hours. After this it increased more slowly until it reached a maximum flow at 08.00 hours. It then started to decrease; there was a small peak at about 11.00 hours, and the flow gradually decreased until it became fairly steady after 20.00 hours, at a greater flow than at the start of the day.

Question 3.10

(a) After 6 minutes the mass of the cucumber was about 145 grams.

(*Note*: the way to find this value is shown in Figure 3.8. First locate 6 minutes on the (horizontal) time axis, indicated by the arrow labelled A; from here move vertically up the graph until you reach the plotted data point, arrow B; then move from arrow B horizontally across the graph to the vertical axis to read off the mass, arrow C. This is $2\frac{1}{2}$ divisions (millimetres) above 140. Since each centimetre on the vertical scale corresponds to 20 g, each millimetre division must correspond to 2 g. So 2.5 mm on the vertical scale corresponds to 2.5 × 2 g, i.e. 5 g. Therefore, arrow C is at (140 + 5) g = 145 g.)

(b) It took 10.6 minutes for the mass to fall to 82 grams.

(*Note*: here you have to start by locating 82 g on the (vertical) mass axis. This is one division above the 80 g line and is indicated by the arrow labelled D in Figure 3.8. From arrow D move horizontally across the graph to reach the plotted line, arrow E, and from there move vertically down to the time axis, arrow F. This is three divisions to the right of the 10 minute mark on the scale. Each centimetre on the time axis corresponds to 2 minutes, so each millimetre division must be

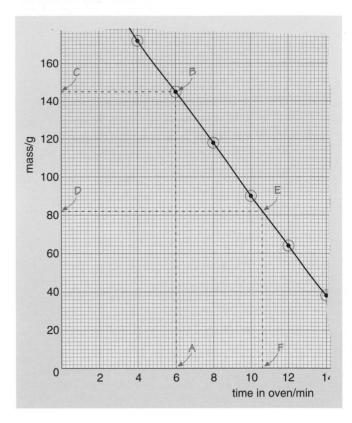

Figure 3.8   How to read values from Figure 3.5 to get the answers to Question 3.10.

0.2 minutes. Three divisions is therefore 0.6 minutes, so the time corresponding to arrow F is 10 minutes + 0.6 minutes = 10.6 minutes.)

Question 3.11

(a) The initial mass is the mass at zero minutes, which is the value on the vertical axis. This mass is 216 grams. The mass of the dried cucumber corresponds to the value at times greater than 20 minutes; all of the water has been removed by this stage, so the mass is approximately constant (the graph levels off) and has a value of about 7 grams. The difference between these two masses 216 grams – 7 grams = 209 grams, is the mass of water in the cucumber.

(b) The percentage of cucumber that was water is calculated in exactly the same way as for the potato:

$$\text{percentage water} = \frac{\text{mass of water in cucumber}}{\text{initial mass of cucumber}} \times 100\%$$

From part (a), the mass of water in the cucumber was 209 grams, and the initial mass of cucumber was 216 grams, so

$$\text{percentage water} = \frac{209 \; \cancel{\text{grams}}}{216 \; \cancel{\text{grams}}} \times 100\%$$

$$= 96.75925926\%$$

The accuracy with which the masses can be read from the graph does not justify quoting the answer to eight decimal places, and so it is more appropriate to round the answer to the nearest whole number, that is 97%.

Question 4.1

A solid, such as a piece of iron, is rigid: it has a shape and a volume that stay the same when you pick it up and handle it, and it keeps its shape irrespective of where it is placed. A liquid, such as cooking oil, has a fixed volume but no shape of its own; its shape depends on the shape of the container into which it is put.

(*Note*: you can't pick up oil without using some sort of container. When you pour it from a bottle into a pan, the oil flows and changes its shape but the volume of the oil doesn't change; it has the same volume in the pan as it had in the bottle.)

A gas, such as air, has no fixed shape, and nor does it have a fixed volume. It also flows, like a liquid, and takes the shape of its container: for example, think of inflating a balloon. What distinguishes a gas from a liquid is that a gas fills the whole volume of its container *completely*: it doesn't just remain in a fixed volume at the bottom of the container.

Question 4.2

Starting with the lowest temperature, and then in order of increasing temperature, the values are: −210 °C, −85 °C, −27 °C, −26 °C, 0 °C, 85 °C, 210 °C, 1750 °C.

Question 4.3

(a) $(-3) + (-4) = (-3) - 4 = -7$

(b) $(-10) - (-5) = (-10) + 5 = -5$

(c) $6 \div (-2) = -3$

(d) $(-12) \div (-6) = 2$

Question 4.4

(a) $117 - (-38) + (-286) = -131$

(b) $(-1624) \div (-29) = 56$

(c) $(-123) \times (-24) = 2952$

Question 4.5

(a) 65 °C is warmer than 57 °C.

(b) 57 °C is warmer than −65 °C.

(c) −57 °C is warmer than −65 °C.

(d) 65 °C is warmer than −57 °C.

Question 4.6

Subtracting −210 °C from −196 °C gives
$(-196 \text{ °C}) - (-210 \text{ °C}) = -196 \text{ °C} + 210 \text{ °C} = 14 \text{ °C}.$

Thus the difference is 14 °C. (*Note*: if you had difficulty in obtaining this answer you are strongly advised to study Box 4.2.)

Question 4.7

(a) Start by converting the lengths of the sides into m: 978 mm = 0.978 m; 622 mm = 0.622 m; 610 mm = 0.610 m.

To find the volume of the tank, multiply the lengths of the sides together:

$$\text{volume} = 0.978 \text{ m} \times 0.622 \text{ m} \times 0.610$$

$$= 0.371 \text{ m}^3 \text{ to three decimal places.}$$

(b) 1 m^3 = 1000 litres and, from part (a), the volume of the tank is 0.371 m^3. So

$$\text{volume} = 0.371 \times 1000 \text{ litres}$$

$$= 371 \text{ litres}$$

(*Note*: alternatively, you can convert the units of each side into decimetres (dm) and then recall that a litre is the volume of a 1 dm^3 cube:

978 mm = 97.8 cm = 9.78 dm

622 mm = 62.2 cm = 6.22 dm

610 mm = 61.0 cm = 6.10 dm

$$\text{volume} = 9.78 \text{ dm} \times 6.22 \text{ dm} \times 6.10 \text{ dm}$$

$$= 371 \text{ dm}^3 \text{ to the nearest whole number}$$

$$= 371 \text{ litres})$$

Question 4.8

(a) To find the area in m^2:

the top of the box has sides of length 1.2 m and 80 cm = 0.80 m

so the area = 1.2 m × 0.80 m = 0.96 m^2

To find the area in cm^2:

the top of the box has sides of length 1.2 m = 120 cm and 80 cm

so the area = 120 cm × 80 cm = 9600 cm^2

(b) To find the volume in m^3:

the box has length of 1.2 m, width of 80 cm = 0.80 m and height 30 cm = 0.30 m

so the volume = 1.2 m × 0.80 m × 0.30 m = 0.288 m^3

To find the volume in cm^3:

the box has length of 1.2 m = 120 cm, width of 80 cm and height 30 cm

so the volume = 120 cm × 80 cm × 30 cm = 288 000 cm^3

Question 4.9

Since 1 m^3 = 1000 litres,

$$
\begin{aligned}
2.5 \text{ million litres} &= 2500\,000 \text{ litres} \\
&= 2500 \times 1000 \text{ litres} \\
&= 2500 \times 1 \text{ m}^3 \\
&= 2500 \text{ m}^3.
\end{aligned}
$$

Question 4.10

The mass of the aluminium block is 81 kg and its volume is 0.50 m × 0.30 m × 0.20 m = 0.030 m^3, so:

$$
\begin{aligned}
\text{density of aluminium} &= \frac{\text{mass}}{\text{volume}} \\
&= \frac{81 \text{ kg}}{0.030 \text{ m}^3} = 2700 \text{ kg/m}^3
\end{aligned}
$$

The mass of the lead block is 570 kg and its volume is 0.50 m × 0.50 m × 0.20 m = 0.050 m^3, so:

$$
\begin{aligned}
\text{density of lead} &= \frac{\text{mass}}{\text{volume}} \\
&= \frac{570 \text{ kg}}{0.050 \text{ m}^3} = 11\,400 \text{ kg/m}^3
\end{aligned}
$$

Both blocks will sink because their density is greater than that of water. Record these values in Table 4.1.

Question 4.11

Water can evaporate at temperatures other than the boiling temperature – wet washing left out to dry is an obvious example. Several examples in the text illustrate this: evaporation of sweat from the body; evaporation of perfume or aftershave from the skin; cooling a carton of milk by wrapping it in a wet cloth; and the drying out of a puddle. In all these examples evaporation occurs at various temperatures that are below the normal boiling temperature of 100 °C.

Question 4.12

Water (a) contains 117 mg/litre of calcium, while water (b) contains 30 mg/litre. So water (a) contains

$$
\frac{117 \text{ mg per litre}}{30 \text{ mg per litre}} = 3.9 \text{ times as much calcium as water}
$$

(b) (*Note*: the unit cancels out.)

The ratio of the quantities of calcium in water (a) and water (b) is 117 : 30 or 3.9 : 1. (*Note*: ratios do not have units; look back at Box 2.5 if you had difficulty with this question.)

(*Note*: it is much easier to read label (b) than label (a) because the information is laid out in columns in a table.)

Question 4.13

Water is taken in both in food and in drink and is lost from the body in sweat, in the air exhaled from the lungs, in faeces and in urine.

(*Note*: this can be written as a word equation:

water in food + water in drink
= water in sweat + water in exhaled air + water in faeces + water in urine.)

Question 5.1

(a) The start of a sentence is signalled by a capital letter; the end of a sentence is signalled by a full stop.

(b) Besides signalling the start of sentences, capital letters are also used for the first letter of proper nouns, i.e. names of people (including the personal pronoun 'I') and places.

(c) A sentence must have a verb and a subject; a quick way to check whether a group of words is a sentence is to ask yourself whether it makes sense on its own.

(d) (ii) is a sentence; (i), (iii) and (iv) are phrases; (i) and (iv) have no verb; (iii) has no subject.

(e) The *student* [subject] *reads* [verb] the *course textbook* [object].

(f) You may have thought of using commas to (i) separate items in a list or (ii) to mark out a less important or non-essential part of a sentence.

If you got these answers right with no trouble, you probably don't need to study Box 5.1 in great detail.

Question 5.2

The original passage is in Chapter 4, Section 4.5. You should look at this to see how closely your results compare with the author's intentions.

Question 5.3

Words, or pairs of words, that begin with a capital letter are: Celsius (Celsius was the name of the scientist who devised the Celsius scale); Sahara Desert; Arctic Circle (in each case the two words together form the names of specific parts of the world); and Earth, when it applies to the name of this planet. Note, however, that when 'earth' is used to mean soil, no capital letter is used.

The word 'scale' in 'Celsius scale' does not have a capital letter because it is not unique; there are many different scales. Similarly, oxygen and desert (when the word is not part of the name of a place) do not begin with capital letters; these are countless billions of particles of oxygen and several different deserts. Barrel cactus, the common (rather than scientific) name of a plant, is more problematic and you are likely to see it written both with and without capitals.

Question 5.4

(a) (1) There is only one verb in this sentence, has. The subject of 'has' is Switzerland and its object is snowfall.

(2) In this sentence there are two verbs, thaws and forms. The subject of 'thaws' is snow and the subject of 'forms' is it, which refers to the thawed snow of the first part of the sentence. 'Thaws' has no object, because none is needed; the object of 'forms' is torrents. The phrase 'of water' describes the torrents; 'water' is not the object of the verb.

(b) There are two incomplete sentences, the second and the fourth. The simplest way to make them complete is to use 'joins' instead of 'joining', 'returns' instead of 'returning' and 'continues' instead of 'continuing'. Alternatively, you could make the second (incomplete) sentence part of the first, and the fourth (incomplete) sentence part of the third, as follows.

From a stream the water might be drunk by a cow or join other streams or lakes, the water eventually joining the rivers and returning back to the sea. From here the droplet moves back to the oceans, the Earth's reservoirs, the cycle continuing indefinitely.

Question 5.5

Do you agree with the position of the commas below?

In order to carry out the experiment I used some kitchen scales, a sponge tin, kitchen foil, a sharp knife, a chopping board, around 500 grams of potatoes, an oven glove and a gas oven. To begin with I cut the potatoes, which were quite large, into thin slices using the knife. Next I placed the slices, making sure that they were lying flat and spread out so that they were separated, on kitchen foil, on top of a metal sponge tin which had a raised, patterned, rough base to help evaporate the water given off.

Commas are used to separate the items of equipment given in the first sentence. Note that there is no comma between the last two items which are joined by 'and'. Paired commas are also used in the second sentence, around the phrase 'which were quite large', which is used to describe the potatoes and which also separates the phrase 'cut the potatoes' from the description of how they were cut, 'into thin slices using the knife'. The same is done around the very long phrase in the third sentence beginning 'making sure that they …'. This phrase describes how the slices were placed and also separates the 'slices' from where they were placed, 'on kitchen foil'. The comma after kitchen foil separates the two stages of the operation, namely, 'on kitchen foil' and 'on top of a metal sponge tin'.

Finally, commas are put in between the list of adjectives, 'raised', 'patterned' and 'rough', which are used to describe the base of the sponge tin.

In addition, you might have put a comma after 'base', near the end of the last sentence, to separate the description of the sponge tin from the activity of separating the slices in order to help evaporation.

Question 5.6

The words and phrases that are underlined are redundant in the sentence below. The numbers in brackets, e.g. (1), refer to the explanations that follow of why the preceding words and phrases are redundant. You may have a different amended sentence; there is more than one way of shortening a sentence.

The process of evaporation, <u>when it occurs</u> (1), is important because <u>not only does it result in</u> (2) water <u>being</u> (2) evaporated <u>into the air where it</u> (2) may condense <u>into water droplets</u> (3) to form clouds which may lead eventually to rain <u>which will fall onto the land surface</u> (4), but also because it leads to the water <u>evaporated, if it is</u> (5) evaporated from the oceans, being separated from all the dissolved and solid substances.

(1) The preceding phrase, 'process of evaporation' implies that evaporation is occurring, so this is unnecessary repetition.

(2) The two phrases are repetitious and state the obvious. Where else does the evaporated water go, if not into the air? The really important point has been retained that the water condenses to form clouds. Removal of the two phrases makes the word 'being' redundant; the sentence reads more easily without it.

(3) The condensation of water vapour (evaporated water) implies that water droplets form, so there is no need to state this.

(4) Again, this is stating the obvious as rain goes down, not up. (A lot of rain falls over the oceans, too.)

(5) 'Evaporated' does not need to be repeated. (In fact, the whole of 'the water evaporated, if it is evaporated from the oceans' could have been summed up in just two words 'evaporated seawater'.)

The amended sentence now reads as follows.

> The process of evaporation is important because water evaporated may condense to form clouds which may eventually lead to rain, and also because it leads to the water evaporated from the oceans being separated from all the dissolved and solid substances.

Note that, to make sense of this sentence, the word 'but' after 'rain' has been changed to 'and'. This is still a very long sentence. Other words would have to be changed completely (see, for example, note 5 above) to make it still more concise, and yet retain the two main points: that evaporation leads to water being cycled and to the separation of water from dissolved and solid substances.

Question 5.7

The most logical reordering follows the natural progression of the water from its initial intake through the mouth, to the ultimate expulsion of some of it from the rectum. Namely: 6, 1, 7, 5, 3, 2, 4.

Question 5.8

(a) The first paragraph introduces the reader to thinking about writing. The second is about communicating in note form. The third deals with communicating more formally, such as by letter. The fourth covers writing assignment answers. The fifth draws attention to the need to consider the purpose of each piece of writing. The last one invites the reader to diagnose their own understanding of correct sentence construction.

(b) In each case, a new paragraph begins where there is a change of topic.

Question 6.1

From Table 6.1, the volume of water stored in ice and snow is 43 000 000 km^3. Expressing this as a fraction of the total volume gives $\dfrac{43\,000\,000 \text{ km}^3}{1460\,000\,000 \text{ km}^3}$.

Six zeros (and the unit) can be cancelled from the top and the bottom of this fraction, so the percentage is $\dfrac{43}{1460} \times 100\% = 2.9\%$.

(Note that 43 is exactly the same percentage of 1460 as 43 000 000 is of 1460 000 000.)

Question 6.2

(a) $100\,000\,000 = 1 \times 10^8$

(b) $35\,000 = 3.5 \times 10^4$

(c) $95 \times 10^5 = 9.5 \times 10^6$

(d) $0.51 \times 10^3 = 5.1 \times 10^2$

Question 6.3

(a) $7.3 \times 10^4 = 73\,000$

(b) $4.44 \times 10^5 = 444\,000$

(c) $6.05 \times 10^3 = 6050$

Question 6.4

(a) $(4.5 \times 10^4) \times (4.0 \times 10^{11}) = 1.8 \times 10^{16}$

(b) $10^{12} - (5.66 \times 10^{11}) = 4.34 \times 10^{11}$

(*Note*: if you got the incorrect answer 9.434×10^{12} you probably entered 10 EXP 12 instead of 1 EXP 12 on your calculator. Remember that 10^{12} can be written as 1×10^{12}.)

Question 6.5

The boxes should read as follows:
ice and snow, 4.3×10^7; underground water, 1.5×10^7; lakes and rivers, 3.6×10^5; plants and animals, 2.0×10^3; atmosphere, 1.5×10^4; oceans, 1.4×10^9.

Question 6.6

(a) The starting point for quoting 0.000 000 0002 in scientific notation is 2.0 (the number between 1.0 and 9.9). The decimal point has to be moved ten places to the left to reach 0.000 000 0002, so the power of ten must be -10 and the answer 2×10^{-10} m.

(b) 2.5×10^{-4} m.

(c) First, convert the fraction into a decimal. This is 0.000 001. In scientific notation, this is 1×10^{-6} m. Alternatively,

$$\frac{1\,m}{1000\,000} = \frac{1\,m}{10^6} = 1 \times 10^{-6}\ m$$

(d) $0.0035\ m = 3.5 \times 10^{-3}$ m.

Question 6.7

(a) To find the decimal number corresponding to 7.3×10^{-4}, the decimal point in 7.3 has to be moved four places to the left to give 0.000 73. The alternative approach is to think of, and work out, $7.3 \div 10 \div 10 \div 10 \div 10$.

(b) 0.000 000 29

Question 6.8

(a) 1.3×10^{-40}

(b) 5×10^{24}

Question 6.9

Water and protein are compounds because they consist of different types of atom bonded together. Hydrogen, nitrogen and carbon are elements because they each consist of only one type of atom.

Question 6.10

Two answers are equally correct. Either fill in the blanks with elements/hydrogen/compound *or* with atoms/hydrogen/compound.

Question 6.11

(a) Carbon dioxide is a compound; (b) nitrogen is an element.

Question 6.12

A gold atom has 79 electrons. Atoms of gold, like atoms of all other elements, are electrically neutral. The charge carried by a proton is $+1$ so the charge on the nucleus of a gold atom is $+79$. To balance this, there must be 79 electrons each with a charge of -1.

Question 6.13

There are seven protons in the nucleus of a nitrogen atom. This can be deduced as follows: as there are seven electrons surrounding the nucleus in a nitrogen atom, the total negative charge is -7. Since the atom is electrically neutral, and the charge on a proton is $+1$, there must be seven protons altogether.

Similarly, the number of protons per atomic nucleus in each of the other elements is: oxygen, 8; argon, 18; neon, 10; helium, 2; krypton, 36; and xenon, 54.

Note, for interest, there is nearly 1% of argon in the air you breathe.

Question 6.14

(a) and (b) are likely to exist and in fact *do* exist as covalent compounds; (c) is most unlikely as carbon forms four and not five covalent bonds.

Question 6.15

$$O = O$$
$$N \equiv N$$

You may have gone through the stage of drawing linked hooks to get to these molecular structures showing double and triple covalent bonds, respectively. (*Note*: a triple covalent bond is the maximum allowed between two atoms; quadruple bonds between two atoms do not exist.)

Question 6.16

(a) Nitrogen and hydrogen: the atoms are in the ratio of 1 : 3 within the molecule of NH_3 (called ammonia).

(b) Hydrogen and sulfur: the atoms are in the ratio of 2 : 1, respectively, within the molecule of H_2S (called hydrogen sulfide).

Question 6.17

The chemical symbol for: (a) hydrogen is H, bromine is Br; (b) silicon is Si, oxygen is O; (c) nitrogen is N, chlorine is Cl.

Question 6.18

The chemical symbol for hydrogen bromide is HBr, silicon dioxide is SiO_2, nitrogen trichloride is NCl_3.

(This ties in with their names, with the meaning of 'di-' and 'tri-', and with the idea of a 'preferred' number of covalent bonds.)

Question 6.19

Remember that the number of atoms of each element must be the same on both sides of the 'balanced' equation.

$$2Mg + O_2 = 2MgO$$
$$C + 2Cl_2 = CCl_4$$
$$4K + O_2 = 2K_2O$$
$$H_2 + Cl_2 = 2HCl$$

Question 6.20

1 The first step is to put the formulas of the reactants on the left and the product on the right.

$$N_2 + H_2 \longrightarrow NH_3$$

2 Now balance the number of atoms of nitrogen. With two atoms of nitrogen on the left, two ammonia molecules are needed on the right. (Remember, N_2 means two atoms of nitrogen joined as a molecule.)

$$N_2 + H_2 \longrightarrow 2NH_3$$

3 The next problem is the number of hydrogen atoms: there is a total of six on the right (three in each of the two ammonia molecules) and only two hydrogen atoms in the single hydrogen molecule on the left. To correct this, three hydrogen molecules are needed on the left (to give a total of six atoms).

$$N_2 + 3H_2 = 2NH_3$$

The result is a balanced chemical equation for a process in which one molecule of nitrogen reacts with three molecules of hydrogen to give two molecules of ammonia.

Question 6.21

(a) Calcium oxide, (b) potassium chloride, (c) sodium sulfate, (d) magnesium oxide.

Question 6.22

Ca^{2+} and O^{2-} in the ratio 1 : 1; K^+ and Cl^- in the ratio 1 : 1; Na^+ and SO_4^{2-} in the ratio 2 : 1; Mg^{2+} and O^{2-} in the ratio 1 : 1.

Although Mg^{2+} is not in Table 6.7, you can deduce it from the formula MgO, knowing that the oxide ion is O^{2-}.

Question 6.23

The formula for calcium sulfate is $CaSO_4$ (one Ca^{2+} ion and one SO_4^{2-} ion).

The formula for potassium sulfate is K_2SO_4 (two K^+ ions and one SO_4^{2-} ion).

Question 6.24

Mg^{2+} and SO_4^{2-} are in the ratio of 1 : 1. You know from Question 6.22 that the ion of magnesium is Mg^{2+}. Hence, magnesium sulfate is $MgSO_4$; the charge of 2+ on the magnesium ion balances the charge of 2− on the sulfate ion (SO_4^{2-}).

Question 7.1

(a) The domestic use per person in developing countries is 10 litres per day, and that in the UK is 150 litres per day. As a percentage, this is:

$$\frac{10 \text{ litres per day}}{150 \text{ litres per day}} \times 100\% = 6.67\%$$

or 6.7% when rounded up to one decimal place.

(b) The water used for domestic purposes in the UK as a percentage of the total use is:

$$\frac{150 \text{ litres}}{3411 \text{ litres}} \times 100\% = 4.398\%$$

Rounding this up to one decimal place gives 4.4%.

Question 7.2

The dissolved oxygen level at this point was about 25% of that at saturation.

(*Note*: if you didn't obtain this answer, check by following the line vertically upwards from the 20 km downstream marker on the horizontal axis to the point where it meets the curve for 1893. Now draw a line horizontally across the page from this point to where it meets the vertical axis. This should be about halfway between 20% and the next grid line (30%), i.e. at 25%.)

Question 8.1

(a)(i) The volume is the independent variable, so this should be plotted on the horizontal axis. The mass is the dependent variable (it depends on volume), so this should be plotted on the vertical axis.

(ii) The axes should be labelled 'volume/m^3' (horizontal axis) and 'mass/kg' (vertical axis).

(iii) On the horizontal axis, volumes from 0 to 0.050 m^3 can be represented by a scale which has 1 cm corresponding to 0.005 m^3 (so the scale would be labelled 0, 0.005, 0.010, 0.015, etc., up to 0.050). On the vertical axis, masses from 0 to 140 kg can be represented by a scale which has 1 cm corresponding to 10 kg (so the scale would be labelled 0, 10, 20, 30, etc., up to 140).

(b)(i) The baby's age is the independent variable (since the ages at which mass was to be measured were decided in advance), so this should be plotted on the horizontal axis, labelled 'age/months'. The baby's mass is the dependent variable (it depends on age), so this should be plotted on the vertical axis, labelled 'mass/kg'. On the horizontal axis, ages from 0 to 24 months can be represented by a scale which has 1 cm corresponding to two months. On the vertical axis, masses from 0 to 13 kg can be represented by a scale which has 1 cm corresponding to 1 kg. This scale could start at, say, 3 kg instead of 0 kg, but there is no obvious advantage in doing so here. The data are plotted in Figure 8.19 (overleaf).

(ii) A baby's weight gain with time would normally be expected to fall on a curve. Looking first at Figure 8.19a, this baby's mass might seem to be rather higher than expected at 6 months and 14 months. The data points are correctly plotted (always worth checking!) so there must be other explanations for these 'high' readings. There are several possibilities: for example, the baby may have been fed just before being weighed, or the baby was wearing more clothes than previously, or the scales used might be reading 'high', or the value was incorrectly recorded. However, if you now look at Figure 8.19b, where a smooth curve has been drawn, the apparently 'high' mass at 6 months and 14 months appears to be more of an illusion because of a lower than expected mass gain between 8 months and 12 months. This suggests that the data are a true record of the baby's gain in mass over 24 months.

Question 8.2

(a) Chris appears to have made good use of the graph paper. He has decided that it's not important to show the scale from 0 to 150 ml. However, the units are missing on the axes labels of the graph, and the independent and dependent variables have been plotted on the wrong axes.

(b) Ruth has forgotten to include a title on her graph. She has used a landscape layout which has constrained the amount of graph paper area available for the plot. Ruth has tried to get around this by using an awkward scale on the *y*-axis which has made it difficult for her to plot the points accurately.

(c) Shamim has included a title but has omitted the temperature at which the measurements were taken. She has incorrectly labelled the two axes and forgotten to include units on the time axis.

Question 8.3

(a) The volume of the yeast mixture after 23 minutes is 296 ml.

(b) The volume of the yeast mixture is 150 ml at the start and 265 ml after 20 minutes. The change in volume of the mixture between 0 and 20 minutes is

$$265 \text{ ml} - 150 \text{ ml} = 115 \text{ ml}$$

(c) The point on the graph that looks as though it may have been incorrectly plotted is the value measured after 12 minutes has elapsed. The expected value of the data

Figure 8.19 Graph of a baby's mass against age for the first 24 months. The individual points are plotted in (a) and the best-fit curve is drawn in (b).

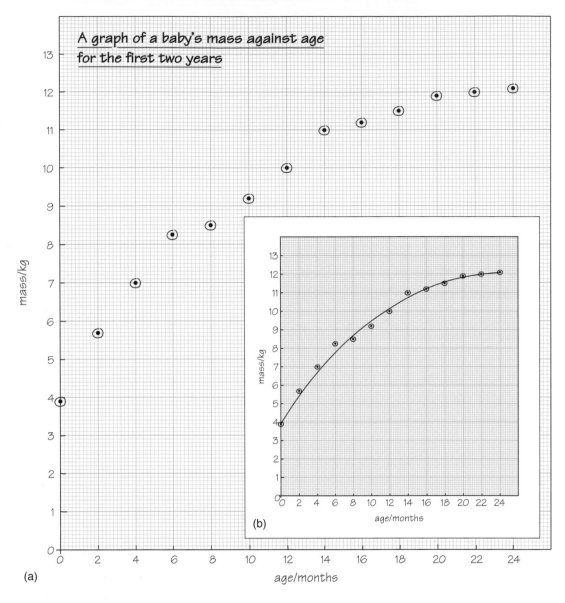

A graph of a baby's mass against age for the first two years

(a)

(b)

mass/kg

age/months

for this point is 190 ml. (It is possible that the volume was measured at the wrong time: for example, the volume noted may have been measured after 13 minutes elapsed time rather than 12 minutes when it should have been measured.)

Question 8.4

Similarities: organisms are made up of cells; they break down food to obtain energy through the process of respiration; they break down chemical compounds assisted by enzymes.

Differences: some organisms are single-celled and others are multicellular; plants obtain energy by trapping the energy of sunlight to produce their own sugars through the process of photosynthesis, whereas animals feed on other organisms; cells of green plants contain chloroplasts; some organisms, such as yeast, can respire anaerobically.

Question 9.1

(a) 1.2×10^{26} m is 10^{26} m to the nearest order of magnitude.

(b) 2×10^{-10} m is 10^{-10} m to the nearest order of magnitude.

(c) 8.7×10^{9} m is closer to 10^{10} m than to 10^{9} m, so it is 10^{10} m to the nearest order of magnitude.

Question 9.2

(a) 72 Tm = 72×10^{12} m. In scientific notation this is 7.2×10^{13} m.

(b) 1.2 pm = 1.2×10^{-12} m.

(c) 36 μm = 36×10^{-6} m. In scientific notation this is 3.6×10^{-5} m.

Question 9.3

(a) $\dfrac{1}{2 \times 2 \times 2 \times 2} = \dfrac{1}{2^4} = 2^{-4}$

(b) $\dfrac{1}{m \times m} = \dfrac{1}{m^2} = m^{-2}$

Question 9.4

(a) $7^0 = 1$ (since any number raised to the power zero is equal to one)

(b) $2^{-3} = \dfrac{1}{2^3} = \dfrac{1}{8} = 0.125$

Question 9.5

(a) $\dfrac{2}{5} + \dfrac{1}{7} = \dfrac{2 \times 7}{5 \times 7} + \dfrac{1 \times 5}{7 \times 5} = \dfrac{14}{35} + \dfrac{5}{35} = \dfrac{19}{35}$

(b) $\dfrac{2}{5} - \dfrac{1}{7} = \dfrac{2 \times 7}{5 \times 7} - \dfrac{1 \times 5}{7 \times 5} = \dfrac{14}{35} - \dfrac{5}{35} = \dfrac{9}{35}$

(c) $\dfrac{2}{5} \times \dfrac{1}{7} = \dfrac{2 \times 1}{5 \times 7} = \dfrac{2}{35}$

(d) $\dfrac{2}{5} \div \dfrac{1}{7} = \dfrac{2}{5} \times \dfrac{7}{1} = \dfrac{2 \times 7}{5 \times 1} = \dfrac{14}{5}$

Question 9.6

(a) $\dfrac{2}{3} + \dfrac{1}{6} = \dfrac{2 \times 6}{3 \times 6} + \dfrac{1 \times 3}{6 \times 3} = \dfrac{12}{18} + \dfrac{3}{18} = \dfrac{15}{18}$

Cancelling by 3 (to express the answer in its simplest form) gives

$$\dfrac{2}{3} + \dfrac{1}{6} = \dfrac{\overset{5}{\cancel{15}}}{\underset{6}{\cancel{18}}} = \dfrac{5}{6}$$

(b) $\dfrac{3}{4} - \dfrac{1}{6} = \dfrac{3 \times 6}{4 \times 6} - \dfrac{1 \times 4}{6 \times 4} = \dfrac{18}{24} - \dfrac{4}{24} = \dfrac{14}{24}$

Cancelling by 2 (to express the answer in its simplest form) gives

$$\dfrac{3}{4} - \dfrac{1}{6} = \dfrac{\overset{7}{\cancel{14}}}{\underset{12}{\cancel{24}}} = \dfrac{7}{12}$$

Question 9.7

(a) $\dfrac{2}{7} \times \dfrac{1}{4} = \dfrac{\overset{1}{\cancel{2}} \times 1}{7 \times \underset{2}{\cancel{4}}} = \dfrac{1 \times 1}{7 \times 2} = \dfrac{1}{14}$

(b) $\dfrac{2}{3} \div \dfrac{3}{4} = \dfrac{2}{3} \times \dfrac{4}{3} = \dfrac{2 \times 4}{3 \times 3} = \dfrac{8}{9}$

(c) $\dfrac{3}{4} \div 5 = \dfrac{3}{4} \div \dfrac{5}{1} = \dfrac{3}{4} \times \dfrac{1}{5} = \dfrac{3 \times 1}{4 \times 5} = \dfrac{3}{20}$

Question 9.8

Figure 9.16 (overleaf) shows that, as the horizontal value increases from 2 s to 20 s, the vertical value increases from 1.2 m to 12.0 m. Thus the run is $(20 - 2)$ s = 18 s and the rise is $(12.0 - 1.2)$ m = 10.8 m and the gradient is given by:

$$\text{gradient} = \dfrac{\text{rise}}{\text{run}} = \dfrac{10.8 \text{ m}}{18 \text{ s}} = 0.60 \text{ m s}^{-1}$$

(You may have taken readings at different points on the graph and so obtained different values for the rise and the run. However, your value for the gradient should be similar.)

Question 9.9

(a) $V = lwh$

where V is volume, l is length, w is width and h is height.

In this case:

$l = 3$ cm

$w = 2$ cm

$h = 15$ mm = 1.5 cm

Figure 9.16 Finding the gradient of the graph in Figure 9.13.

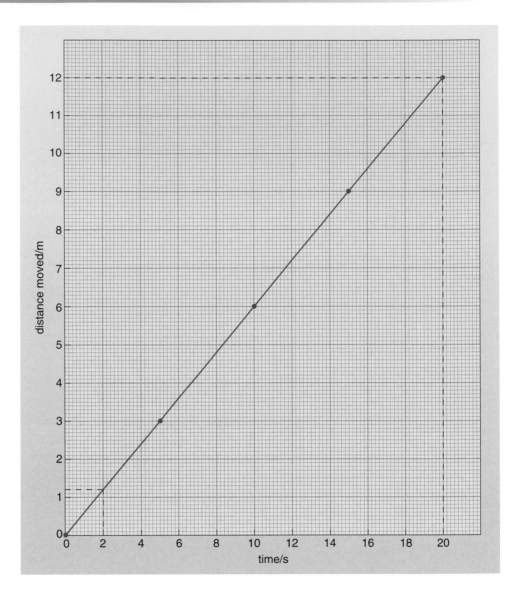

$V = lwh$

$= 3 \text{ cm} \times 2 \text{ cm} \times 1.5 \text{ cm}$

$= 9 \text{ cm}^3$

So, the volume of the 'cube' of olive oil is 9 cm³.

Alternatively, you could start by converting the length, width and height to metres:

$l = 3 \text{ cm} = 3 \times 10^{-2} \text{ m}$

$w = 2 \text{ cm} = 2 \times 10^{-2} \text{ m}$

$h = 15 \text{ mm} = 15 \times 10^{-3} \text{ m} = 1.5 \times 10^{-2} \text{ m}$

$V = lwh$

$= (3 \times 10^{-2} \text{ m}) \times (2 \times 10^{-2} \text{ m}) \times (1.5 \times 10^{-2} \text{ m})$

$= (3 \times 10^{-2}) \times (2 \times 10^{-2}) \times (1.5 \times 10^{-2}) \text{ m}^3$

$= 9 \times 10^{-6} \text{ m}^3$

So, the volume of the 'cube' of olive oil is 9 × 10⁻⁶ m³.

Since 1 cm = 1 × 10⁻² m,
1 cm³ = (1 × 10⁻² m)³ = 1 × 10⁻⁶ m³, so the answers obtained by the two methods are equivalent. An answer of 9000 mm³ (9 × 10³ mm³) is also acceptable.

(b) $V = lwh$

where V is volume, l is length, w is width and h is height.

In this case:

$l = 13$ km

$w = 6$ km

$h = 125$ m $= 0.125$ km

$$V = lwh$$
$$= 13 \text{ km} \times 6 \text{ km} \times 0.125 \text{ km}$$
$$= 9.75 \text{ km}^3$$

So, the volume of the iceberg is 9.75 km³, i.e. about 10 km³.

Alternatively, you could start by converting the length, width and height to metres:

$l = 13$ km $= 13 \times 10^3$ m $= 1.3 \times 10^4$ m

$w = 6$ km $= 6 \times 10^3$ m

$h = 125$ m

$$V - lwh$$
$$= (1.3 \times 10^4 \text{ m}) \times (6 \times 10^3 \text{ m}) \times 125 \text{ m}$$
$$= 9.75 \times 10^9 \text{ m}^3$$

So, the volume of the iceberg is 9.75×10^9 m³.

Since 1 km $= 1 \times 10^3$ m,

1 km³ $= (1 \times 10^3 \text{ m})^3 = 1 \times 10^9$ m³,

so the answers obtained by the two methods are equivalent.

Question 9.10

(a) The expression is $b + f + c$.

(b) The equation is $T = p \times (b + f + c)$

It is also acceptable to write this as $T = p(b + f + c)$

where T is the family's water use per day

$\quad$ p is the number of people in the family

$\quad$ b is the daily use per person for baths and showers

$\quad$ f is the daily use per person for flushing toilets

$\quad$ c is the daily use per person for washing clothes.

Compare your answer with the one you got for Question 2.8(b). If you substitute values for b, f and c from Table 2.1 and $p = 4$, you should obtain the same numerical answer.

Question 9.11

The diameter of the hailstone is 1 cm, so its radius is 0.5 cm.

$$V = \frac{4}{3}\pi r^3$$
$$= \frac{4}{3} \times \pi \times (0.5 \text{ cm})^3$$
$$= 0.523\,598\,775 \text{ cm}^3$$

So, the volume of the hailstone is about 0.5 cm³.

Alternatively, you might have started by converting the radius to a value in metres:

$$r = 0.5 \text{ cm} = 0.5 \times 10^{-2} \text{ m} = 5 \times 10^{-3} \text{ m}$$

$$V = \frac{4}{3}\pi r^3$$
$$= \frac{4}{3} \times \pi \times (5 \times 10^{-3} \text{ m})^3$$
$$= 5 \times 10^{-7} \text{ m}^3$$

The answers obtained by the two methods are equivalent. It is also reasonable to give a value for the volume of the hailstone in mm³ (about 500 mm³).

Index

Entries and page numbers in **bold type** refer to key words which are printed in **bold** in the text and which are defined in the Glossary. Where the page number is given in *italics*, the indexed information is carried mainly or wholly in an illustration, table or box.

Acknowledgements

Among the many people who helped in various ways with the production of this book, the S154 course team would particularly like to thank the Course Assessor, Dr Andy Platt (University of Staffordshire), for his helpful comments and suggestions. The authors also gratefully acknowledge the contribution of members of the S103 course team, in particular Evelyn Brown, Stuart Freake, Judith Metcalfe and Malcolm Rose, and members of the "Into Science" course team, in particular Stuart Bennett, for previous materials on which this text is based.

Grateful acknowledgement is made to the following sources:

Cover: Courtesy of Ruth Williams;

Figures 1.1a, 1.1b, 6.1, 7.1b, 7.9b: Courtesy of Linda Fowler; *Figures 2.1, 2.2*: copyright © George Gerster/Panos Pictures; *Figure 3.1a*: copyright © Holt Studios International Ltd/Alamy; *Figures 3.1b, 4.5a, 4.5b, 9.3, 10.3*: Courtesy of Sally Jordan; *Figures 3.6a, 4.2, 4.4a*: copyright © Dr Andy Sutton, www.andysuttonphotography.com; *Figure 3.6b*: Courtesy of Dr Colin Walker; *Figure 4.19a*: DeWitt, William, (1989) From *Human Biology: Form, Function and Adaptation*, Copyright © 1989 by Scott, Foresman; *Figures 4.1b, 6.1c*: copyright © GeoScience Features Picture Library; *Figures 4.3a, 4.3b*: copyright © Adam Hart-Davis, http://www.adam-hart-davis.org/; *Figure 4.17*: Courtesy of the Library and Information Centre, Royal Society of Chemistry; *Figure 4.21*: copyright © Terry Fincher.Photo Int/Alamy; *Figure 6.1a*: NOAA; *Figure 6.2*: NASA; *Figure 6.5*: copyright © Tom Payne/Alamy; *Figures 6.7, 6.8b, 6.18c, 6.19c, 6.20b, 6.21b, 6.22b, 7.1a*: Courtesy of Ruth Williams; *Figure 6.11*: Courtesy of Dr Elaine McPherson; *Figure 7.1c*: copyright © Charlotte Thege/Alamy; *Figure 7.2*: Map taken from http://en.wikipedia.org/wiki/Image: HDImap_current.png; *Figure 7.3a*: copyright © Woodfall Wild Images/Alamy; *Figure 7.3b*: copyright © Robert Brook/Alamy; *Figure 7.4*: Courtesy of Richardson Photography; *Figure 7.5a*: copyright © Mark Edwards/Still Pictures; *Figure 7.5b*: copyright © Suzanne Long/Alamy; *Figure 7.8*: Warner, Sir F., 1994, *Conference Paper No. 4, Industry and Society*, HRH The Duke of Edinburgh's Study Conference, July 1994; *Figure 7.9*: copyright © Mike Goldwater/Alamy; *Figure 8.1a*: copyright © Microfield Scientific Limited/Science Photo Library; *Figure 8.16*: copyright © Food Alan King/Alamy; *Figure 8.17c*: copyright © J.C. Revy/Science Photo Library; *Figure 9.4*: Courtesy of Treak Cliff Cavern, Castleton, Derbyshire; *Figures 9.6a, 9.6b*: Courtesy of Stuart Bennett; *Figure 10.1a*: copyright © Neil Cooper/Alamy; *Figure 10.1b*: copyright © WildPictures/ Alamy; *Figure 10.2*: copyright © Mario Tama/Getty Images; *Figure 10.4*: copyright © Jochen Track/Alamy; *Figure 10.5*: copyright © Pam Owen.

Every effort has been made to contact copyright holders. If any have been inadvertently overlooked the publishers will be pleased to make the necessary arrangements at the first opportunity.